An Introduction to Using Theory in Social Work Practice

D0223726

An Introduction to Using Theory in Social Work Practice equips the reader to use fourteen key social work theories to guide each phase of the planned change process, from engagement through to evaluation. Suitable for a generalist approach, this book illustrates the value of applying theory to practice in a variety of social work roles, across diverse fields and facing assorted challenges.

- The first section provides a practical foundation for beginning to use theory in your social work practice.
- Section two looks at how you can translate and integrate fourteen theories commonly found in social work across each phase of the planned change process. The theories discussed are: behavioral, interpretive anthropology, psychodynamic, evolutionary biology, cognitive, symbolic interactionism, strengths, social constructionism, exchange economics, role, ecological, critical, feminist, and systems theory.
- Sections three and four address some key issues for real-life social work practice, including common barriers to using theory in practice, the potential for multi-professional communication and theory-sharing, and developing an integrative theoretical model for your own personal practice.

Linking to core competencies identified by the Council on Social Work Education, this text supports social work students and practitioners in developing vital skills, including critical thinking, applying theory, and the effective use of the planned change process.

James A. Forte is Professor of Social Work at Salisbury University, Maryland, USA.

An Introduction to Using Theory in Social Work Practice

James A. Forte

 Routledge
Taylor & Francis Group

LONDON AND NEW YORK

First published 2014
by Routledge
2 Park Square, Milton Park, Abingdon, Oxon OX14 4RN

and by Routledge
711 Third Avenue, New York, NY 10017

Routledge is an imprint of the Taylor & Francis Group, an informa business

British Library Cataloguing in Publication Data
A catalogue record for this book is available from the British Library

Library of Congress Cataloging-in-Publication Data
Forte, James A.
An introduction to using theory in social work practice/James Forte.
pages cm
1. Social service. 2. Social service--Great Britain. I. Title.
HV40.F672 2014
361.3'2--dc23
2013028778

ISBN13: 978-0-415-72669-6 (hbk)
ISBN13: 978-0-415-72671-9 (pbk)
ISBN13: 978-1-315-85605-6 (ebk)

Typeset in Sabon
by GreenGate Publishing Services, Tonbridge, Kent

To my students—near and far, young and old, recent and past, very attentive and less attentive, with thanks for their encouragement, insight, participation, openness, and patience.

Contents

Figures

Tables

Foreword

We must find a theory that will work; and that means something extremely difficult; for our theory must mediate between all previous truths and certain new experiences.

(William James, Pragmatism, 1907/1946, p. 76)

Theory and the reflective practitioner

The critical root of "theory," I remind my students, is the Greek *theamai*, meaning "I behold." In the most fundamental sense, theories enlarge our fields of observation and broaden ways of seeing, understanding, and acting. In the course of our training as social workers, I emphasize in my teaching, we must come to terms with irreducible tensions between more pure conceptions of the helping process and more limited, fragmentary renderings of what we do as we carry out our day to day practice. Although some of us are moved to search for an encompassing point of view that would promise to unify our understandings of vulnerability and problems in living, most of us come to develop a pluralist or integrative approach, refusing to privilege any single explanatory system. Grand theories, we realize, inevitably fail us as we move into the concrete particulars of our work. What is missing is certainty, we find, and the remedy lies in risk: we must carry out what Donald Winnicott called experiments in adapting to need, and have faith in the outcomes of experiential learning. Our theories are tools for thinking, as William James reminds us, and what matters is what works—the "cash value" of our ideas, as he put it.

The pragmatic attitude has been a defining feature of social work, from the start of the profession, and clinicians have called upon ideas and methods across a divergent range of intellectual traditions and disciplines. Surveys show that most workers come to characterize their fundamental orientation as "eclectic" or "integrative." And yet, as our reviews of the literature show, we continue to find remarkably little consideration of the ways in which practitioners actually engage differing theories, empirical findings, and technical procedures over the course of intervention. If we are to avoid a willy-nilly eclecticism, I have argued, we must develop an orienting perspective—what I think of as a home base—and formulate basic considerations and principles that guide us in our efforts to make use of differing ideas, research findings, and methods (Borden, 2010). As practitioners we must justify and defend the choices we make in light of the guiding values of the social work tradition and the particular circumstances of the clinical situation.

James Forte has a deep appreciation of the foregoing concerns, as we see in the following pages, and he realizes the crucial role of theory in critical thinking and reflective practice. Although the translational research movement has helped clinicians make realistic and sensible use of empirical findings, there is as yet little exploration of the ways in which clinicians translate theories and engage differing ideas over the course of their work. More than ever, Forte emphasizes, clinicians are expected to master multiple theories, therapeutic languages, and technical procedures. In doing so, however, as Forte realizes, we must establish a center of gravity, a personal practice model, that provides points of reference as we work to integrate differing ideas, empirical findings, and technical procedures.

In light of these challenges, Forte sets out to help students and practitioners develop what he has come to call an integrative multi-theory practice model. Ever attuned to the complexities and ambiguities of the clinical situation, he introduces a framework and a method that promise to guide us in our efforts to translate theories and bring ideas to bear over the course of intervention. He outlines a series of translation strategies in an effort to help us broaden our use of theoretical perspectives across the phases of the helping process, from engagement to evaluation, and he provides learning and reflection activities to facilitate mastery of the core competencies of "theory use" as outlined by the Council on Social Work Education. In each of the lessons in this book we follow a journey of exploration as we consider potential points of entry into the helping process, establish our "home base," and locate ourselves in the broader surrounds of the profession.

Having taught clinical theory for many years, Forte has developed a supple understanding of the paradigms and languages that inform social work practice, and his presentations of explanatory systems encompass divergent domains of inquiry, including evolutionary biology, interpretive anthropology, cognitive and behavioral psychology, psychodynamic thought, ecological and systems perspectives, and feminist studies.

Forte's accounts reflect the energy and the richness of theorizing in our time, and his conceptions of integrative practice bring rigor, precision, flexibility, and common sense to the clinical situation. He emphasizes the importance of pluralist approaches to understanding; the place of experiential learning over the course of intervention, and the practical outcomes of ideas in a given situation. He has an energy and clarity of mind all his own, and his model has a wide range of application in our efforts to help vulnerable groups across the domains of social work practice. This book serves as a wonderful introduction to the fundamentals of generalist social work, and it promises to enrich the work of advanced practitioners as well.

William Borden, PhD

William Borden is Senior Lecturer in the School of Social Service Administration and Lecturer in the Department of Psychiatry at the University of Chicago.

Borden, W. (2010). Taking multiplicity seriously. In W. Borden (Ed.), *Reshaping theory in contemporary social work: Toward a critical pluralism in clinical practice* (pp. 3–27). New York: Columbia University Press.
James, W. (1907/1946). *Pragmatism*. New York: Longmans, Green.

Preface

Two components are necessary for sound social work practice. First, practice needs to be in theory—a theory related to the people served. But, theory also needs to be operational. Theory about the function and the role of social work needs to be translated into the actual workings of an agency, the structure designed for the delivery of services.

(Lee and Swenson, 1978, p. 359)

Need for fluency in multiple languages

What language should North American social workers speak? English, only? No, Bloom and his colleagues (1991) argued that competent social workers must achieve fluency in many additional languages. Besides our native language, professional practitioners must learn to converse in the language of clients, of research, of ethics and values, and of social work practice and scientific theory. Social workers must learn and respond to the lay languages of their clients. Many social workers, for example, are learning a second natural language such as Spanish to communicate better with their service users and community members. Social work practitioners must also be able to make sense of the folk theories about life challenges and problems that clients bring to the helping setting. Increasingly, social workers use the empirical language of scientific research. Many have embraced, for instance, the tenets and vocabulary of the empirical practice movement and are speaking more often about "best practices," "rapid assessment instruments," and the "evidence" supporting their policy and practice judgments. These social workers have become "bilingual" as indicated by their familiarity with the languages and cultures of both research and practice (Palinkas and Soydan, 2012). The profession has transformed its ideals into a distinctive language of values and ethical guidelines. Social workers who fail to master our ethical code and stay current with the new terms and principles frequently added to this lexicon risk their reputations and their careers. Beside learning the profession's shared language of practice, effective social workers must also acquire and use the jargon specific to their field of practice or professional specialty, like the many technical terms that I learned to use when working in the criminal justice system. The abstract language of theory also serves as an important tool for social workers. Contemporary social workers must learn multiple theoretical languages and also how to translate theoretical languages into the idiomatic English, Spanish, Chinese, or other native language spoken by some clients and collaterals.

Often, these languages seem foreign, their words incomprehensible, and the mastery of a new vocabulary, grammar, and syntax seems a daunting task. Scientific theory is a component of the knowledge base for contemporary social work but a tough one to learn. This book, *An Introduction to Using Theory in Social Work Practice,* will treat the acquisition of scientific theoretical knowledge as like the mastery of a new language and provide tools and experiences to increase the reader's theoretical fluency and literacy.

Science as language

Scientists develop a distinctive "universe of discourse" or communication system (Mead, 1934). A collective of scientists working on similar projects can be characterized by its unique vocabulary (a shared set of significant symbols), rules of grammar, standards for pronunciation, habits of communication, and norms for appropriate interaction with each other using the shared symbol system. This common language enables the members of the scientific group to understand each other and to collaborate efficiently. Theories are a major part of the communication system that scientists and applied scientists use for scientific problem solving (Fararo, 1989). Each theoretical tradition within science, then, can be conceptualized as a distinctive language with its own central metaphors, core concepts, common categories, typical sentences, implicit and explicit rules of grammar, preferred pronunciations, dialects, and diagramming conventions. Social work students often struggle with their first theory survey classes, I think, because this course requires the study of the complex language of scientific theory. Let's expand on the linguistic notion of scientific theory.

Brown (1992) suggests "like all of human experience, science is a conversation that takes place over time in which accounts of what is, what has occurred and what is true of the past and present are negotiated through symbolic interaction" (p. 227). Effective symbolic interaction occurs when scientists can act together thanks to the words, images, objects, diagrams, and other symbols available in scientific institutions (Halliday and Martin, 1993). They share the discoveries generated by these conversations in scientific journals, technical books, and conference workshops.

Joas (1993) conceives of science as a language for practical inquiry and action, and argues that members of a scientific community agree to a set of communication principles. Scientists make a commitment to the free and unrestricted scientific speech among members of the community of inquirers using this language. Even unpopular theories deserve a hearing. Scientists pledge to honor shared standards such as honesty, rationality in arguments, and the use of evidence to support written and verbal claims. Peer review processes monitor adherence to these standards. Scientific members of a particular community of inquiry talk to themselves often as they ponder theoretical puzzles but they accept the obligation to share the discoveries and insights emergent during self-talk with others in the joint enterprise of solving problems of collective concern. Scientists promise to use journals, websites, conferences, and other forums for intellectual exchange to share, revise, and improve continually their personal and shared thinking, talking, and experimenting about life processes and structures.

Since the founding era of the profession, social workers have wrestled with the linguistic difficulties associated with "speaking science." Communicating with scientists lodged in research centers or housed in universities distant from field sites; reading and understanding scientific texts; and persuading scientists to listen to and learn from the talk of practitioners and clients takes effort. Greenwood's (1955) classic observation is still germane. He wrote:

> the plain truth is that social work practitioners are unable to understand the language of social science. To expect a social worker to become familiar with the social sciences sufficiently to translate their practical contribution into his practice is, in effect, to ask him to master a series of languages.
>
> (p. 29)

However, you won't hear social work's professional leaders, expert practitioners, or founding figures ever call for the renunciation of science as a communication system that informs practical/theoretical work. The language of science makes possible quality service and the profession's success.

Science as a society with many languages

Traveling across Europe, the tourist must interact with people who speak many different foreign languages. Travel across the United States and you will encounter many English-speaking Americans who converse in regional dialects. Adding to the difficulty of mastering the language of science, we must recognize that science is also a pluralistic assembly of diverse sub-societies. Distinctive scientific groups and networks form with reference to discipline, profession, theoretical allegiance, role (researcher, theorist, practitioner, client or consumer), and work project (Sarukkai, 2001, 2002).

Referring to scientific specialties, Morris (1946, p. 509) summarized this position. He wrote:

> Each science expresses its results in a terminology and system of laws largely unrelated to the terminology and laws of the other sciences. Continuous collaboration among members of an interpretive network results in an order and communication predictability. This facilitates within group interaction but differentiates the network from others.

Talking and doing science, Lemke (1990) adds, always creates or re-creates a pluralistic society, a complex field of social interaction. Each scientific community or "symbol system" within the larger society develops its own register (an approach to language use tailored to particular purposes in specific settings), favored genres (explanation, biography, reports referencing current knowledge, how to, and narrative), and preferred communication practices (approaches to generating, disseminating, judging and accumulating knowledge). Novices learn a language of scientific theory by association with full members of their disciplinary or theoretical community (Gergen, 1982). Membership in a particular practice association or scientific network (ego-psychological clinical therapists or behaviorally-oriented correction workers, for instance) includes the obligation to use the "right" language in the right way (Wagner-Pacific and Bershady, 1993). A polyglot science challenges science users like social workers to become multilingual and capable of decoding and using multiple theoretical languages.

Speakers of a theoretical language often interact in networks of like speaking scholars, researchers, and practitioners (Watson, 1985). However, social work has a historical and mission-driven need to cross the boundaries of scientific and natural language and communities and cooperate with a wide range of partners. The social work profession like the world of science is characterized by the use of multiple theoretical languages also (Bloom, Wood, and Chambon, 1991). Let's just consider the interface of the profession of social work and science. Members of different disciplinary and professional groups speak different scientific languages and have difficulty communicating across theory-based language communities (King and Fawcett, 1997). In relation to disciplines, for instance, social workers might learn from colleagues well versed in the scientific languages of anthropology, biology, earth sciences, economics, geography, political science, psychology, and sociology. In the field, we may feel adept at the use of social work terms but struggle when communicating with allied professionals like nurses, attorneys, or accountants who use different and specialized theoretical languages. Mead's single universe of discourse has fragmented into multiple communities of discourse. Later in this book, we will discuss the proliferation of explanatory or "human behavior and the environment" theoretical languages and of practice languages.

Difficulties mastering the languages of science

Novice social workers face an apparent mountain (the language of science) with numerous peaks (disciplinary and professional theoretical languages) that must be traversed during the trek toward competent professionalism. Several obstacles complicate our journeys.

First, the language of science is very complex compared to native languages like English or Spanish. Scientific communication systems, languages, evolve in specialized ways. Mathematics-oriented scientists, for example, use a register (a specific configuration of meanings) quite different from an everyday language, and this impedes efforts by non-mathematicians to grasp the register because of its high degree of definitional precision, its high degree of technicality, and its specific use of notation (Halliday, 1978). You may remember a college statistics course and troubles understanding "weird" concepts like median, standard deviation, analysis of variance, and multiple regression procedures as illustrative of the alien nature of the language of mathematics.

Halliday and Martin (1993) estimate that a branch of a scientific discipline may have 50,000 to 100,000 distinctive concepts, and many of these concepts are hard to understand. Scientists tend to compress much information into one word, a word that replaces more cumbersome but perhaps clearer plain English words. Scientists are also prone to "lexical density," the packing of many ideas and themes into each passage of text or turn of conversation. Scientists change commonsense understandings into technical understandings, and they communicate using terms defined by the interlocking of multiple concepts and by very complex technical taxonomies. Scientists create and use "special expressions" not found in everyday speech like "solving the open sentence over D." A scientific language is built of "abstractions" and "objectifications" (processes turned into objects named by nouns like "fission"), "complex nominalizations" (the creative naming of phenomena like "energy instability" by blending everyday words—words from diverse fields of study or new words—and attaching specialized meanings to the blend), and "grammatical metaphors" (the substitution of one image or symbol for another).

Second, science communicators follow different rules and conventions than citizens engaged in daily discourse. The scientific English used in written reports, textbooks, laboratory discourses, and other forms of scientific communication also differs greatly in complexity from that in non-scientific writing (Lemke, 1990; Roth, 2005). Science writing tends to be verbally explicit, technical, serious, authoritative, and oriented toward causal logic. Science writers tend to avoid the informal forms of language, personal feelings, personification, colorful and value-laden phrases, first-person pronouns, reference to fantasy or fiction, and history or historical personalities common to non-scientific discourse. Yet, the demands of life-long profes-sional growth require social workers to read cutting-edge books and studies, attend workshops by scientific experts, and consult with researchers and theorists.

Third, scientists are part of social and cultural worlds quite alien to non-scientists. As members of different racial and ethnic groups differ in language and language use conventions, members of different scientific social worlds differ in symbol sets and symbol use (Duncker, 2001). Therefore, symbols—scientific terms, in this case—can have multiple potential meanings and one needs to understand the culture and context of their use (Gottdiener, 1995). In conversations across science and non-science divides, citizens and scien-tists must communicate with persons of unfamiliar cultural backgrounds. Such cultural differences often contribute to communication failures includ-ing failures in taking the perspective of others, failures in gesturing, failures in coordinating verbal meanings, and failures, generally, in using symbolic resources in ways that facilitate the aligning of individuals lines of action. Misunderstanding is common and conflict may follow. Consider how the brain scientist, the pharmacist, the clinical social worker, and the support group member all assign different, and perhaps conflicting, definitions to the word depression. Culture and language issues often hinder efforts at collaboration among members of a diverse interdisciplinary team.

Translation is necessary but difficult when some theoretical language communities are isolated from other communities like the community of Tangier Island in the Chesapeake Bay, United States. Its residents speak a version of English common to their ancestors and quite unlike the main-stream English. Opportunities for refining meanings based on cross-theory conversations are limited. Work teams may be composed of professional members who speak different theoretical languages and have limited con-tact with each other. Helping groups are composed of social workers speaking an applied scientific language and clients who speak their every-day language. Work teams and helping groups are prone to communication breakdowns. Misunderstandings, instances of non-comprehension, and belated understanding become common. The esoteric and idiosyncratic parts of the different scientific, professional, and layperson languages cannot be brought together easily. In summary, language differences usually indicate underlying cultural differences. A translation between scientific theoretical languages, and native languages then, is not a simple matter because it takes extra efforts to translate both the words and the cultural particularities of diverse language users (Duncker, 2001).

Fourth, power and status issues can also block effective communication and collaborative inquiry (Fujimura, 1991). Scheff (1995), for example, commented on translation and cooperation across university departments. He likened professors to gangsters adopting academic codes similar to the codes of the street. Professors align themselves with a "school of thought" and abide by its norms. Disciplines are super-gangs competing for influence, and the department is the gang's turf. Members signal loyalty to their groups by using its specialized jargon and members secure their prestige and their attachments by distancing themselves discursively from other gangs. This is signaled by hostile and competitive interaction, verbal attacks, or non-recognition of those showing enemy colors.

Expanding on this metaphor, social workers seeking assistance from academic and scientifically oriented sociologists or psychologists may be like foreign travelers venturing naively into dangerous gang territory. Political jockeying undermines efforts to communicate and collaborate successfully across different language communities. These and other barriers to the mastery of scientific theories, and strategies for penetrating the barriers, will be discussed in greater detail in Lesson 15.

Translational research and the need for translational theory

Because of the complexities of the language of science, the proliferation of scientific languages, and the communication and interaction barriers to cooperation between users of different languages, social workers need theory translation. Translation makes communication possible between diverse theoretical communities and between theory specialists, users, testers, and beneficiaries.

The translation research movement has recognized the problems of communication between scientific theorists, science researchers, and knowledge users. The Canadian Institutes of Health Research (2013) recommend concerted efforts to promote knowledge translation, "the exchange, synthesis and ethically-sound application of knowledge—within a complex system of interactions among researchers and users—to accelerate the capture of the benefits of research for Canadians through improved health, more effective services and products, and a strengthened health care system." Some social workers have joined this movement and recommended the emulation of translation researchers and their "practice of translating basic science data or discoveries from the laboratory bench into clinical applications aimed at treating various diseases" (Hudgins and Allen-Meares, 2000, p. 2).

Palinkas and Soydan (2012) offer a working definition of translation as "the rendering from one language or representational system into another, such as from research to practice" (p. 86). Other social workers have developed conceptual frameworks and strategies for translating the language of research into practice (Allen-Meares, Hudgins, Engberg, and Lessnau, 2005; Hudgins and Allen-Meares, 2000). Borrowed from the field of medical science, social workers are beginning to use translation research to builds bridges (or translation centers) connecting the professional arenas of practitioners and researchers.

But progress has been slow. Palinkas and Soydan (2012) report "social work is often excluded in lists of disciplines engaged in translational social science research" (p. 87). Although theory is an important component of professional social work, and, as Fargion (2007) notes theorists and practitioners belong to completely different language groups, the translation research movement generally focuses on the translation of research findings for use. The movement ignores the need to translate theory. Additionally, most translation researchers give limited attention to translation except in the very limited sense of "use." The Canadian Institutes' display of the "Knowledge to Action Process" doesn't even include the term translation. Translation researchers also tend to minimize the complexities of translation from one language to another language. Translational science offers few methodological directives guiding the transformation of theoretical knowledge developed by disciplinary or professional specialists for assessment intervention use.

This failure oddly neglects our history (Forte, 2002). Guided by Jane Addams, settlement workers partnered with University of Chicago academics in the early twentieth century and translated interactionist theories for practical use. During this period, social work became the profession with the distinctive function of "intersystem translation" including the translation of knowledge from the academy for the field (Abbott, 1995). More than fifty years ago, Herzog (1951) conducted an influential survey of social workers and the questions related to daily practice that needed further study. She found four types of important questions and highlighted the fourth need. She wrote: "this fourth group of questions differs from the others in the extent to which it reveals a prerequisite need to translate the concepts of the social sciences into terms more visibly and cogently applicable to social casework" (p. 71).

Social workers have created many frameworks for the integration of theory and practice (ITP) (Forte and LaMade, 2011) but none accounts fully for the barriers of language. In this book, we offer a novel theory translation approach. Assuming that social workers, like all humans, are "symboling" beings who use symbols while interacting with the environment (White, 1962), we conceptualize the planned change process as sense-making translation work and practitioners as translators who can transform and make use of fourteen major theoretical languages (Forte, 2006, 2007, 2009).

Translation in trading zones

A visual aid may help us depict the multi-language terrain where contemporary social workers serve. Figure 0.1 displays the conventional model provided by translation researchers for knowledge utilization. There are three major regions. On the left side, we find theorists, laboratory scientists, and field researchers. These specialists create basic scientific knowledge (not a focus of social work translation) and applied knowledge: research and theory for use in understanding and ameliorating personal and public problems. These knowledge creators work in knowledge production settings: academic departments of universities, scientific laboratories, and research centers. Medical translation experts often refer to these sites as the "bench" referring to the image of a workbench in a lab. The right side is where we find most social workers. The knowledge generated is not ready for use at the hospital bedside (or the private practice office or public service organization). Knowledge must be translated so policy makers, practitioners, and clients can benefit from the advances in science.

How might scientists and applied scientists including social workers from different language communities learn to talk to each other and share knowledge? Here, we need to focus on the middle territory: the places where knowledge creators and knowledge users interact. I will refer to this as the region of trading zones.

The conventional model has several limitations. Participation in trade across disciplinary, specialty, and theoretical boundaries has nuances not captured in Figure 0.1. Galison (1997) developed the concept of "trading zones" while studying conflicts among members of teams of physicists doing "high energy" research. He realized that cooperation was impeded because the scientists were speaking different theoretical languages. Scientific *trading zones* are places where envoys from each social world met to barter and trade their special goods: discoveries, inventions, and tentative theories. In these trading zones, actors cross boundaries, and began to learn their counterparts' language, or, at least, create new words and devices for

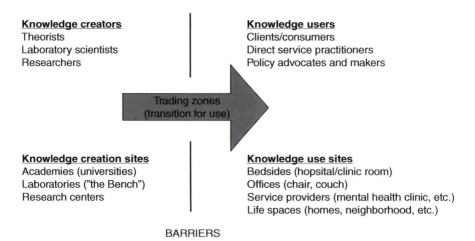

Knowledge creators
Theorists
Laboratory scientists
Researchers

Knowledge users
Clients/consumers
Direct service practitioners
Policy advocates and makers

Trading zones
(transition for use)

Knowledge creation sites
Academies (universities)
Laboratories ("the Bench")
Research centers

Knowledge use sites
Bedsides (hopsital/clinic room)
Offices (chair, couch)
Service providers (mental health clinic, etc.)
Life spaces (homes, neighborhood, etc.)

BARRIERS

Figure 0.1 Knowledge sites and translation

communicating. The common language was like a Creole, a communication system originating from contact between two different speech communities. Even when trading agents held totally different viewpoints and spoke distinctive scientific languages, the common language built up in the trading zone made cooperation and exchange possible.

If we update the translational research model using the concept of trading zones, we must make several more additions. First, trade is a two-way and reciprocal process. Social work practitioners make use of academic and research knowledge but they also report back on the quality of the knowledge and on ideas of how it might be refined for better use at the bedside, couch, or clinic. The arrow should point in both directions. Specifically, practitioners generate knowledge too, knowledge grounded in specific contexts and particular problem solving projects. This knowledge should be communicated to and used by theorists and researchers.

Second, the conventional model leaves out important contributors to successful trades, translators. Thagard (2005) summarizes the findings about successful trading zones for transactions between members of intersecting scientific social worlds. Successful trades require the presence of adventurous traders or envoys, people who model the processes of initiating, negotiating, communicating, and trading across language differences and symbolic boundaries. Kuhn (1970) summarized this stance neatly. In examining interaction between adherents to different theoretical paradigms, Kuhn argued "briefly put, what the participants in a communication breakdown can do is recognize each other as members of different language communities and become translators" (p. 202). For example, in the case of social work, classroom educators, field liaisons, and supervisors can assume the role of translator and facilitate trading processes. They translate the texts of knowledge creators and expedite knowledge exchange between knowledge creation (university classrooms) and knowledge use sites (agency settings). Additionally, translators can create hospitable places that encourage communication and collaboration across social worlds – seminars in agencies including academic experts, researchers, and practitioners, for instance. Translators might create organizations and journals that support and reward theoretical translation work and mutually beneficial trade encounters.

Third, although Thagard (2005) doesn't use the notion of "translation devices" (an omission common to translational researchers, too), he notes that successful trading zones were characterized by the use of communication tools. These tools or *translation devices* included concepts and metaphors that enabled trading partners to transcend their differences and conduct satisfying business. In this book, I will model the role of translator, introduce a set of seven translation devices, and use these devices to translate fourteen theoretical languages for use by social work practitioners.

A sense-making approach to translation

I would like to take a brief but important detour and summarize my approach to theory translation. It blends ideas from two closely related theoretical traditions: semiotics and symbolic interactionism.

Semiotics is the science of all systems of signs, and *social semiotics* is the study of how people use signs in specific social and cultural circumstances to construct the life of a community (Halliday, 1978; Lemke, 1990). A *sign* is an inclusive concept defined as "anything that stands for something (the object) in such a way as to generate another sign (its interpretant)" (Colapietro, 1993, p. 180). There are three commonly identified signs or types of representations: icon, index, and symbol. Scientists use diagrams, for example, as *icons*: representations with important similarities or resemblances to the studied aspect of reality. Science teachers use their fingers to *index* or point to an object important to the laboratory experiment. A *symbol* is anything—a word, nonverbal gesture, object, action, or style of appearance—that by agreement is used to represent something else. Symbols are signs connected by social convention to that which they represent. The term, chronic depression, has an agreed upon meaning, for example, to clinical social workers at a specific mental health agency.

Symbolic interactionism is a theoretical perspective with origins in the social philosophy and psychology of George Herbert Mead and the practice experiments of Jane Addams at Hull-House (Forte, 2006). Interactionists prioritize the study of symbols especially as critical components of language, and make less frequent reference to the concept, sign, or to sign systems constituted of elements other than words and gestures. The symbolic interactionist perspective focuses on the symbolic and the interactive together as they are experienced in everyday life. It looks at how the meanings attached to symbols emerge during social interaction and how people use these shared and conventional meanings to do things together.

We might refer to the combined tradition as *semiotic interactionism* (Forte, 2006), a theoretical perspective that merges elements from symbolic interactionism and semiotics and provides useful conceptual and methodological tools for theory translation work. However, this is a cumbersome term. Instead, lets refer to this blended framework as *a sense-making approach*. This refers neatly to the process by which people attach meaning to objects, events, words, and experiences and affirms the work of an important pioneer in theorizing and theory translation, Karl Weick (1995).

The work of making sense of scientific theories can take three forms (Jakobson, 1965; Sarukkai, 2001). *Intralingual translation* is a process of translation within a single language: the rewording or paraphrasing of concepts (significant symbols) or phrases by means of other concepts (significant symbols) or phrases from the same language. For instance, the translator uses different interactionist words and phases to communicate the same meanings assigned to the interactionist notion of "self" by a formalizer of the tradition, Herbert Blumer.

Interlinqual translation is translation across languages, the rewording of texts (sets of symbols) in one theoretical language by mean of sets of symbols from another language. For instance, great theorists wrote many classical texts on human behavior in foreign languages (German by Sigmund Freud or Russian by Lev Vygotsky, for examples) and their books had to be translated into English for use by North American theorists and theory users. In a second example, we could consider the work of some ambitious behaviorists who offered translations from the source language of psychoanalysis into the target language of behaviorism.

Our last type of translation is called *intersemiotic translation*, the translation from one type of sign to another type of sign. Science uses many different types of sciences, and scientists are familiar with varied scientific representations including words, pictures, diagrams, and mathematical formulas. A common act of intersemiotic translation involves rendering the verbal content of a theory text (symbols) into diagrams of the theory (icons). We will return to this idea of translation types later when we review the major translation devices.

Figure 0.2 expands on the discussion so far of science as a language and of theory–practice integration as a translation process. It also relates semiotic interactionism, our sense-making approach, to the planned change process. The display was inspired by Barnard's conceptualization (2004) of the processes common to the practical application of science.

The first column focuses on the process of hearing and making sense of *client representations*. These are the words, images, gestures, and so on that clients use to characterize their personal dimensions, their environmental contexts, their interaction with these contexts, and the challenges that bring them to the helping professional. Translation begins at the first exchange between worker and client.

The second column refers to the *scientific representations* that the worker offers as resources for informing the inquiry into the puzzle experienced by the client and for identifying possible puzzle solutions or interventions. These representations are parts of interpretive frameworks or theoretical traditions that influence perception, conceptualization, and communication during the planned change process. William James (1907/1955) articulated this view of science when he argued:

> no theory is absolutely a transcript of reality, but that any one of them may from some point of view be useful. Their great use is to summarize old facts and to lead to new ones. They are only a man-made language, a conceptual shorthand, as some one calls them, in which we write our reports of nature.

(p. 48)

Client's construction of experiences as a system interacting with environment. Facing Puzzling challenges (events and structures)	Theories (tools) (14 interpretive frameworks) Theories to inform Theories to intervene	Partipatory discovery translation – nature of challenge Partipatory prescriptive translation – possible actions	Translation products Working hypotheses and plans of action
Client representations	Science representations	Bridging representations	Mutually constructed puzzle–resolving representations

Moment-to-moment co-translation of client/helping team communication

Science representations (interpretive frameworks) = Perceptual-conceptual symbol systems (theoretical languages) for perceiving, understanding, acting and communicating
Bridging representations = Universal translation devices

Participatory discovery translation uses engagement via metaphor, information gathering via major terms, problem spcification via middle-range causal theories, assessment summary via eco-maps, and so on
and
Particpatory prescriptive translation uses intervention selection via exemplary models, intervention specification via mapping if/then generalizations, evaluation planning via major terms and middle-range theorizing, and so on.

Figure 0.2 A translation approach to theory–practice integration

Planned change processes can be grouped into two major categories: discovery and prescription. Translation devices such as metaphorical imagining, middle-range theorizing, and theory/person-in-environment (PIE) mapping are ways of translating client and scientific representations into *bridging representations,* provisional formulations of the detailed nature of the challenge. Translation devices such as exemplar profiling, mapping interventions, and evaluation with reference to major theoretical terms are ways of translating client and scientific representations into provisional prescriptions for problem solving or ameliorative action.

In a process of dialogue, the practitioner and client consider the bridging representations that merge translations of clients representations and translations of scientific representations and from these construct together their preferred puzzle explaining (explanatory hypotheses) and *puzzle resolving representations* (plans of action). Of course, other sources of knowledge— client and worker's intuition, personal wisdom, and research base—enhance this mutual construction work on the project of making sense of the PIE challenge and taking sensible action to address effectively the challenge.

Universal translators

Universal translators are devices for translating theoretical languages into words, phrases, narratives, images, displays, and into combined symbols such as directives for inquiry (the nature of the challenge) or judgments for use (possible intervention actions) by practitioners. They are universal in that they serve to translate any scientific theory in ways that bridge client representations, the science representations, and worker-client representations of explanatory hypotheses and action plans. Figure 0.3 summarizes the universal devices presented in this book for translating fourteen theoretical languages. The first row represents the possible target or source of knowledge including articles, studies, books, elements of theses texts (paragraphs, sentences, words, diagrams, images), and secondary literature including biographies of theorists, studies of theories and their use, critiques of theories and theoretical arguments. In the second row, I summarize the translation device. Translation devices are presented in alphabetical order from left to right. Following the use of translation devices, knowledge is transformed creatively into the products listed in the third row; products that can guide the planned change process such as dictionaries of major terms or theory displays.

Target (icon, indices, symbols, combos)	Theory paragraph sentence, word	Theory books, articles, exegeses	Theory test-cases, studies, critiques	Theorist writings and quotes	Theory canon with figures of speech images	Applied theory articles, books, studies	Theorist history and bios
Translation device	Major terms	Maps (eco-maps and structure maps)	Marks of excellence	Memorable words	Metaphors – root and conveyance	Middle range theory – concepts, propositions	Models-role
Product	Dictionary	Display of theory elements	Judgment of quality	Directives practical theorizing	Portraits of client, worker, change, setting	Report – causes or effects, relations, links: themes	Profiles with lessons for inquiry and action

Translation for use

Theory-informed constructions for each phase of planned change including
Working hypotheses
(about nature of puzzling challenge)
and
Plans of action
(for resolution of puzzle

Figure 0.3 Knowledge translation devices

Major term interpreting

Major term interpreting is a translation process of identifying the major terms or key words of a theoretical language and rendering them into other words from the theory (intralinqual translation, into Standard English terms or into the idiomatic language preferred by the client (interlingual translation). When studying a culture, linguists attempt to identify its major terms or key words. These are the words that "are particularly important and revealing in a given culture" (Wierzbicka, 1997, pp. 15–16). Major terms are used frequently and serve often as the center of many clusters of phrases. For example, "freedom" is a very important concept in the United States. It is commonly used by politicians, by advertisers, and by citizens and it is associated with many common phrases like freedom of speech, freedom from hunger or poverty, and freedom to act. Key words can be studied as focal points, Wierzbicka (a linguist) recommends, to understand particular domains of a culture. Fargion (2007) asserts that the mastery of theoretical language also requires training in the use of the key words recognized by full members of the language community.

Each theoretical language includes key concepts or words, and those who speak the theoretical language must understand and be able to use these key concepts. Theory understanding and use requires mastery of a theory's vocabulary. The dictionary of the symbolic interactionist language, for instance, includes major terms like meaning, situation, definition of the situation, role, role taking, identity, self, symbol, and coordinated action. This and other theories can be revealingly studied and used through study of its major terms.

The new word or phrase will be consistently used to represent the original and to make sense of the theoretical knowledge in the helping content; like words in a conventional dictionary, however, a theoretical term may have several meanings (Albert and Anderson, 2009). The practitioner as translator can create a "listeners' dictionary." This includes the list of major terms, their abbreviations and their meanings, and instructions for transforming strange theoretical expressions into familiar expressions (Duncker, 2001). Heise (2007), for example, provided nominal definitions of 45 interactionist concepts central to his Affect Control Theory of role performances and identities in a plain English dictionary. The social work translator might create dictionaries of varied technical precision depending on perceptions of the threshold competencies of the client in understanding and using scientific theories.

Mapping theory

Mapping theory is the visual representation of a theory and its elements to guide assessment formulation and intervention planning. Mapping theoretical structure is an intersemiotic translation process (across two different types of sign systems) when the translation product is a diagram and an intralingual process (within the same language) when the product is a narrative. There are two major variants of this translation approach.

Translation by a structural map is a sense-making tool inspired by the pragmatist philosopher Charles Sanders Peirce's use of the term architectonic to describe the systematic form of a body of knowledge (Forte, 2007). Theorists create a structure or systematic form on which the detailed elements of their approach to understanding human conduct are built. An architectonic or structural map identifies all the major components of a scientific text or canon (assumptions, concepts, propositions, and theories) and the paths connecting these components. Familiarity with the overall theoretical structure facilitates generalized discourse among those interested in the framework and supports effective use of the theory.

Translation by eco-maps is a way of representing visually how multiple theoretical insights inform a comprehensive assessment summary of a "person interacting in an environment to meet a challenge". During the information gathering and assessment phase, the practitioner can translate theory-informed observations into the visual language of the eco-map and supplement this with a written narrative.

The "mapping theory" translation device recognizes that theory users think and work with concepts but they are also think and work with visual tools. Maps, diagrams, charts, and other displays can usefully and concisely represent theories. Maps incorporate elements of a sign system naturally and easily understood by humans. Such maps make theory-based information gathering and hypothesis formulation explicit. Such maps can guide theoretical reasoning during later problem solving intervention and effectiveness evaluation.

Marking excellence

Marking excellence involves the critical reflection on theories by referring to standards including the standards of science, practical standards like relevance, and professional standards such as the affirmation of difference in social work. These are normative statements about how to appraise the quality of theoretical knowledge. The standards transcend any particular theory.

These three types of standards can be used as an interlingual translation process (from theoretical language to standard English) across theories to enrich critical thinking about issues of quality. Scientific standards are based on notions of ideal scientific practice and include parsimony, testability, explanatory power, predictive power, and scope. Professional social work standards are derived from the profession's identity and core commitments.

They include a strengths orientation, appreciation of social justice, affirmation of difference, holistic or bio-psycho-social-spiritual explanations, ethical and values integrity, attention to varied size-systems and life stages, and empirical support. Practical standards emerge from the need to use theoretical knowledge to complete particular tasks in specific settings. They include degree of articulation of theory elements and communicability, relevance, and ease of use (Forte, 2006).

Memorable word exegesis

Memorable word exegesis refers to the critical reflection on quotations from exemplary theorists and scholarly practitioners. Exegesis is a term from studies of the bible and other sacred texts. Scholars contend that careful interpretation of particular biblical passages can produce insights into their meanings. These insights can guide searchers for spiritual revelations and comforts.

Theory users can interpret and translate memorable words interlinqually from theoretical texts about the importance of theory to practitioners. Quotations can provide general inspiration for practical theorizing endeavors. For example, Bruce Thyer (2008), a leading social work educator and research promoter wrote: "the integration of theory and practice is one of the hallmarks of a fully developed professional" (pp. xiii–xxvi). Or theory users might find inspiration for specific helping tasks or particular phases of the helping process by reflecting on the memorable words of great theorists and theory users. I will begin each lesson in this book with a suitable quotation.

Metaphorical imagining

Metaphorical imagining is the comparison of theoretical ideas to everyday objects. Pepper (1942), a philosopher, brought direction to the decoding of complicated theoretical languages. He argued that each framework of thought is built on a root metaphor. *Root metaphors* are basic comparisons that a theorist uses to make sense of an overall theoretical framework or disciplinary stance toward human development. Some theorists compare society to a machine; some to a living organism; some to one type among many types of social organization; and some to the historical process. Understanding a theory's root metaphors can deepen our conceptual grasp of the person, the environment, the change process, and the social worker as we imagine and extend the core comparison. For instance, if society is like a machine, then the person is like a mechanical part. If the person is a part in a social machine, then the social worker is somewhat like a mechanic.

These metaphorical comparisons are common among social workers using structural functionalist theory.

Conveyance metaphors are comparisons of more limited scope that theorists use to make sense of a selective aspect of human development or behavior (MacCormac, 1985). Human development theorists, for instance, have used varied conveyance metaphors (Forte, 2009). Development has been compared to advances in argumentative ability (Kohlberg), to competition for survival in a jungle (Darwin), to the gradual mastery associated with an apprenticeship process (George Herbert Mead), and to the developing of friendships and other reciprocal, caring relationships (Gilligan).

Translation by metaphorical imagining is an interlingual (across two or more languages) translation process (Jakobson, 1965). It requires the examination of scientific texts for words, phrases, and themes indicating the theorist's or the researcher's use of symbols from everyday English (objects, events, processes, places, and so on) to represent important elements of the scientific theory or research.

Translation by metaphorical imagining metaphors helps social worker practitioners understand various human behavior and developmental theories as theory groups organized by similarities in foundational metaphors. Likewise, metaphorical imagining helps social workers differentiate and judge theories by an examination of distinctive metaphorical underpinnings and associated basic assumptions (Albert and Anderson, 2009). In practice situations, the worker and the client can use metaphorical imagining to decide which theories might be used sequentially during inquiry; each focuses information gathering on different aspects of the person-environment-time configuration. Drawing from reviewed literature, preliminary information gathering and analysis, and hunches, the worker can engage in the metaphorical imagining of varied theory-based images and phrases to produce trial representations of client problem, worker role, and other aspects of planned change process (Cornelissen, 2006). Translation by metaphorical imagining can also prepare clients for communicating with help providers and other collaterals committed to varied theoretical languages.

Middle-range theorizing

Middle-range theorizing is the creation of conceptualizations and narratives of small-scale theoretical models that represent a theory-informed case. Such theorizing is an intralingual translation process of transforming a scientific text into a theoretical or conceptual statement, and an intersemiotic translation process when accompanied by a diagram or map. Middle-range theoretical models with visual displays employ symbols (terms and their meanings) but also have an iconic function (a design meant to represent an object or process in important ways) and an indexical function (notation indicating and pointing to persons, processes, relationships, organizations).

Middle-range theorizing falls in level of abstraction between the specific observations and minor generalizations that emerge during daily practice and the all inclusive and systematic theories designed to explain all the uniformities of society. Middle-range theories are built with a limited number of concepts (less than seven, for instance) and a limited number of relationships between these concepts. A middle-range theory may include, for example, only four or five propositions.

Translation by middle-range theorizing may produce a causal theoretical model summarizing the major causes of a client problem or challenge. Translation by middle-range theorizing might also produce a process model summarizing the key personal and social processes leading to a turning point. Middle-range theoretical translations can help practitioners guide the process of gathering information about biological, psychological, social, and spiritual factors relevant to a case; organize their observations; connect case details to a theory and its elements; generate possible intervention hypotheses for change process; structure the evaluation of helping effectiveness; and present their theoretical work concisely to clients and colleagues.

Model profiling

Model profiling is the characterizing and imitating of exemplary theorists with reference to their contributions to the assessment or intervention process. Much can be learned, for example, from studies of the lives of practical theorists like Jane Addams, Patricia Hill Collins, William Edward Burghardt "W. E. B." Du Bois, Carol Gilligan, or Erik Erikson. Such lessons, however, need to be translated for practical use.

Translation by profiling is an interlingual translation process. The record of the lives of useful theorists and scholarly practitioners including their classic texts, their quotations, their public service history, and their accounts of practical theorizing are studied for their value as a guide to helping work. A profile of a role model or exemplar translates into everyday English, for example, what the exemplar's life represents as a model for knowledge creation and knowledge use. The profile may show how the archaic language of an original and important article by the theorist translates into contemporary verbiage, or how a particular text by an exemplar translates into directives for helping tasks like engaging a client, setting helping goals, or fostering mutual inquiry into person–problem–context interconnections. A profile may show the ways that the life of an exemplar signifies a sympathetic commitment to the ideals of the social work tradition (appreciation of diversity, promotion of democratic principles, advocacy for at-risk groups) or the ways the life signifies an abandonment of such ideals.

Translation by profiling exemplary theorists is also a strategy for translating a theory for intervention purposes. This sense-making task requires the practitioner to imagine that he or she could ask a theory's exemplars for intervention advice and then after immersing himself or herself in the accounts of the exemplar's professional life use this imagined advice to increase professional effectiveness. For example, we might ask "What would Jane Addams and perhaps a team including Addams and her theoretical colleagues at the University of Chicago (John Dewey, George Herbert Mead, William Isaac Thomas) do to deal with current inequities, violence, or hate?"

Translation and the planned change process

There are many different ways that theorists talk about and explain the predicaments faced by our clients. Each theoretical language provides a distinctive vocabulary for gathering information, formulating an assessment, and developing explanatory hypotheses about the puzzling challenge. For example, psychoanalytic theorists talk about the use of "free association" to identify "repressed impulses," while feminists prefer a strategy involving "liberating social criticism" of the pervasive negative effects of "sexism." Each theoretical language also recommends distinctive action strategies for resolving the PIE puzzle and improving the PIE situation (lengthy psychoanalysis versus collective social action, for instance), and each offers a theoretically based discourse for conceptualizing the worker role (passive or active, expert or partner, detached or involved, and so on) and how the worker engages, supports, and ends with the client system.

However, each theoretical language must be translated from technical and complex abstractions into specific and comprehensible words, sentences, paragraphs, and images for practical use during the helping process (Forte, 2006). Specifically, a theory translator can interpret theoretical knowledge to direct every phase of the planned change process including engagement, assessment, intervention, and evaluative activities. Universal translators will make the job of translation manageable.

Figure 0.4 provides illustrations of how translation devices can be used differentially across the major phases of the helping process with consideration of multiple theoretical languages.

Multi-theoretical engagement involves the selective and purposeful use of diverse styles of relationship in reaching out to vulnerable populations and allies and in challenging villains. Metaphoric imagining can be used to compare and contrast fourteen approaches to the engagement phase, and to select the approach or approaches most suitable for a particular case.

Planned change	Theory guidance
Engagement	Use *metaphors* to guide role selection and performance
Assessment	Use PIE metatheory *map* to guide into gathering Use *major terms* from theory to focus inquiry Use *major terms* and mapped proposition sto inquire Use *metaphors* of theory to generate expanations Use *map* of theory assumptions to prioritize explanations Create theory-based *map* of PIE configuration Forulate *middle range theory* of causes or processes
Goal setting	Contrast actual and ideal eco *map* to suggest goals
Intervention	Transform *major terms* into action directives *Map* elements of theory of change and change logic Create interventions from *Map's* if-then propositions Select interventions by profiles of theory *models* Judge interventions by theory *marks of excellence*
Evaluation	Use theory *major terms* to set outcome and criteria Develop *middle-range theory* for evaluation Judge overall effectiveness of theory use by *marks*
Ending	Use theory *metaphors* to guide ending conceptualization
Overall	Use *memorable words* to inform MTSW

Figure 0.4 Translation tools and the planned change process

Multi-theoretical assessment deepens PIE contexts information gathering and understanding by using polytheoretical inquiry focused on the processes facilitating and restraining individual and collective fulfillment. Our fourteen theories can be used to investigate the liberating and constraining dimensions of personal functioning (biological for sensations, behavioral for actions, cognitive for thoughts, faith tradition for spiritual convictions, and psychodynamic for feelings), transactions between the person and environment (symbolic interactionism for such communication), and the contextual influences on functioning (constructionist for cultural, critical and feminist theories for political, role theory for organizational, social exchange for economic, strengths and resilience perspective for communal contexts, and systems theory for social structure and network influences). Translation devices including the use of major terms, eco-maps, metaphors, and middle-range theories can facilitate information gathering and assessment formulation processes.

Multi-theoretical goal setting uses the major theoretical languages to generate and state images of ideal and desired outcomes for members and communities. Translation of case details into theory-informed actual and ideal eco-maps, for example, can help practitioners identify fourteen different possible and desirable end-states for the helping work.

Multi-theoretical intervention assembles and integrates personal and social action strategies from fourteen theories suitably responsive to the challenges or problems identified during the case formulation. The use of major terms can render concepts from the fourteen theories into change directives. Theoretical mapping helps in the specification of if–then propositions (intervention hypotheses) and in the articulation of the overall change logic. Interventions might be creatively identified by use of profiles of exemplary theorists and judged for suitability by considering salient marks of excellence.

Multi-theoretical evaluation offers the resources of fourteen theories to the practitioner for designing a plan to evaluate effectiveness, efficiency, or satisfaction. Theoretical languages might be translated into specific outcome targets and specific criteria for success using major theoretical terms. Marks of excellence can help social workers and clients judge the theory-informed helping process in line with scientific, practical, and professional standards

Multi-theoretical ending requires the identification of possible complications related to the termination process from multiple theoretical frameworks. Multi-theoretical ending suggests strategies for skilled pluralistic guidance in resolving these issues, ceasing the helping process, and preparing the client system for the future. Conveyance and root metaphors translate fourteen theoretical languages so each serves as a resource for understanding and handing the ending phase.

Finally, memorable quotations from exemplary theorists and scholarly practitioners can provide guidance across the planned change process and at each phase. As indicated earlier, the preface and each lesson in this book will begin with an illuminating quotation to demonstrate this kind of guidance.

Multi-theoretical social work, social work education and competencies

The Council on Social Work Education (CSWE) expects educators to prepare social work students for careers as practitioners who can demonstrate their expertise in reflective and competent action. CSWE defines competencies as "measurable practice behaviors that are comprised of knowledge, values, and skills" (Council on Social Work Education, 2008, p. 3). CSWE has developed guidelines for educational programs. These identify ten core competencies. The competent social worker can demonstrate mastery in the following realms: professional identity and conduct, the use of ethical principles, critical thinking, the engagement of diversity, the advancement of rights and justice, research usage, knowledge application, policy practice, responsiveness to practice contexts, and the use of the planned change process.

CSWE has also identified the specific practice behaviors associated with each competency. For example, Educational Policy and Accreditation

Standard (EPAS) 2.1.7, knowledge application, mandates that social workers achieve the competency necessary "to apply theories and knowledge from the liberal arts to understand biological, social, cultural, psychological, and spiritual development" (p. 6). Such mastery should be demonstrated by two identified practice behaviors: utilizing conceptual frameworks to guide the processes of assessment, intervention, and evaluation and critique and applying knowledge to understand person and environment. EPAS 2.1.10 specifies that competent social workers can "engage, assess, intervene, and evaluate with individuals, families, groups, organizations, and communities" and specific practice behaviors are listed for each of the four phases.

Chambers recommended long ago:

> a call to the National Association of Social Workers committee on certification of competence to insure that, among other things, certification is based on the ability of the candidate to cognitively command *rival* explanatory sets, choose among them, and extrapolate them to practice behaviors, policy formulations, or program designs.
>
> (1973, p. 42; italics in original)

The CSWE statement offers minimal guidance in response to this mandate to teach practitioners to manage theoretical pluralism. Additionally, the Council chose to remain mute on the details of the specific knowledge, skills, techniques, and attitudes that constitute each practice behavior. This book begins to remedy the problems caused by these omissions.

Purpose of this book

From the starting point of CSWE Core Competency 2.1.7 and Core Competency 2.1.10, my approach prepares students for expertise in the use of multiple frameworks or theories and theorizing skills across the phases of the planned change process. This primer will increase the reader's adept use of multiple theoretical languages to guide processes of engagement, goal setting, information gathering and assessment formulation, intervention, evaluation, and ending. For example, the reader will learn new ways to use contemporary theories in a reflective and critical way to address the personal and public problems of varied client systems. The book will also help the reader better understand the relationship between theory, theorizing, practice choices, and effective outcomes, and the book will help make the reader's practice more theoretical.

Let me make a few comments here on my adaptations of the CSWE competencies statement. First, I include some additional processes of the planned change such as information gathering, goal setting, and ending.

The Council didn't specify these processes but they are important phases of helping work and merit attention.

Second, the Council on Social Work Education uses the term "conceptual framework." This term has multiple meanings. It can refer to a set of ideas and related assumptions about human behavior and the environment in a usage that is broader and less precise than the term "theory" (Weis, 1998). Or it can follow Levy (1978) who recommends the use of the term "conceptual framework" as a variation of the term, practice theory: an organized constellation of concepts used to guide inquiry, assessment, and intervention. Researchers use the term "conceptual framework" as a theoretical framework that guides important phases of the research process including problem definition, methodological design, data gathering, and data analysis. Sheafor and Horesji (2008) define conceptual framework as a framework "composed of a coherent set of concepts, beliefs, values, propositions, assumptions, hypotheses, and principles. Such a framework can be thought of as an outline of ideas that help one to understand people, how people function, and how people change" (p. 46). They consider it an umbrella term that includes orienting and explanatory "Human Behavior and the Social Environment" theory, practice theory, and theoretical orientation (the practitioner's synthesis of explanatory and practice theories). I am sympathetic to this definition, and will use conceptual framework as a term equivalent to theoretical framework or language.

Finally, I assume that social work's territory is vast and the profession serves in a wide range of fields while addressing numerous different and complex personal and public problems. There has been a proliferation of theoretical languages in the last thirty years and many of these are valuable resources for practice. Therefore, contemporary social workers will improve their competence and effectiveness if they make use of multiple theories.

Lessons

Each lesson is focused on a particular theorizing skill necessary for multi-theoretical social work; a skill is knowledge combined with a set of actions designed to accomplish a particular outcome (Sheafor and Horesji, 2008). Each of the eighteen lessons provides detailed information about the knowledge and action components (and in some cases, attitude components) of the skill while referencing the relevant practice behavior(s) attached to the Council on Social Work Education's core competencies. Each lesson includes a title, a commentary synthesizing necessary information about the skill, learning and reflection activities, and related references. The title includes a skill name, a number, and linkage to the core competencies/practice behaviors addressed by the lesson. The commentary provides the knowledge necessary to understand the skill and to use it effectively. Following the commentary are included a set of learning/reflection activities. Most lessons include learning activities focused on the use of fourteen human behavior theories and on the use of fourteen major human development theories.

Doing these lessons with fellow students, colleagues, mentors, or teachers provides the practice necessary to transform the skills into habitual ways of thinking, communicating, and acting. Talking about and practicing the skills with more expert social workers can help the reader develop the professional dispositions for their adept use in specific practice circumstances. Each lesson also includes a set of references for further exploration of the relevant knowledge and skill information. Key terms are included in the lessons, printed in italics, and listed in an appendix. The set of key terms included as this appendix represents a multi-theoretical vocabulary for practical theorizing. Many lessons include a figure or display to guide multi-theoretical social work and enhance the reader's understanding of the lesson's content.

Section 1 lessons provide a foundation for multi-theoretical social work. Lessons focus on skills related to the general uses of theoretical knowledge, the identification of factors influencing one's preferred theoretical orientation, the alternative approaches to the proliferation of scientific theories, the suitability of a pluralistic stance to modern practice, and the use of a PIE metatheory to organize theory-informed practice.

Section 2 lessons focus on skills related to the use of fourteen theoretical languages or frameworks across the phases of the planned change process. These include the selective and purposeful use of theoretical languages to guide engagement, information gathering and assessment formulation processes; goal setting; the use of theories to guide the selection of intervention strategies and to specify the change theory and logic for a given case; and the use of theoretical languages to guide the evaluation and ending processes. Commentaries and learning activities for these lessons also focus on the adaptation of theories to client membership factors and to features of the helping context.

Section 3 offers lessons relevant to a career as a multi-theoretical social worker. These include lessons on overcoming barriers to knowledge exchange, participating in multidisciplinary teams, and developing integrative multi-theory personal practice models. The book closes with section 4, a presentation on the role of multi-theory translators in the advancement of our professional careers and the social work profession.

Audience

This book, *An Introduction to Using Theory in Social Work Practice*, will be useful to varied readers. Social work educators eager to teach a multi-theoretical stance toward social work practice can use this book fruitfully.

These lessons include learning activities and useful tables. Therefore, the book could be used in a practice with individuals course and in advanced practice courses. Human behavior educators can make productive use of this book. I use this book in my Human Behavior and the Social Environment (HBSE) theory survey course to demonstrate the application of theory to practice. Students work on one to two lessons per week in class for face-to-face sections, and my students work on these lessons online as part of a discussion board in my hybrid sections.

Novice practitioners can read the book, study the commentaries, and complete the learning/reflection activities as a way to begin to master and speak fourteen different theoretical languages. Experienced practitioners can speed their progress toward *theoretical multilingualism*, the ability to converse fluently about a particular client and with particular colleagues in a number of theoretical languages (Clarkson, 1992), by reading this book and completing the learning activities.

Conclusion: translating theories for practice

Translation is the act of translating from one language into another, rendering meanings intelligible across languages (Forte, 2002). A *translator* is a person who specializes in providing equivalent terms in a target language for the terms in a source language (Sarukkai, 2002). Social work theory translators can provide translations for practical use that are logically consistent, supported by evidence, and useful for applications in relevant contexts. In this preface, I have suggested repeatedly that theoretical languages are indispensible tools for speaking and doing social work, and that contemporary social work practitioners need to learn to use many different theoretical languages. This book offers readers an opportunity to add the role of theory translator to their repertoire of professional roles. Here I will preview the potential benefits of theory translation. We will return to many of these ideas in later lessons.

As a translator using a multi-theory orientation, the practitioner is more likely to develop a comprehensive and detailed depiction of the many aspects of the client-concern-context configuration than by using no theory or one theory (Greene, 1999). This improves client assessment work. The practitioner conversant and fluent in many theoretical languages (and in marks of excellence for theory critique) can avoid the theories that have been shown to cause harm to clients (Turner, 1999). Translation of multiple theories can also increase worker effectiveness because the worker selects from a variety of theoretical languages the ones that provide the deepest understanding and the ones that work best in the particular situation (Rosen, 1988). More theoretical choices for the worker means more possibilities for understanding and generating ameliorative action (Payne, 1997) and more likelihood of a maximal positive impact based on the differential use of theories (Turner,

1996). Practitioners adept at multi-theory translation, in short, are likely to provide better service to their clients (Reid, 1998).

As a translator, the practitioner can render theoretical terms and other professional jargon into plain English for the sake of clients. Thus reduces confusion, lessons the distance between practitioner and client, and is likely to increase client commitment to the working agreement. Practitioners adept at theory translation can communicate appropriately in writing and orally to judges, administrators, family members of a client, and non-professional colleagues because the practitioner can use the audience members' preferred language and can translate scientific terminology work into a language appropriate to the recipient of the communication.

Multi-lingual practitioners can use the appropriate theoretical languages to explain their practice choices at case conferences and in supervisory meetings with helpers from other theoretical backgrounds. As translators, these practitioners can aid participants of work teams and helping groups as they try to take each other's perspective and understand what the other is trying to say. The translator can help participants learn the basics of each other's language. The translator can convert the theoretical language of one subgroup into the terms of the other group. The translator can help participants develop a common and shared vocabulary. The translator can also help the participants in a multi-theory dialogue begin to learn the craft of translation so they can undertake efforts on their own to clarify misunderstandings.

As a translator, the practitioner can translate scientific languages into language understandable by the general public so that the knowledge and skills developed by social workers can be shared with a wide audience. Additionally, practitioners might translate lessons from their revisions of theoretical knowledge in the practice setting for use by knowledge creators at academic and research sites.

Social work has a special need for all practitioners and educators to become theory translators. Let's return to our starting conception of the profession. Social work, according to Bloom, Wood, and Chambon (1991):

> may be the multilingual profession par excellence because it deals with many dialects of lay language, borrows heavily from many basic sciences, uses research findings and methods from a variety of disciplines, is involved in value considerations from diverse points of view, and has chaotic and uncontrolled jargon.
>
> (p. 530)

Coady and Lehmann (2001) concur, and they "support the long-range goal of translating theories into ordinary English in order to further demystification and to facilitate cross-theory dialogue" (p. 415). This book addresses these concerns, and provides resources for the cultivation of the multi-theoretical social workers deemed essential to our profession's growth.

References

Abbott, A. (1995). Boundaries of social work or social work of boundaries? *Social Service Review, 69*, 545–562.

Albert, S. and Anderson, M. H. (2009). Conceptual translation: A metatheoretical program for construction, critique, and integration of theory. *Journal of Management Inquiry, 19* (1), 34–46.

Allen-Meares, P., Hudgins, C. A., Engberg, M. E. and Lessnau, B. (2005). Using a collaboratory model to translate social work research into practice and policy. *Research on Social Work Practice, 15* (1), 29–40.

Barnard, P. J. (2004). Bridging between basic theory and clinical practice. *Behavior Research and Therapy, 42*, 977–1000.

Bloom, M., Wood, K. and Chambon, A. (1991). The six languages of social work. *Social Work, 36* (6), 530–534.

Brown, R. H. (1992). Science and society as discourse: Toward a sociology of civic competence. In S. Seidman and D. G. Wagner (Eds), *Postmodernism and social theory: The debate over general theory* (pp. 223–243). Cambridge, MA: Basil Blackwell.

Canadian Institutes of Health Research (2013). Knowledge translation publications. Retrieved July 3, 2013 from http://cihr-irsc.gc.ca/e/39128.html.

Chambers, D. E. (1973). Three principles of a knowledge-guided social work practice. *Journal of Social Welfare, 11*, 35–43.

Clarkson, P. (1992). Systemic integrative psychotherapy training. In W. Dryden (Ed.), *Integrative and eclectic psychotherapy: A handbook* (pp. 269–295). Buckingham: Open University Press.

Coady, N. and Lehmann, P. (2001). Revisiting the generalist-eclectic approach. In P. Lehmann and N. Coady (Eds), *Theoretical perspectives for direct social work practice: A generalist-eclectic approach* (pp. 405–420). New York: Springer.

Colapietro, V. M. (1993). *Glossary of semiotics.* New York: Paragon House.

Cornelissen, J. P. (2006). Making sense of theory construction: Metaphor and disciplined imagination. *Organization Studies, 27* (11), 1579–1597.

Council on Social Work Education (2008). *Educational policy and accreditation standards.* Retrieved June 16, 2010, from www.cswe.org/Accreditation/Reaffirmation.aspx.

Duncker, E. (2001). Symbolic communication in multidisciplinary cooperations. *Science, Technology, and Human Values, 26*, pp. 349–386.

Fararo, T. J. (1989). The spirit of unification in sociological theory. *Sociological Theory, 7* (2), 175–190.

Fargion, S. (2007). Theory and practice: A matter of words, language, knowledge and professional community in social work. *Social Work and Society, 5* (1), 62–77.

Forte, J. A. (2002). Mead, contemporary metatheory, and twenty-first-century interdisciplinary team work. *Sociological Practice: A Journal of Clinical and Applied Sociology, 4*, 315–334.

Forte, J. A. (2006). *Human behavior and the social environment: Models, metaphors, and maps for applying theoretical perspectives to practice.* Belmont, CA: Thomson Brooks/Cole.

Forte, J. A. (2007). Using a semiotic metatheory for theory understanding, appraisal, and use: An illustrative social work translation of the affect control theory of emotions. *Advances in Social Work, 8* (1), 1–18.

Forte, J. A. (2009). Translating theory and research for interactionist practice: A signs, symbols, and social worlds approach. *Humboldt Journal of Social Relations, 32* (1), 86–122.

Forte, J. A. and LaMade, J. (2011). The center cannot hold: A survey of field instructors' theoretical preferences and propensities. *The Clinical Supervisor, 30* (1), 72–94.

Fujimura, J. H. (1991). On methods, ontologies, and representation in the sociology of science: Where do we stand? In D. R. Maines (Ed.), *Social organization and social process: Essays in honor of Anselm Strauss* (pp. 207–247). Hawthorne, NY: Aldine de Gruyter.

Galison, P. (1997). *Image and logic: A material culture of microphysics.* Chicago: The University of Chicago Press.

Gergen, K. J. (1982). *Toward transformation in social knowledge.* New York: Springer-Verlag.

Gottdiener, M. (1995). *Postmodern semiotics: Material culture and the forms of postmodern life.* Cambridge, MA: Blackwell.

Greene, R. R. (1999). *Human behavior theory and social work practice* (2nd ed.). New York: Aldine de Gruyter.

Greenwood, E. G. (1955). Social science and social work: A theory of their relationship. *Social Service Review, 29* (1), 20–33.

Halliday, M. A. K. (1978). *Language as social semiotic: The social interpretation of language and meaning.* Baltimore, MD: University Park Press.

Halliday, M. A. K. and Martin, J. R. (1993). *Writing science: Literacy and discursive power.* Pittsburgh, PA: University of Pittsburgh Press.

Heise, D. R. (2007). *Expressive order: Confirming sentiments in social actions.* New York: Springer.

Herzog, E. G. (1951). What social casework wants of social science research. *American Sociological Review, 16* (1), 68–73.

Hudgins, C. A. and Allen-Meares, P. (2000). Translation research: A new solution to an old problem. *Journal of Social Work Education, 36* (1), 2–5

Jakobson, R. (1965). On linguistic aspects of translation. In R. A. Brower (Ed.), *On translation* (pp. 223–239). New York: Oxford University Press.

James, W. (1907/1955). What pragmatism means. In *Pragmatism and four essays from "The Meaning of Truth"* (pp. 41–62). New York: Meridian.

Joas, H. (1993). *Pragmatism and American sociology.* Chicago: University of Chicago Press.

King, I. M. and Fawcett, J. (1997). *The language of nursing theory and metatheory.* Indianapolis, IN: Sigma Theta Tau International.

Kuhn, T. S. (1970). *The structure of scientific revolutions* (2nd ed.). Chicago: University of Chicago Press.

Lee, J. A. and Swensen, C. R. (1978). Theory in action: A community social service agency. *Social Casework, 59,* 359–370.

Lemke, J. (1990). *Talking science.* Westport, CT: Ablex.

Levy, C. (1978). On concepts, conceptualization, and conceptual frameworks. *Social Work, 23* (5), 351–353.

MacCormac, E. R. (1985). *A cognitive theory of metaphor*. Cambridge, MA: MIT.

Mead, G. H. (1934). *Mind, self and society*. Chicago: University of Chicago Press.

Morris, C. (1946). The significance of the unity of science movement. *Philosophy and Phenomenological Research*, 6 (4), 508–515.

Palinkas, L. A. and Soydan, H. (2012). New horizons of translational research and research translation in social work. *Research on Social Work Practice*, 22 (1), 85–92.

Payne, M. (1997). *Modern social work theory* (2nd ed.). Chicago: Lyceum.

Pepper, S. C. (1942). *World hypotheses: A study in evidence*. Berkeley: University of California Press.

Reid, W. J. (1998). The paradigms and long-term trends in clinical social work. In R. A. Dorfman (Ed.), *Paradigms of clinical social work* (Vol. 2, pp. 337–351). New York: Brunner/Mazel.

Rosen, H. (1988). Evolving a personal philosophy of practice: Towards eclecticism. In R. A. Dorfman (Ed.), *Paradigms of clinical social work* (pp. 388–412). New York: Brunner/Mazel.

Roth, W-M. (2005). *Talking science: Language and learning in science classrooms*. Lanham, MD: Rowman and Littlefield.

Sarukkai, S. (2001). Translation and science. *Meta, XLVI* (4), 646–663.

Sarukkai, S. (2002). *Translating the world: Science and language*. Lanham, MD: University Press of America.

Scheff, T. (1995). Academic gangs. *Crime, Law, and Social Change, 23*, 157–162.

Sheafor, B. W. and Horejsi, C. R. (2008). *Techniques and guidelines for social work practice* (5th ed.). Boston: Pearson/Allyn and Bacon.

Thagard, P. (2005). Being interdisciplinary: Trading zones in cognitive science. In S. J. Derry, C. D. Schunn and M. A. Gernsbacher (Eds), *Interdisciplinary collaboration: An emerging cognitive science* (pp. 317–339). Mahwah, NJ: Lawrence Erlbaum Associates.

Thyer, B. A. (2008). Preface. In K. M. Sowers and C. N. Dulmus (Eds). *Comprehensive handbook of social work and social welfare: Volume 2, Human behavior in the social environment* (pp. xiii–xxvi). Hoboken, NJ: John Wiley & Sons.

Turner, F. J. (1996). An interlocking perspective for treatment. In F. J. Turner (Ed.), *Social work treatment: Interlocking theoretical approaches* (4th ed., pp. 699–711). New York: Free Press.

Turner, F. J. (1999). Theories of practice with vulnerable populations. In D. E. Biegel and A. Blum (Eds), *Innovations in practice and service delivery across the lifespan* (pp. 13–31). New York: Oxford University Press.

Wagner-Pacific, R. and Bershady, H. (1993). Portents or confessions: Authoritative readings of a dream text. *Symbolic Interaction, 16* (2), 129–143.

Watson, W. (1985). *The architectonics of meaning: Foundations of the new pluralism*. Albany: State University of New York Press.

Weick, K. E. (1995). *Sensemaking in organizations*. Thousand Oaks, CA: Sage.

Weis, D. L. (1998). The use of theory in sexuality research. *The Journal of Sex Research, 35* (1), 1–9.

White, L. A. (1962). Symboling: A kind of behavior. *Journal of Psychology, 53*, pp. 311–317.

Wierzbicka, A. (1997). *Understanding cultures through their key words: English, Russian, Polish, German, and Japanese*. New York: Oxford University Press.

Section 1

Multi-theoretical social work: basics

1

Use theories
for professional
purposes

(EPAS 2.1.7 Apply knowledge; EPAS 2.1.1 Identify
as social worker)

Social workers have an ethical and professional responsibility to have knowledge of established and researched theories that are grounded in social work values and to draw continually upon these theories in social work practice.
(Teater, 2010, p. 1)

Most social workers begin their careers as generalists. Generalist social workers can work with client systems of different sizes. Generalist social workers can enact a variety of roles. Generalist social workers can adapt to diverse practice settings including urban, suburban, town, and rural environments. Generalist social workers can make use of a range of social science and practice theories.

Theoretical knowledge has many important uses for the generalist social worker, for the social worker who specializes later in his or her career, and for the profession of social work. The use of sound and scientific knowledge adds value to the generalist and specialist social worker (see Figure 1.1) and to the profession, and helps distinguish us from amateurs, technicians, volunteers, and other non-professionals. In this lesson, we will examine some of the specific uses of theory for social workers and for the profession.

To make better sense of and understand practice situations.	To provide a guide to thinking and action during all phases of the helping process including engagement, assessment, intervention, and evaluation. Theory is ike a blueprint for a collaborative worker–client construction project.	To communicate clearly and precisely with all those involved in a helping enterprise.
To assist in the selection of relevant knowledge about the case from all possible sources.		To increase worker's professional knowledge and the confidence to figure out complex person-in-environment challenges andcase dynamics

Figure 1.1 Why translate theories for practice?

Uses of theories for the professional social worker

Theories are like tools. Professional socialization involves the acquisition of many different tools (theoretical models, propositions, concepts, and displays, for examples), and the mastery of their use. Theory tools help us do a variety of jobs. The professional social worker with a box of many "high quality" theory tools is better prepared for the challenges of contemporary practice than the worker who brings the same hammer and screwdriver to each job.

Deepens understanding

Effective practitioners are curious about their clients, the clients' environments, and the challenges these clients confront. Human curiosity has deep evolutionary roots, and the impulse to solve the client and organizational problems that emerge in daily practice may be as fundamental as the impulse to meet needs for clothing, food and liquids. Theories are instruments or tools that enable practitioners to satisfy this core curiosity, the need to understand events, objects, people, processes, and situations. For example, theories assist workers in making sense of the very complex situations and person-in-environment (PIE) puzzles common to professional activity. The behavioral theory can enhance our understanding of a child's destructive behaviors in the home. The interactionist theory can enhance our understanding of repeated communication problems between a supervisor and a worker. The critical perspective can help us understand the difficulties experienced by city mayors attempting to pass gun control legislation. From this position emphasizing the use of theories as instrumentalities for comprehension, Laudan (1977) even argues: "the repudiation of theoretical scientific inquiry is tantamount to a denial of what may be our most characteristic human trait" (p. 225).

Aids in knowledge selection

For any particular case, there is a multitude of information that a practitioner might consider in understanding the person-/system-in-environment configuration. Three illustrations of this challenge follow. First, the PIE framework challenges the worker to learn about the person and his or her qualities, the transactions between the person and the environment, and the specific contexts in the environment (cultural, economic, political, and so on) relevant to a focal challenge. I was trained as a social group worker. Second, clinical social workers often attempt to gather and organize much bio-psycho-social information shared by clients with mental health concerns, and accurately categorize the troubling patterns. Third, and on a personal note, I soon realized that in work with small groups, the leader must struggle to make sense of an abundant data including information about eight or ten members, their problems, and their styles of participation; about the interaction of each of these members with each other and with the whole group; about a range of group processes and structures; and about the agency and community context of the group services.

Social workers serving families, communities, and international organizations face information management demands that also make them vulnerable to information overload. For all social workers, the mandate to complete the cognitive tasks necessary for competent information gathering and assessment formulation can seem overwhelming. Theories help the worker select the knowledge that is most relevant to the case. Theories serve as a guide to what to look and listen for but also as a guide to what to ignore (Coser, 1981).

Guides thinking and action

Theoretical knowledge provides a blueprint to guide thinking and acting during each phase of the helping process (Bowen, 1976). Our choice of a particular theory or set of theories can have positive consequences for all that follows. For instance, during the information gathering and assessment phase, theories help the worker organize data into patterns and possibilities for action as recommended by the theoretical frameworks. A useful theory of change, for example, will point to the mechanisms or processes that must be identified and altered to realize desired outcomes. During the intervention-planning phase, theory directs the worker and client's selection or creation of effective interventions (Johnson and Svensson, 2005). With a toolbox of multiple theories, the practitioner can help clients by selecting from a large set of intervention tools rather than settling on just one tool. Problems and their causes vary and one tool may be insufficient for the diverse caseloads of many practitioners (Coser, 1981). During the evaluation-planning phase, theory helps the practitioner and client set targets for change, determine criteria for success, and devise suitable evaluation procedures.

Facilitates professional communication

Theoretical knowledge and theorizing competencies can inform our helping work, ethical analyses, research projects, and policy advocacy. These endeavors are generally collaborative. Social workers must communicate and cooperate with colleagues, clients, collaterals, supervisors, and many others. Theoretical knowledge provides the social worker with a vocabulary for talking clearly and precisely about practice challenges. This vocabulary enhances communication between the worker and all stakeholders in the task at hand. The theoretically fluent social worker, for example, can explain the agency's theoretical orientation in simple terms to a couple seeking marriage counseling. The worker able to translate theoretical jargon into plain English or Spanish can justify his or her assessment formulation and intervention plan and discuss clearly the specifics of the helping process necessary for client progress to the couple, other family members, and significant others. The worker confident in the use of multiple theoretical languages can participate articulately and intelligently on the multi-professional team assisting with family services.

Enhances worker confidence

Social workers often serve persons and social systems attempting to mobilize many inner and outer resources and to meet multiple challenges. In much social work service, we cast a wide net and consider personal, interactional, and environmental factors associated with coping processes. Besides providing increased understanding about PIE dynamics, clarity about the search for relevant information, and directives for action theories can fortify the worker's confidence. Professional theoretical knowledge, a set of effective theorizing skills, and aptitudes for creative and rigorous theory application will supply the equipment, esteem, and confidence for dealing with a range of complex case puzzles and for cooperating adeptly and assuredly with all members of helping teams.

Uses of theories for the profession of social work

Professional groups in contemporary societies compete for task assignments, monetary and other resources, and legitimacy. Mastery of multiple theories and their languages equips the profession of social work for such competition.

Defines professional identity and boundaries

Theoretical knowledge helps establish a profession's identity and its boundaries. Social workers prefer to use theories committed to explaining PIE configurations, and social workers prefer theorizing in ways appreciative of the multiple dimensions of human functioning and the multiple contexts of behavior. This differentiates us from professional groups that prioritize either the person (psychologists) or the social environment (sociologists), and groups that specialize in only one aspect of the person like clergy members emphasizing spirituality or one environmental context like economists assessing market conditions (Hardiker and Barker, 1991).

Social work theorizing also is guided by a distinctive set of ethics and values. The profession, for example, recommends value criteria for judging the appropriateness of theories like strengths orientation, justice promotion, difference affirmation, and so on. The profession's code of ethics provides guidelines relevant to the responsible and sensitive employment of theory in everyday helping situations. Member commitment to and use of these ideals fortifies the profession's distinctive identity and core convictions and differentiate the social work profession from professions with different ethical and value preferences.

Promotes profession's status

What makes social work a profession? A major ingredient is its proclaimed use of scientific knowledge accumulated over time and demonstrated to be useful in ameliorating community and personal problems. In fighting for part of the turf allocated by society to professional organizations, the profession of social work uses empirically sound theoretical knowledge to achieve successes at professional tasks like describing, explaining, predicting, and resolving problems of human membership. The profession works also to document its effectiveness especially compared to professional competitors indifferent to scientific theory (Webster and Whitmeyer, 2001). Could a professional group earn community regard and legitimacy by asserting: "Count on us. Our members have finely developed instincts" or "Assign important social tasks to our profession. We may not know much about science but we have accumulated many trade secrets over the generations"? Not likely. Publicity about the informed use of validated scientific theories improves the reputation and status of the profession of social work in society.

Builds the knowledge base

In a sense, the social work profession is a mutual aid association. Members help each other perform their professional roles. Imagine how hard it would be if each social worker had to start with a blank mind and create new knowledge for each new case. Instead, the profession has created a body of knowledge that can be loaned to every member and a "hardware store" of theory-informed tools for members' acquisition.

Theories borrowed from other disciplines and theories created by social workers become part of this collective resource. Continual and enthusiastic theorizing when shared in communities of applied scientists, for example, stimulates and guides research. Such theorizing helps researchers construct and test theory-based explanatory models that answer important questions identified by the profession (Sztompka, 2004). Evidence-supported theoretical knowledge becomes part of social work's knowledge base.

The knowledge base is like a large library and all professional social workers have a library card. Each can check out the books and journals from the library needed to analyze and understand the particular features of an upcoming job. Switching to the hardware store metaphor, each member of the social work profession can walk through the shelves, check out different tools, and pick the theory-based measurement instruments, explanatory hypotheses, change logic models, interventions, or other tools to do the required job.

Contributes to public problem solving

Finally, theories prepare social worker leaders for participating in the significant role of public intellectual (Widmaier, 2004). Theoretical knowledge can be an instrument, for example, for contributing a theory-informed social work perspective to social and political change projects. We can describe and recommend change strategies related to the socially constructed understandings that societal members have about problems and unmet needs caused by drug abuse, family conflicts, homelessness, intolerance, poverty, and war, for examples. We can also engage citizens in appraising the relevant theoretical reasoning and empirical evidence, and influence public debates and dialogues about these understandings. Theory creation, dissemination, and application can also expand the range of imagined problem solving alternatives for both policy and personal problems. With many options, change agents are more likely to advance the common good. Theorizing practitioners can help stakeholders solve problems and reconstruct social and political realities in ways fair and beneficial to large numbers of people.

Social workers can use theories to provide citizens engaged in projects of human betterment with sound conceptual orientations, a set or reasonable explanations, and enlightenment regarding viable interventions. These contributions improve the discussion, deliberation, and decision-making necessary to the reduction of unmet needs and the realization of democratic ideals (Sztompka, 2004).

Learning activities and reflections

1. Imagine an untrained, non-degreed, novice practitioner who identifies himself as a social worker. This practitioner proudly refrains from using theoretical or research knowledge. He claims that his gut feelings are all the tools needed to effectively help individuals, families, groups, and policy stakeholders. Now shift gears and imagine a highly trained, experienced social worker with a Masters of Social Work degree, a social work license, extensive knowledge of human behavior theories and practice theories, and mastery of numerous theorizing techniques and skills. Compare the likely career paths, accomplishments and failures of each of these imaginary social workers. Brainstorm some of the uses to which the experienced social worker can put theoretical knowledge and theorizing skills that will enhance his or her career progress.

2. Imagine that an untrained practitioner unites with a group of like-minded peers and they agree to call themselves members of a new profession, the "helpers with heart." Now shift gears and think of the social work profession with its commitment to extensive college education and post college continuing education for its members; a profession that expects its members to stay current with scientific knowledge of person and the environment, to competently apply theoretical knowledge to understand person-in-environment" configurations, and to use theoretical knowledge to guide the planned change process. Brainstorm about some of the positive uses to which the profession can put its collective theoretical knowledge. Identify some of the values of competent theorizing for the whole profession. Speculate on some of the likely consequences if social work abandoned its commitment to a theory and research enriched knowledge base.

3. Compare and contrast the experienced and knowledgeable social work professional with the gut feeling, theory-free practitioner who is part of a group claiming professional status despite an aversion to theoretical knowledge. How might the two kinds of practitioners differently approach helping work, interaction with clients, evaluation of their effectiveness, and so on? How might the two kinds of professions differently claim the rights and privileges of the professional status? What advantages and disadvantages might be associated with the theory-free stance and the theory-informed stance to professionalism?

4. Finally, reflect on this learning activity. What have you learned about social work and the basics of competent theorizing?

References

Bowen, M. (1976). Theory in the practice of psychotherapy. In P. J. Guerin (Ed.), *Family therapy: Theory and practice* (pp. 42–90). New York: Gardner Press.

Coser, L. A. (1981). The uses of classical sociological theory. In B. Rhea (Ed.), *The future of the sociological classics* (pp. 170–182). London: George Allen & Unwin.

Drapela, V. J. (1990). The value of theories for counseling practitioners. *International Journal for the Advancement of Counseling, 13*, 19–26.

Hardiker, P. and Barker, M. (1991). Towards social theory for social work. In J. Lishman (Ed.), *Handbook of theory for practice teachers* (pp. 87–119). London: Jessica Kingsley.

Johnson, E. and Svensson, K. (2005). Theory in social work—some reflections on understanding and explaining interventions. *European Journal of Social Work, 8* (4), 419–433.

Laudan, L. (1977). *Progress and its problems: Towards a theory of scientific growth.* Berkeley: University of California Press.

Sztompka, P. (2004). Shaping sociological imagination: The importance of theory. In J. Alexander, G. T. Marx and C. L. Williams (Eds), *Self, structure, and beliefs: Explorations in sociology* (pp. 254–267). Berkeley: University of California Press.

Teater, B. (2010). *Applying social work theories and methods.* Maidenhead: Open University Press.

Webster, M. Jr. and Whitmeyer, J. M. (2001). Applications of theories of group processes. *Sociological Theory, 19* (3), 250–270.

Widmaier, W. W. (2004). Theory as a factor and the theorist as an actor: The "pragmatist constructivist" lessons of John Dewey and John Kenneth Galbraith. *International Studies Review, 6*, 427–445.

2 Identify your theoretical orientation

(EPAS 2.1.7 Apply knowledge; EPAS 2.1.1 Identify as social worker)

While social workers 'ought' to have a relatively coherent, integrated theoretical base from which they work, often they are not clear or unable to specify what constitutes this base.

(Beder, 2000, p. 40)

When I studied in the Masters of Social Work Program at Virginia Commonwealth University, I learned that professional social workers took a test to acquire a license. At that point, the test included a written examination and a panel interview. There was a common hurdle raised by the panel. The candidate read a case, articulated and defended his or her overall theoretical orientation to the case, and then responded to a range of specific case questions inquiring about the practical use of this orientation. Word was that many candidates stuttered; they couldn't speak the language of theory. They had to engage in more theoretical language learning and return at a later date.

In my current home state, Maryland, United States, I have learned that many employers continue this tradition of challenging candidates for a position to show how they would apply their preferred theories to a particular case. The cultivation of a theoretical orientation can prepare social workers for meeting licensing, employment, and other professional hurdles.

Theoretical orientation: An overview

A *theoretical orientation* is an organized set of assumptions, concepts and propositions used by a social work practitioner to understand the "person interacting in an environment," explain client system problems, and guide all phases of the planned change process. Sometimes, an orientation is referred to as a "theoretical approach," a "theoretical framework," a "model," a "perspective on practice," or a "personal practice model." A theoretical orientation may match with one theoretical tradition or the theoretical orientation may reflect a blend of multiple traditions: behavioral, cognitive, and ecological, for instance. The orientation also reflects the worker's distinctive synthesis of various life influences.

See Table 2.1 for a summary of fourteen important theoretical frameworks. The table identifies the dimensional aspect for each person-oriented theory, the focal context for each environment-oriented theory, and symbolic interaction as characterizing transactions between person and environment. For each theory, the table also provides information about exemplary models, root metaphors, major terms, and theoretical models. A comprehensive and integrative theoretical orientation might be built from this collection of theories.

Personal influences on theoretical orientation

Many personal factors influence our choice of an orientation. These include your family of origin, your reference groups, your personal role models (significant others, celebrities, characters in fiction and film, and so on), your philosophy of life, your values, and your personality style. During my doctoral studies, I had the fortune of meeting an applied sociologist devoted to symbolic interactionism, He became a very influential model and I have incorporated symbolic interactionism into the central place in my own orientation.

Personality characteristics including style of thinking (complexity, emphasis on rationality); degree of initiative (on the continuum from active to passive); enjoyment of creative and imaginative processes; value assigned to dreams, emotions, intuition, and insight; inclinations toward empiricism, and comfort with assertiveness are variables that may dispose you toward some theoretical orientations and away from others (Arthur, 2001). For example, behaviorist practitioners tend to like empirical research and want to take an active stance toward helping others while psychodynamic practitioners are often people who appreciate the complexity of the psyche and believe that emotions, dreams, and intuition are critical elements in the human experience (Arthur, 2001).

Sometimes our personal values clash with the core assumptions of a theoretical tradition, and we reject it (Murdock, 1998). We may affirm in our beliefs and actions the value of "self-determination," and feel that a social structural or Marxist theoretical framework's assumption of the conditioning power of political and economic forces clashes with this value. In contrast, an activist political orientation might attract us to neo-Marxist or

Table 2.1 Overview of fourteen theories comprising PIE metatheory

PIE/theory	Exemplars	Root metaphors	Major terms	Theory model
Multi-dimensional person				
Acting (behavioral)	Ivan Pavlov John Watson B. F. Skinner Bruce Thyer	Person like animal in laboratory	Behavior Stimuli Reinforcement Punishment	Substance abuse treatment by changing stimulus-response chains
Faithing (anthropological)	Clifford Geertz Mary Douglas James Fowler Edward Canda	Person like seeker searching web of symbols	Meaning Rituals Sacred Beings Sacred Symbols	Crisis and healing by religious/spiritual rituals
Feeling (psychodynamic)	Sigmund Freud Erik Erikson John Bowlby Florence Hollis	Person like untamed beast in civilizing circus	Attachment Crises Ego Defenses Ego Identity	Loss, grief, and corrective emotional experiences
Sensing (evolutionary biology)	Gregor Mendel Charles Darwin Arnold Gesell Harriette Johnson	Person like ape in jungle	Adaptation Heredity Natural Selection Species	Biological changes to brain related to alcohol
Thinking (cognitive)	Lev Vygotsky Jean Piaget Albert Bandura Paula Nurius	Person like computer networked to other computers	Cognition Information Schemas Thinking	Restructuring neglectful mothers' self cognitions

Continued

PIE/theory	Exemplars	Root metaphors	Major terms	Theory model
Interacting				
Transacting (symbolic interactionism)	John Dewey George H. Mead Norman Denzin Jane Addams	Person like language speaker in multi language settlement house	Interaction Labels Perspective Taking Self	Exploring and managing meanings of depression
In environmental contexts				
Communal (strength-resilience)	Abraham Maslow Carl Rogers Martin Seligman Dennis Saleeby	Person like athlete developing strengths in gym	Potential Protective Factors Resilience Strengths	Adversity and mobilizing inner and outer resources
Cultural (constructionist)	Peter Berger Thomas Luckmann Kenneth Gergen Patricia Hill Collins	Person like a construction built in line with cultural categories	Categories Social Construction Stocks of Knowledge Typifications	Understanding and resisting racial categorizations
Economy (exchange)	Peter Blau George Homans John Thibaut Harry Lloyd Hopkins	Person like buyer and seller at marketplace	Benefits Costs Negotiations Social Exchange	Advocating for social work program by changing cost-benefit ratios
Organization (role)	Robert Linton Erving Goffman Bruce Biddle Helen Harris Perlman	Person like an actor performing a part on the stage	Expectations Position Role Scripts	Socialization for a new role as a volunteer

PIE/theory	Exemplars	Root metaphors	Major terms	Theory model
Physical environment (ecology)	Robert Park Ernest Burgess Urie Bronfenbrenner Carel Germain	Person like other living organisms growing in a niche	Ecosystem Interdependence Niche Sustainability	Identifying territorial issues related to NIMBY problem
Political – class (critical)	C. Wright Mills Jurgen Habermas Bertha C. Reynolds	Person like critic advocating for interests in forum controlled by elite	Conflict Oppression Power Privilege	Increasing capabilities of powerless for political action
Political – gender (feminist)	Simone de Beauvoir Betty Friedan Carol Gilligan Dorothy Smith	Person like speaker voicing identity, desires, moral impulses	Gender Inequality Patriarchy Private Sphere Sexism	Increasing teen girls "voice" despite sexist oppression
Social systems	Ludwig Bertalanffy Talcott Parsons Robert Merton Gordon Hearn	Person like a part of a large and complex machine	Boundary Function Steady State System	Aiding military family systems disorganized and disrupted by war

empowerment theoretical traditions that espouse "taking sides" and fighting for social change. Likewise, certain theoretical orientations resonate with our self-concept. Others don't resonate.

A practitioner's earlier experiences with his or her family of origin, with a spouse or partner, and with significant others can influence the choice of preferred theories (Bitar, Bean, and Bermudez, 2007). For example, a caring and intimate relationship may increase one's sensitivity to issues of communication and set a preference toward a theoretical framework emphasizing verbal and nonverbal communication and communication skills training. Many social work students that I have known report family experiences of conflict between parents, and relate these experiences to their interests in a theoretical framework that includes a family-enhancement component such as family systems theory.

Our cultural heritage has an impact on our theoretical allegiances (Gross, 2002). If we identify with the United States, we may be drawn to pragmatism, a distinctively American orientation to practice. Social workers from other parts of the world are drawn to theoretical frameworks and research with different emphases (Forte, 1994). For instance, Asian social workers and Israeli social workers, in contrast to American social workers, may prioritize theories closer to the collectivist end of the community–person continuum rather than the individualistic end. If we identify with a particular membership community constituted by African Americans, homosexuals, or Christians, for example, we may seek to learn and develop orientations attentive to the perspectives of such communities: the Afrocentric paradigm, queer theory, or a faith-based spirituality framework, respectively.

Professional socialization experiences

Our professional socialization influences our development of a theoretical orientation. Socialization experiences include interaction with your professional role models (teachers, colleagues, mentors, and supervisors), your experiences in the classroom (psychology, sociology, biology, economics, and related classes), and your participation in workshops and continuing education events.

When in graduate or undergraduate school, the classes that you take may influence your theoretical preferences. From the mentor mentioned above, I took a sociology course when in school that focused on the symbolic interactionism approach to human emotions. I found that approach exciting, useful, and relevant to social work and I have been developing this as a primary feature of my theoretical orientation ever since. Continuing education workshops in the community as well as professional development opportunities in an agency may also alert us to theoretical frameworks meriting exploration and study.

By chance, you may be assigned to a supervisor with a passion for a particular theoretical tradition (Feminist Social Work or Cognitive–Behavioral Social Work, for examples). The supervisor's enthusiasm and expertise stimulates your interest and you develop a special appreciation for his or her theoretical orientation. You even begin to use your supervisor as a model for applying the theory or theories. A theoretical framework that we adopt early in our career may be confirmed or augmented by a respected mentor (Guest and Beutler, 1988). Or a valued supervisor, colleague, teacher, or friend may persuasively disparage our theoretical framework prompting us to consider a shift in our theoretical allegiances (Lovinger, 1992).

Field placement and agency influences

The characteristics and dynamics of our workplace strongly influence our professional socialization including our development of theoretical preferences. Relevant workplace factors include the agency mission and goals, the agency funding, the agency training emphases, the agency reward structure, and agency access to equipment, supplies, and other resources.

Garvin (1997), a renowned small groups theorist, suggests that organizational requirements influence the practitioners' choice of theoretical framework(s). If the agency has a tight budget, then the worker may not be able to adopt an orientation that requires extensive post-graduate training, expensive equipment, or the use of high-paid consultants. If the agency is a community center providing most services through small groups, then the worker may be expected to adopt a humanistic, mainstream group work approach.

Our choice of a theory or theories is also influenced by status considerations (Gross, 2002). Issues of professional advancement, increases in salary, and the regard of agency and community leaders are relevant. Psychodynamic social work became very popular in the middle of the twentieth century for some of these reasons. The demonstration of an allegiance to a theoretical framework preferred by the organization's elite members increases our access to and opportunities within their social network. The choice of a particular theoretical foundation may be valued locally (a family strengths and preservation model, for example) and increase our credibility and stature as a professional in the agency's surrounding neighborhood if we endorse the approach.

Client characteristic influences

Characteristics of our typical clients influence our development of a theory base. These include client needs, problems and challenges, client membership features (age, race, gender, nationality, sexual orientation, religion, and so on), and service users' stated preferences regarding theory indicated in agency evaluation data, focus groups, or informal conversations.

As we choose and develop theoretical knowledge for our theoretical orientation, we should do so with consideration of the needs and interests of our clients. Evidence-based social workers consider the research documenting the suitability and effectiveness of particular practice theories with particular clients with particular problems. They often prefer behavioral and cognitive approaches because of extensive empirical support for their applications. Clients may provide direct feedback that a particular theory, theory-based conceptualization, or theory-specific intervention suits them well or doesn't seem to help. Professionals should adjust their theoretical orientations accordingly. Each client brings his or her informal "theory of change," an everyday theory, to the helping encounter. The helping process is a mutual enterprise. If we act from a theoretical orientation alien to the client or contrary to his or her everyday theory, then we are showing disrespect and we are undermining our ability to help.

In summary, please identify and be mindful of the components of your theoretical orientation, and the various influences on your choice and development of this orientation. While there are pressures and constraints that any social work theory user must consider, there are also possibilities for the free and creative crafting of a distinctive theoretical approach to practice. Many of the lessons in this book will help you build systematically your theoretical orientation. In Lesson 18, you will have an opportunity to synthesize what you have learned in the form of an integrative multi-theoretical personal practice model.

Learning activities and reflections

1. Recall our working definition. A "theoretical orientation" is an organized set of assumptions, concepts and propositions used by a social work practitioner to understand the "person and environment," explain client system problems, and guide helping work. Review the social work knowledge that you have mastered so far (assumptions about the person and environment, concepts, guidelines for practice, and theories) and identify the theory or theories that you prefer and have included in your theoretical orientation. Now, reflect on the various possible factors that have influenced and may influence your choice of a theoretical orientation.

    Identify possible personal influences. These include your family of origin, your reference groups, your personal role models (significant others, celebrities, characters in fiction and film, and so on), your philosophy of life, your values, and your personality style. Which influences were relevant in your development of a theoretical orientation? Which factors may become important in the future?

Identify possible professional socialization experiences relevant to your development of a theoretical orientation. These include your professional role models (teachers, colleagues, supervisors, and so on), your experiences in the classroom (psychology, sociology, biology, economics, and related classes), and your participation in workshops and continuing education events. Which influences have been relevant to your development of a theoretical orientation? Which experiences may become important in the future?

Identify possible field placement or agency influences (or organizations where you have volunteered). These include the agency mission and goals, the agency funding, the agency training preferences, the agency reward structure, and agency access to equipment, supplies, and other resources. Which influences have been relevant to your development of a theoretical orientation so far? Which influences may become important in the future?

Identify possible client characteristics that are influences on your choice and refinement of a theoretical orientation. These may include typical client needs, problems and challenges; client membership features (age, race, gender, sexual orientation, religion, and so on); clients' theories of change; and clients' stated preferences indicated in agency evaluation data or during discussions with the clients. Which influences have been relevant to your development of a theoretical orientation so far? Which influences may become important in the future?

2. Identify the negative personal, professional, agency, and client influences: those that have turned you away from a particular theoretical approach. What happened to affect negatively your assembly of this theoretical knowledge for your orientation? How specifically were you "turned off" by the rejected theory?

3. Take a life course /human development perspective. First, scan your past and attempt to construct a history about how your theoretical orientation has changed since your first college class or social work class to the present. Second, consider the present. How are you currently developing your theoretical orientation? Finally, project into the future. What do you anticipate as some possible influences on your cultivation of a theoretical orientation

in the near and distant future? What will you share with a licensing board, employer panel, or colleague who asks you: What is your theoretical orientation?

4. Finally, conclude with reflections on these learning activities. What have you learned that will prepare you to utilize theoretical frameworks to guide the processes of assessment, intervention, and evaluation?

References

Arthur, A. R. (2001). Personality, epistemology and psychotherapists' choice of theoretical models: A review and analysis. *The European Journal of Psychotherapy, Counseling, and Health, 4* (1), 45–64.

Beder, J. (2000). The integration of theory into practice: Suggestions for supervisors. *Professional Development: The International Journal of Continuing Social Work, 3* (2), 40–48.

Bitar, G. W., Bean, R. A. and Bermudez, J. M. (2007). Influences and processes in theoretical orientation development: A grounded theory pilot study. *The American Journal of Family Therapy, 35*, 109–121.

Forte, J. A. (1994). Around the world with social group work: Knowledge and research contributions. *Social Work with Groups, 17* (1–2), 143–162.

Garvin, C. D. (1997). *Contemporary group work* (3rd ed.). Boston: Allyn & Bacon.

Gross, N. (2002). Becoming a pragmatist philosopher: Status, self-concept, and intellectual choice. *American Sociological Review, 67* (1), 52–76.

Guest, P. D. and Beutler, L. E. (1988). Impact of psychotherapy supervision on therapist orientation and values. *Journal of Consulting and Clinical Psychology, 56* (5), 653–658.

Lovinger, R. J. (1992). Theoretical affiliations in psychotherapy. *Psychotherapy, 29* (4), 586–590.

Murdock, N. L. (1998). Joining the club: Factors related to choice of theoretical orientation. *Counselling Psychology Quarterly, 11* (1), 63–78.

3

Cultivate an orientation affirming theoretical pluralism

(EPAS 2.1.7 Apply knowledge)

In the domain of psychosocial intervention, comparative analysis of the theoretical systems clarifies differing conceptions of the helping process; the structure of intervention; the range of application; the functions of the therapeutic relationship and the role of interactive experience; strategies and technical procedures; curative factors, facilitating conditions and change processes; and methods of monitoring progress and evaluative outcomes

(Borden, 2010, p. 6)

For my first social work teaching position, I was expected to teach and also to serve as a field liaison, the person who assists a group of students make connections successfully between the classroom and the agency. We placed one of my students at a highly regarded nursing home affiliated with a Catholic hospital. After a few weeks at the placement, the student reported back her growing fear of failure. The field instructor expected the student to participate in weekly team meetings. The team included professionals with diverse backgrounds: a doctor representing health services, a psychologist who specialized in psychological testing and diagnoses, a priest who was most concerned with the spiritual needs of residents, a business expert who always considered cost issues, and, sometimes, a lawyer to advise on the legal implications of a case. The field instructor expected the student to bring a social work bio-psycho-social strengths perspective to the team meetings and, somehow, to learn to understand and interact with other team members. To the student, her new colleagues seemed to be thinking in alien ways and talking foreign languages. The student found this socialization process very difficult, especially the task of learning the medical jargon of the doctor. For me, this was one of my first practical encounters with theoretical pluralism—each team member at the nursing home had allegiance to a different theoretical tradition—and the fact that social workers must learn to understand and speak many different theoretical languages.

Theoretical pluralism: overview

Theoretical pluralism is a philosophical position comprised of the convictions that a theoretical framework is a representation of reality created by a theorist, that no theoretical framework is the "true" or only representation, and that there are many useful theoretical frameworks. From the viewpoint of theoretical pluralism, science can be characterized as an enterprise with many different paradigms, theories, conceptual frameworks, ideas, and hypotheses (Merton, 1996). For contemporary social workers, there are competing explanations rather than one single or dominant explanation available to understand "human behavior and the environment."

We can compare science to a large city. New York, Los Angeles, Mexico City, Sydney, Toronto, and London are all pluralistic urban communities. Their populations are composed of diverse cultural groups and languages. Someone familiar with the neighborhoods of cities would notice the identification of different groups with different locations in the cities. Science is also best understood as a plurality of thought communities, cultures, and languages (Duncker, 2001). Universities and other academic settings, scientific conferences, and human service arenas are some of the ecological settings where scientific knowledge is applied; each convenes members of different thought communities and these members include theory users aligned with many different disciplines and professions.

Applied scientists all share "science" as a reference point as the residents of New York City share an identity as New Yorkers. However, each discipline and profession cultivates a distinctive identity, builds a special assemblage of theoretical knowledge, and develops a unique culture and scientific language: their own Harlem, Little Italy or Chinatown. Within a scientific community, communication is generally fast and effective. However, there may also be some overlap between the languages of theoretical communities like the similarities between the Spanish and Italian languages spoken in neighboring city enclaves. Behavioral and social exchange theorists, for instance, make similar assumptions, share some terminology, and understand easily each other's theoretical propositions.

There are also clear and identifiable differences in the ways that members of each scientific community interpret and talk about human behavior and the social environment. Communication across boundaries of scientific communities is difficult. Symbolic interactionists hold that humans are qualitatively different from all other animals and human symbol-using capacities make creative, self-fulfilling action possible even for clients in harsh environments. Radical behaviorists hold that humans are very similar to mice, pigeons, dogs and other animals. A client like other behaving animals does what is reinforced; the learning environment powerfully determines behavioral patterns. Interactionists and behaviorists may feel like foreigners to each other. Due to language differences, interaction between members of such different scientific communities is slow and fraught with misunderstandings.

Theoretical pluralism: the proliferation of theories

There is clear evidence that social workers now draw concepts from a theoretically pluralistic knowledge base. In her detailed history of the development of theoretical approaches to social work practice, Germain (1983) profiled the profession in the 1950s. There were only three major models of casework: the Freudian diagnostic model, the functional school, and Perlman's problem solving approach. Group workers were limited basically to the social goals, interactionist, and remedial models. The social work knowledge base has grown significantly in the past fifty years. Educators and practitioners are drawing from a larger number of theoretical traditions to guide their professional action.

More than twenty years ago, Frances Turner (1999), a theory expert, estimated that there were thirty different practice theories useful to social workers. In Forte's (2006) recent content analysis of eighteen social work theory survey textbooks, forty different theoretical approaches were identified as relevant to the social work knowledge base. In the meta-analysis of studies of practitioners' theoretical preferences between 1980 and 1994 in the same book, nineteen different theoretical preferences were identified. Theoretical pluralism characterizes the contemporary knowledge base, and social workers can now make use of theoretical contributions to our knowledge base from multiple disciplines, professions, and theoretical communities. For professionals overwhelmed by the knowledge explosion, the image of employment at the Tower of Babel is apt.

Complexity theory and theoretical pluralism

Complexity theory offers a conceptual justification for my endorsement of a pluralistic approach to theoretical knowledge. *Complexity theory* is a multi-disciplinary branch of science developed through the investigation in fields like biology and meteorology of complex behavior in adaptive systems (Remington and Pollack, 2007). Applied to social work, the theory posits that social workers provide services to complex systems composed of numerous interacting subsystems, and these subsystems influence each other through "multiple, recursive, nonlinear feedback loops" (Sanger and Giddings, 2012, p. 371). Advocates argue that complexity theory provides new ways to advance the profession's eco-systems paradigm while affirming our commitment to a person-in-environment (PIE) metatheory, that is, an overall framework for understanding multi-dimensional persons interacting in a range of interrelated environmental contexts (Hudson, 2000). Complexity theory offers orienting tenets such as "small system changes in initial conditions may lead eventually to large changes," "a complex system exhibits a degree of chaos and order," and "human systems are generally so complexly linked to other systems that a practitioner can't predict with certainty the outcome of a specific intervention."

Summarizing the concepts of complexity theory (complexity, edge of chaos, emergence, non-linearity, phase transition, sensitive dependence on initial conditions, and so on) in greater detail would divert us from the focus of this lesson. However, we need to consider one important implication. If we accept that social workers often deal with complex systems, then we need to provide social workers a set of intellectual tools appropriate to the tasks of making sense of and helping complex systems. Complexity theorists endorse this kind of complexity thinking. They argue that there may be a large number of theoretical frameworks that fit the available evidence and provide useful, valid but different descriptions or explanations of the focal complex system (Richardson, 2004). Scientific thinking about complex PIE configurations requires, then, the adoption of theoretical pluralism, and cultivation of the ability to observe interrelated systems from many different perspectives using a wide range of theoretical tools and research tools (Remington and Pollack, 2007).

Stances toward theory proliferation

There are several different ways that social workers can approach the multiplicity of theoretical languages. We can compare them by using metaphors of religious belief, language mastery, and eyeglass lenses.

No theory

Some practitioners, educators, and administrators are *atheoretical* or theory free. They are like atheists who do not believe in God or a higher being. They don't recommend training in theories and theorizing. Theory-free practitioners are not interested in intellectual conversation about theory and claim that good social work can be practiced effectively without reference to theory. Atheoretical practitioners don't talk about concepts, propositions, models or other theoretical elements of theoretical language as essential guide to practice. Theories have little relevance to the necessities of day-to-day practice. For some who endorse the "no theory" stance, practice wisdom and maxims, intuition, and feelings rather than theorizing and theoretical concepts are the lenses that best guide work. Such practitioners prefer to respond to the immediate helping experience and its challenges without reflection on and critical thinking about theoretical knowledge. Other atheoretical social workers argue that research especially findings derived from the evidence-based practice movement best guides practice. Only helping actions and their demonstrated effectiveness in achieving desired outcomes are necessary considerations. When it comes to speaking about theory, the theory-free practitioner is inarticulate or "arrested at the level of justifying dogmas" (Bailey, 1980, p. 108).

In advocating a negative stance toward theory, some philosophers, practitioners, and scientists are very active and assertive. Like Stanley Fish (1982), they argue that theory and theorizing have no useful consequences for policy, public problem solving, or therapy. They also argue against the use of theoretical propositions and principles because they are too abstract, general, and distant from the contexts, diversity issues, and historical constraints that social workers face in local and dynamic helping situations. The anti-theorist social workers look forward to the fading away of theoretical assumptions, concepts, and guidelines. Rules of thumb, not theoretical rules, they argue, should be the only guides to understanding and acting when helping specific clients.

I have objections to the no theory approach to the growth of theoretical knowledge. The profession of social work is reviled by some political leaders and barely tolerated by others. In the competition for support, the no theory approach, a rejection of the traditional belief that groups achieve professional status by demonstrating the use of scientific knowledge, reduces our chances of effectively competing. There is also growing evidence that practitioners who choose interventions informed by behavioral and social science theories are more effective than those who reject theory (Glanz and Bishop, 2010). How can we advance the interests of our profession by endorsing methods of trial and error, science-free intuition, or the imitation of colleagues?

For the practitioner, theoretical self-consciousness is necessary. The proliferation of theories means theoretical knowledge permeates our everyday lives as well as our professional culture. Theories influence our perceiving, thinking, and action. Better to be aware rather than unaware of such influences. As lenses, different theories help us see and focus on different aspects of person-in-environment configurations. Why try to understand and help others encumbered by blurred vision, a vision that can be sharpened?

One theory

Some social workers are purists and prefer to immerse themselves in one theoretical tradition. They might make some of the following arguments for their one-angle approach. There are too many risks in mixing theories: many theories are incompatible; it's harder to use and to talk about many theories than one theory; multiple theory use leads to a lack of consistency in practice; and learning multiple theories takes too much time. The embrace of one theoretical approach or language makes for clearer, more consistent, and more competent practice (Percy and Sprenkle, 1985–86).

Theoretical monism is the term used by Merton (1996) to refer to the preference for a single conceptual scheme. In this comparison to faith orientations, theoretical monists talk but they prefer monologues, and they will only speak one theoretical language. They are dogmatic about their faith and believe in one true God while assuming that all other gods and religious beliefs are false. Theoretical monists are content with their choice of a framework, the righteous religion (Romaine, 2000). Monists have found the best theory. Open and reciprocal exchanges with those who speak other languages are discouraged as pointless, or as hazardous and contaminating (Turner, 1996). Complete and life-long loyalty to the theory is expected, and the disciple is challenged to master the one-true theory and its distinctive assumptions and beliefs (Payne, 1997). Monists are very protective about their ideas (Payne, 2002). They are convinced that the theoretical lenses provided by their belief tradition can explain every kind of practice situation or challenge. Some one-theory social workers are prone to dualistic or either/or thinking (Prochaska and Norcross, 1999). Their approach is good and all other approaches are bad. Either you are a true believer like them or you are deluded and condemned to a life without the possibility of salvation.

Some one-theory practitioners are proselytizers and even fanatics. They have found the best theory and are determined to convert everyone else to this theory. Theoretical proselytizers always define their own theory as superior when contrasted to others (Safran and Messer, 1997). Theoretical proselytizers want to monopolize and control the search for understanding (Merton, 1975). They are struggling for the supremacy of their theoretical framework and embrace the "wheeling and dealing, personal manipulation, threats, and cajolery involved in promoting that worldview" (Rule, 1997, p. 195). A social work educator recently told me, for example, that political leaders in a mid western state were demanding that all social workers embrace a solution-oriented conceptual model for practice. The government will not support any other approach. Theoretical proselytizers prefer one theory and prefer a competitive, aggressive, and forced conversion to gentle persuasion. As champions of a theoretical framework, they eagerly seek opportunities for debate. However, instead of offering carefully developed arguments about how their theoretical perspective best solves social work's theoretical puzzles and practical problems, they exhort or entice potential converts. Thus, the superiority of their affiliation (and inferiority of that of their rivals) is arrogantly and continually claimed but not demonstrated in official edicts (Payne, 1997). Missionary work to convert others to the correct doctrine and the political campaign for theoretical dominance are never ending. Influence seeking, name calling, grand promising, and disciplining those who stray from the line of the faithful are additional tools for jockeying for glory (Rule, 1997).

Let me begin my challenge to the one theory approach by returning to the toolbox metaphor. Theories are tools, and different social work jobs require different tools. My handyman brings tools for electric work, plumbing work, and carpentry work to every work site. Why restrict professional practitioners to one tool? Using the comparison to lenses, we need a different lens depending on the focal system. A cognitive-behavioral lens brings clarity to some individual level processes but social networking theory helps us see the clients connection to supportive others and organizations clearly and an economic theory can help us visualize the market forces that are complicating coping efforts of numerous clients.

Many theories

Some theory users appreciate the proliferation of theoretical frameworks and endorse many theories. In their view, there is value to the theoretical diversity because such diversity increases the resources available for assessment and intervention (Bailey, 1980). Moreover, in the multi-theoretical stance Kaplan (1964, p. 309) proposes, "we need not look for the true theory, but countenance and encourage various theories, and without thinking of them only as so many candidates for the single post to be filled."

Social work is a broad profession with a mandate to deal with many different collective and individual problems. Our PIE professional paradigm assumes that social life is very complex, that humans are multi-dimensional beings, that the environment includes many different contexts and systems, and that social systems are dynamic, continually changing entities. Advocates of a multi-theory stance argue that we are more likely to grasp the whole pie and each of its special slices if we use many different theoretical approaches. The complexity and multiplicity of problems justifies the integration of multiple theoretical frameworks. Limiting the profession to one theory is likely to increase helping failures.

A theoretical framework is not the discovery of a hidden fact but a way of looking at the facts, a way of organizing facts, and a way of representing facts to others. From this stance, the more lenses or angles on PIE configurations, the better. The advocates of multiple theory use might recommend a triangulation process modeled after the work of surveyors, for example, and encourage the practitioner to look at a case by scanning for issues related to the personal dimension, scanning for interaction between person and environment issues, and scanning for forces and factors related to various environmental contexts. From the merger of theoretical insights obtained at these three different vantage points, errors in characterizing the case are reduced. C. Wright Mills (1959) used imagery similar to that of triangulation. He referred to a prism to characterize the craft of applied science from a multi-theory stance. He wrote:

> The idea is to use a variety of viewpoints: you will, for instance ask yourself how would a political scientist whom you have recently read approach this, and how would that experimental psychologist, or this historian? You try to think in terms of a variety of viewpoints and in this way to let your mind become a moving prism catching light from as many angles as possible.
>
> (Mills, 1959, p. 214)

Opponents of the multi-theory stance doubt that social workers can master a large number of theoretical languages and speak each effectively. Moreover, there is little agreement in the profession on the preferred theories, and the profession adds and drops theories from its knowledge base often.

There are several strategies for adopting multiple theories. The following is a very brief review of each.

An *eclectic approach* means either that the social worker select parts of different theoretical traditions and tries to use these parts together in one helping situation, or that the worker uses different theories for different practice situations depending on the fit between the theory and the case (Payne, 2002). Many eclectic theory users are somewhat familiar with a variety of theories but they may not possess the complete set of knowledge and the in-depth vocabulary for demonstrating mastery of any one theoretical framework. Some practitioners take a disciplined approach to their eclecticism. They use critical thinking when selecting theoretical knowledge and combining theoretical parts. They appraise theoretical candidates on their internal merits and on their usefulness in guiding planned change with particular problems before making a selection.

Some multi-theory users are *theoretical dilettantes* and take eclecticism to the extreme. Allegiances to any one theoretical tradition are short lived. Dilettantes prefer talking the latest theoretical trend one season but soon forget it and move onto the next glamorous fad. Dilettantes prefer speaking the transactional analysis talk one season and the vocabulary of the new favorite, neuroscience, the next season. Or dilettantes may mix and match theoretical frameworks with little awareness of or attention to their compatibility. They are like religious cultists following the latest system of religious beliefs and rituals for a while, then losing interest and moving on to the next fad. They are also like movie stars shifting regularly from one pair of sunglasses to another with a different style and lenses.

Some multi-theory social workers are *theoretical integrationists* (Forte, 2006). They can be compared to people who speak multiple languages and enjoy world travel. They are like ecumenical religious believers who accept those with other faiths as having a legitimate conception of ultimate reality and who are eager to worship respectfully with and learn from devotees of other traditions. Contact with different theoretical societies presents exciting challenge, not dread or disdain. Boundaries to communication between rival theoretical traditions should be removed, and bridges for respectful encounters built. As skilled diplomats, the theoretical integrationist aims to understand the "culture" of other theoreticians on their own terms. Each theory can contribute to a dialogue that helps social workers better solve membership problems. Rigid segregation of theories by discipline, tradition, and conventional occupational categories stifles the social work imagination.

Theoretical integrationists believe that practitioners who seriously and carefully look at and listen to those from diverse conceptual traditions avoid wasteful work duplication, stay informed about social science developments, increase their theoretical understanding through contrast and comparison, cultivate a reflective and critical approach to their preferred theoretical orientation, and most importantly, broaden the repertoire of theoretical tools that they can bring to practice (Payne, 1997; Turner, 1983, 1996). The integrated toolbox contains a carefully organized set of lenses. Each is useful for perceiving certain PIE phenomena. Theoretical integrationists value an open, inclusive, tolerant, and non-dogmatic attitude toward social workers aligned with different theoretical traditions (Sztompka, 2004).

I will be promoting a theoretical integration approach in the remainder of this book. The alternative methods for using multiple theories—common factors, the eclectic approach, assimilative integration, and client-directed integration—as championed by various theory users aligned with the Society for the Exploration of Psychotherapy Integration (Feixas and Bottella, 2004) or the theory integration movement, will be discussed in Lesson 17.

Integrationist metaphors of multi-theory practice

Let's use some metaphors to understand better the idea of multi-theoretical social work practice. I am going to develop some comparisons between multi-theory social work and everyday jobs and activities.

First, the multi-theory social worker is like a linguist or translator who has expert knowledge of a native language, has become fluent in several additional languages, can converse effectively with persons from various speech communities, and can translate the communication of non-English speaking persons to English listeners. The social work linguist can participate in a family assessment planning team with representatives from five different departments and from multiple professional groups in a large hospital. The social work linguist can understand the language of the priest from the pastoral counseling center speaking of a patient's faith-based beliefs and convictions related to after life. This social worker can understand the physician speaking in terms of disease, medication, medical treatments, and prognosis. Finally, the multilingual social worker can even understand the program administrator who articulates an agency policy position using the language of tight budgets, fiscal accountability, sliding scale fees, and reimbursement plans.

Second, the multi-theory social worker is like a skilled handyman or handywoman with a large toolbox. In everyday life, a tool is a physical device designed to serve a particular purpose. Theories are the social worker's tools. They serve specific purposes like the production of knowledge for use. The handyman selects the right tools (hammer and nails, power saw and ruler, or screwdriver and screws) for each job; so does the multi-theory social worker. The handywoman knows that tools (like theories) may need replacing at some time, and the social work generalist knows the importance of replacing old tools, and that new tools are available at the profession's "hardware" store. Theories are available in the professional literature. Here are a few concrete images of the multi-theory social worker as tool user. The social work theory user can implement an ego psychological life review to help nursing home residents give new meanings to their lives. She can use a behavioral observation checklist to help teachers who are tracking progress toward appropriate classroom behavior by their special education students. She can use a family-oriented eco-map to identify the environmental stressors and supports, the internal family subsystems, and the boundary regulation issues faced by a family joined by a former member returning from a state mental hospital. She can use economics and create a marketing plan as a tool to publicize and promote a program teaching safe sex practices to adolescents.

The multi-theory social worker can also be compared to an actor who continually expands the repertoire of parts mastered integrating more and more roles so he is invited to perform in many different theoretical performances. He can use the economic framework as administrator to guide the board of directors as it conducts a cost–benefit analysis of a new program to divert nonviolent offenders from the criminal justice system. He can learn the critical theory scripts and perform as an advocate to document laws regarding drug use that treat differentially members of minority cultural groups (crack users) compared to members of mainstream groups in suburbia (cocaine users). He can refer to social learning and role theory screenplays as a coach who prepares those recently released from prison for community roles of worker, tenant, roommate, and friend.

The multi-theory social worker is like a camera operator who can shift lenses during a photo shoot depending on the changing conditions, the goals of the client, and the light. The social worker can use a certain lens for close ups, the applied biological approach, to capture micro-level images of body chemistry associated with a client's anger management problems. The social worker as photographer can use a lens for standard range photos, applied symbolic interactionism, for example, to study the patterns of interaction between the angry client and his family. This social worker can use a special lens for long distance, applied critical theory, to snap shots capturing the ways that social structural variables like social class and minority group membership relate to individual member problems with rage, resentment, and barely repressed feelings of humiliation.

The multi-theory social worker is like an experienced map user who has integrated knowledge of many different kinds of maps and can select the map that best describes the terrain where she is traveling: a street map, a map of navigable waters, or a map of trails through the woods. So too, the multi-theory social worker can use different maps: a physical ecology map that traces the homeless client's daily routines in a neighborhood, locates resources in the community space, identifies dangerous spots, and describes paths for travel, physical features, and major buildings; or a systems map that identifies all the large systems that indirectly influence family functioning of a recently evicted client family, and characterizes the nature of family system connections to the larger systems; or a map of the client's brain function-ing presented in simplified form by the medical consultant to the homeless shelter to help workers understand the impact of Alzheimer's disease on an elderly alcoholic who has wandered repeatedly from the agency's house.

Finally, the multi-theory social worker can be compared to a perspective taker. Think of the proverbial elephant handlers who all took a look at the elephant from a different perspective and defined the animal in ways that fit their perspectives (snout like a hose, leg like a tree trunk, tail like a fly swatter, etc). The multi-theory social worker can also use different theoreti-cal frameworks in an integrated and intentional way to shift perspectives on the client–environment configuration. She can use the applied ego psycho-logical framework to aid in taking the perspective of the client's intimate others, mother, father, and siblings, and in even taking client perspectives of which the client may not have full awareness. She can use the applied sym-bolic interactionist framework to aid in taking the perspective of significant others (teachers, best friends, lovers and spouses) who have influenced the client's identity formation process, the reference group others who the client uses to develop standards for success and life aspirations, and the general-ized others (religious organizations, the legal system, etc) who the client uses to appraise appropriateness of varied lines of conduct. She can use the critical or feminist frameworks to help take the perspective of marginal, exploited, oppressed, or powerless group members.

Learning activities and reflections

1. In the last three decades, social workers have seen a proliferation of theoretical frameworks and theories. The contemporary social worker must develop a position on this trend toward theoretical pluralism. He or she might attempt to practice with no or minimal reference to theoretical knowledge. The theory-oriented social worker might select, master, and affirm one theoretical tradition as critical to her in her theoretical orientation. The social worker might embrace theoretical pluralism and work hard to learn and use many theories.

   Today's social worker may make other decisions regarding theoretical knowledge. He or she may make a strong commitment to one theoretical framework or to a set of theories and choose to honor this commitment for years. In contrast, the social worker might be fickle and shift theoretical allegiances often. Additionally, the social worker may make choices regarding theoretical advocacy and fight hard to convince others of the merit of his or her preferred theory, avoid any promotion or selling of theoretical ideas, or only rise to defend favored theoretical knowledge when attacked.

   First, brainstorm some possible arguments for each of the three major stances toward theoretical knowledge—no theory, one theory, multiple theories. What are the arguments in favor of each stance and the arguments against each stance? What might be the practical consequences, good and bad, following the adoption of each of the stances?

2. Identify your preferred stance towards theoretical proliferation and the other choices that you have made or are likely to make regarding a stance toward theoretical knowledge—likely length of commitment and degree of advocacy, in particular. Provide some arguments justifying your overall stance toward theory proliferation. How has this stance served you well? In what ways has sticking to the stance presented you tough challenges?

3. Finally, conclude with reflections on these learning activities. What have you learned that will prepare you to utilize theoretical frameworks to guide the processes of assessment, intervention, and evaluation?

References

Bailey, J. (1980). *Ideas and intervention: Social theory for practice*. London: Routledge & Kegan Paul.

Borden, W. (2010). Taking multiplicity seriously. In W. Borden (Ed.), *Reshaping theory in contemporary social work practice: Toward a critical pluralism in clinical practice* (pp. 3–27). New York: Columbia.

Duncker, E. (2001). Symbolic communication in multidisciplinary cooperation. *Science, Technology, and Human Values, 26* (3), 349–386.

Feixas, G. and Botella, L. (2004). Psychotherapy integration: Reflections and contributions from a constructivist epistemology. *Journal of Psychotherapy Integration, 14* (2), 192–222.

Fish, S. (1982). Consequences. In W. J. T. Mitchell (Ed.), *Against theory* (pp. 106–131). Chicago: University of Chicago Press.

Forte, J. A. (2006). *Human behavior and the social environment: Models, metaphors, and maps for applying theoretical perspectives to practice*. Belmont, CA: Thomson Brooks/Cole.

Germain, C. B. (1983). Technological advances. In A. Rosenblatt and D. Waldfogel (Eds), *Handbook of clinical social work* (pp. 26–57) San Francisco: Jossey Bass.

Glanz, K. and Bishop, D. B. (2010). The role of behavioral science theory in the development and implementation of public health interventions. *Annual Review of Public Health, 31*, 399–418.

Hudson, C. G. (2000). At the edge of chaos: A new paradigm for social work? *Journal of Social Work Education, 36* (2), 215–230.

Kaplan, A. (1964). *The conduct of inquiry: Methodology for behavioral science*. San Francisco: Chandler.

Merton, R. K. (1975). Structural analysis in sociology. In P. M. Blau (Ed.), *Approaches to the study of social structure* (pp. 21–52). New York: Free Press.

Merton, R. K. (1996). Theoretical pluralism. In R. K. Merton and P. Sztompka (Eds), *On social structure and science* (pp. 34–40). Chicago: University of Chicago Press.

Mills, C. W. (1959). *The sociological imagination*. New York: Oxford University Press.

Payne, M. (1997). *Modern social work theory* (2nd ed.). Chicago: Lyceum.

Payne, M. (2002). Social work theories and reflective practice. In R. Adams, L. Dominelli and M. Payne (Eds), *Social work: Themes, issues and critical debates* (pp. 123–138). Basingstoke: Palgrave.

Percy, F. P. and Sprenkle, D. H. (1985–86). Family therapy theory building: An integrative training approach. *Journal of Psychotherapy and the Family, 1* (4), 5–14.

Prochaska, J. O. and Norcross, J. C. (1999). *Systems of psychotherapy: A transtheoretical analysis* (4th ed.). Pacific Grove, CA: Brooks/Cole.

Remington, K. and Pollack, J. (2007). *Tools for complex projects*. Farnham: Ashgate Publishing.

Richardson, K. A. (2004). Systems theory and complexity: Part 1. *Emergence: Complexity and Organization, 6* (3), 75–79.

Romaine, S. (2000). *Language in environment: An introduction to sociolinguistics*. Oxford: Oxford University Press.

Rule, J. B. (1997). *Theory and progress in social science.* Cambridge: Cambridge University Press.

Safran, J. D. and Messer, S. B. (1997). Psychotherapy integration: A postmodern critique. *Clinical Psychology: Science and Practice, 4* (2), 140–152.

Sanger, M. and Giddings, M. C. (2012). A simple approach to complexity theory. *Journal of Social Work Education, 48* (2), 369–376.

Sztompka, P. (2004). Shaping sociological imagination: The importance of theory. In J. Alexander, G. T. Marx and C. L. Williams (Eds), *Self, structure, and beliefs: Explorations in sociology* (pp. 254–267). Berkeley: University of California Press.

Turner, F. J. (1983). Directions for social work education: The challenge of developing a comprehensive, coherent and flexible integrating network of theories. In L. S. Bandler (Ed.), *Education for clinical social work practice* (pp. 125–141). Oxford: Pergamon Press.

Turner, F. J. (1996). An interlocking perspective for treatment. In F. J. Turner (Ed.), *Social work treatment: Interlocking theoretical approaches* (4th ed., pp. 699–711). New York: Free Press.

Turner, F. J. (1999). Theories of practice with vulnerable populations. In D. E. Biegel and A. Blum (Eds), *Innovations in practice and service delivery across the lifespan* (pp. 13–31). New York: Oxford University Press.

4

Use theories to guide helping processes in six ways

(EPAS 2.1.7 Apply knowledge; EPAS 2.1.10 Engage, assess, intervene, evaluate)

The social work profession draws on theories of human development and behaviour and social systems to analyse complex situations and to facilitate individual, organisational, social and cultural changes (original spelling)
(International Federation of Social Workers, 2012)

Theories have many specific and practical uses. Theories can help social workers answer important "why," "how," "when," "what," and "which" questions. Theories can also enhance the speed and precision of professional communication.

Six practical uses of theory

Social work helping activities are enriched when practitioners use relevant research especially research about effective information-gathering instruments and effective interventions and programs. Professional helping work is also enriched when practitioners draw on the practice wisdom accumulated by the profession, by their field of service, by the agency, and by the reflective practitioner. In this book, we are concentrating our attention on theoretical knowledge, and attempting to show that theories and their elements can serve practitioners in many practical ways. In Lesson 1, we examined some of the general uses of theoretical knowledge. Additionally, theory experts have identified six specific functions or uses of theory related to practice and the planned change process (Buchanan, 1998; Burr, 1995; Howe, 1997). We will discuss each in this lesson. See Figure 4.1 for a summary of these uses.

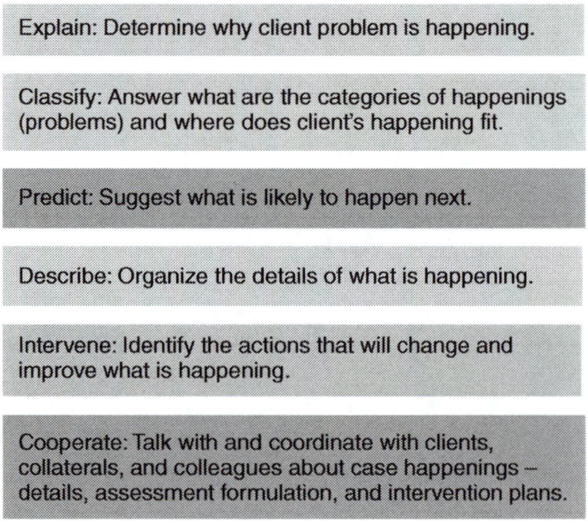

Explain: Determine why client problem is happening.

Classify: Answer what are the categories of happenings (problems) and where does client's happening fit.

Predict: Suggest what is likely to happen next.

Describe: Organize the details of what is happening.

Intervene: Identify the actions that will change and improve what is happening.

Cooperate: Talk with and coordinate with clients, collaterals, and colleagues about case happenings – details, assessment formulation, and intervention plans.

Figure 4.1 Six uses of translated theory

To explain (why is it happening?)

Theories can answer practitioner's questions such as why is this happening to the client or what is triggering this kind of troubling or joyful event? Such theorizing is used to generate specific explanations about events, processes, and social arrangements. Theoretical explanations often take a causal form. Causes are events that precede effects (that which is caused). Causes are associated statistically with that which is caused (as one value—eating fast food—changes, the other value—overall body weight—changes), and causes have been established by research as the best explanation for the effects; alternative or spurious causal explanations have been ruled out. Causal theoretical explanations summarize concisely much relevant information answering why questions.

Development theories, for example, assist social workers in explaining client system challenges that have their sources in developmental experiences. These theories can specify the key explanatory variables or causes and the relationships between these variables. Smith-Osborne (2005) blended two developmental theories, ego psychology and feminist theory, to explain shoplifting by female teenagers. Erikson's ego psychological theory articulates why some adolescents steal. This theory suggests that such behavior is a response to an identity crisis and the teenager's exploration and trial adoption of the attractive "thief" identity. The feminist theory indicates that there is a gender feature of this act of delinquency. Female teens feeling alienated from the self and disempowered because of sexist patterns in their community use shoplifting to make statements about their power aspirations.

Burton and Meezan (2004) used social learning theory to explain the behavioral patterns of sexually abusive male teenagers. Their deviant behavior is learned primarily in the family and during interaction in media environments. Relevant learning processes explaining the behaviors included the modeling of the sexual abuse the teenagers experienced, learning sexual actions via pornography, learning rule-breaking via observing family members, and learning aggression by imitating the father's violence.

Human behavior theories derived from sociology, psychology, anthropology, and other related disciplines offer explanations of a range of personal and public challenges and problems. These explain human and collective patterns and processes associated with crime, delinquency, disasters, disease, drug use, eating disorders, hate crime, homelessness, immigration, mental illness, poverty, prostitution, social isolation, suicide, and unemployment among others. Strengths-oriented theorists are beginning to develop theoretical explanations for patterns and processes associated with positive experiences, emotions, relationships, and organizations.

To classify (what are the categories of happenings?)

Theories can answer the practitioner's question: how does this case, problem, process, or event fit into a larger pattern or set of cases, problems, processes, or events? Theories can help social workers thereby categorize data, and place observed phenomena into different categories based on resemblances and differences (Turner, 2010). A *typology* is a "classification scheme developed systematically by specifying a series of attributes and creating categories that exhaust the logical combinations of those attributes" (Chafetz, 1978, p. 67). Classification systems or typologies provide a method for organizing and categorizing phenomena that aims to be exhaustive—inclusive of all the things being classified. There is no item that doesn't fit in the scheme. Classification schemes also use categories that are mutually exclusive—each thing clearly fits into only one category (Reynolds, 1971).

Social workers have made use of a family systems theory approach, Olson's Circumplex Model of Family Functioning (Olson et al., 1989), for example, to categorize families by central system attributes and organize these into categories (levels) of adaptability and cohesion (healthy, moderately healthy, unhealthy). Based on this classification system, workers can make judgments about the likely vulnerability to stressors of specific families at specific family stages.

Attachment theorists classify children in terms of their attachment style. The categories include secure, avoidant, ambivalent/resistant and disorganized. Social workers in mental health settings and health settings often use diagnostic category systems to identify, understand, and treat clients reporting mental health and physical health problems. Social workers in justice settings use crime categories or the degree of a crime's severity to classify offenders. Macro social workers use community type (city, town, suburb, rural area, and so on) to make sense of the particular ecological challenges and opportunities presented to community residents in different residential settlements.

To predict (what is likely to happen next?)

Theories can answer the practitioner's question: what comes next for this client and when might changes be anticipated? What outcomes are likely to follow a specific intervention? Theorizing is used to make predictions about events or sequences of events in the future. Knowledge about past and current events and their likely impact can be used to make tentative statements about anticipated choices, careers, challenges, and trajectories of clients.

For example, development theories assist social workers in predicting trajectories of behavioral patterns based on a developmental history. Stacy (2006) used attachment theory and information about childhood attachment experiences with parents and friends to predict delinquency, substance misuse, and high school performance of siblings. Children who had certain types of negative attachment experiences early in life were more likely to engage in delinquency, substance misuse, and unsuccessful high school behavior than children who experienced secure attachments. Forte (2006) reviewed the interactionist approach to gender that connects childhood socialization experiences (labeling by parents, appearance management, peer interaction, play with toys, and so on) to the development of later-life gender ideals and gender behavior preferences. Social workers in community correction centers need to predict the likelihood that an offender will soon engage in violent crime, and health social workers offer predictions about the likely course of a disease to concerned family members. Theories help with such prognostic tasks.

To describe and organize (how can the details of what is happening be best organized?)

Theories provide a degree of precision and rigor in descriptions of person-in-environment (PIE) configurations not available in everyday language (Turner, 2010). With theories practitioner's can answer important assessment questions: what should I look for when I am gathering information about the client, the environment, transactions between the client and environment, and the focal problem; how can I use this information to determine what is going on here; and how should I organize and report all the data? Personal and situational factors relevant to a problem or stimuli to personal growth are discovered and prioritized. Theories can guide the processes of information collection, organization, and summary necessary to such assessment work.

A developmental theory, for example, provides a framework for assembling "person interacting in an environment and changing over time" data, for judging the relative importance of the information collected during the assessment process, and for discerning developmental patterns. Turton, McGauley, Marin-Avellan, and Hughes (2001) employed an attachment-theory based tool to gather and organize detailed information obtained about adult offenders with personality disorders. Havighurst's developmental stage theory with its delineation of stage tasks and normative behavior has been used to facilitate the effective information-gathering process and the assessment of adolescent clients (Rubenstein, 1991).

Social workers deal in information. In everyday practice, they write reports about information on a client system's progress. They confer with supervisors using information about advances or setbacks experienced with particular cases. Assuming information release policies have been followed, they share information with colleagues to understand and help clients who are stuck or who have many needs. Theories are useful tools for completing such tasks.

To intervene (what actions will change what is happening?)

Theories can answer the practitioner's questions: what is to be done to help and which specific interventions and techniques are likely to achieve the desired consequences. Many theoretical traditions include a "theory of change," a conception of what independent and mediating variables need to be changed to address a troubling condition. Theories suggest worker actions that will produce positive client system change. Specifically, theorizing can direct social workers in decision-making processes, and in the selection of and implementation of theory-informed intervention procedures.

Useful and scientifically validated theory-based interventions increase our power as practitioners to change social systems and to help small-scale client systems achieve desired outcomes. Competent practitioners adapt such helping actions so that they are sensitive to developmental stages and ecological characteristics. Theories can guide mezzo or macro-oriented reform efforts also, by suggesting interventions designed to make a difference in the lives of many community members by changing social structures, patterns of power and resource distribution, or shared culture. These theories contribute to a better world in line with the social work value of advancing political, social, and economic justice.

Applied development science, for example, includes theories that help answer questions about "what to change" and "how to make the change." Cummings, Bride and Rawlins-Shaw (2006) reported on the rationale for and the use of age-specific, cognitive-behavioral practice theory to guide intervention with elderly persons abusing alcohol. Drumm, Pittman and Perry, (2003) demonstrated how social workers could employ Bronfenbrenner's ecological theoretical approach to select and implement interventions in United Nation camps for Kosovar refugees, and thus to minimize trauma. These notions of theories of change and theory-informed intervention will be described more fully in later lessons.

To cooperate (how can we meaningfully interact in relation to relevant happenings using theoretical language?)

Effective social workers can use theoretical languages when cooperating with experts in particular theoretical languages. For example, as a group worker in a community mental health center I learned to confer with a consulting psychiatrist who met with the staff each week. His specialty was the therapeutic use of psychotropic medication and he spoke commonly using a biomedical language. Many of the center members were complying with medication prescriptions and my conversations with the psychiatrist enabled me to help members better understand the likely impact of the medication, monitor the physical and psychological effects of the medication, avoid substances that mixed poorly with the medication, and collect information for their monthly meetings with case managers where dosage and medication changes were considered.

Later as a correctional social worker, I needed to learn the legal language of judges, lawyers, and probation workers to cooperate with them on behalf of my clients. I also led a bi-weekly orientation group for 15 or more new nonviolent offenders. Besides fostering mutual aid processes during our ninety-minute session, I worked hard to help group members understand the terms of their contract with the court. A grasp of the intended meanings of the judge and his agent, the probation worker, and a commitment to responsible action to fulfill the contract would spare dutiful group members incarceration in the cities overcrowded and dangerous jail.

Effective social workers also must cooperate with those who don't specialize in professional and disciplinary languages, for example, clients and their families. Knowledge of the theoretical language deepens such social workers' understanding of client concerns and problems, and knowledge of translation procedures makes it possible to translate such knowledge into the everyday language familiar to the client, family, and significant others. My wife worked as a director of a Ronald McDonald House for a decade. Families with children dealing with cancer—often from distant and rural areas with limited health services—stayed at the home while their children received treatment at the local teaching hospital. The families would meet occasionally with the medical specialists to discuss their children's diagnosis and treatment plans. Without translation help, they reported that these encounters were incomprehensible. My wife and the medical social workers frequently translated the busy doctors' talk, a use of jargon derived from sophisticated, complex, and technical theories and research about cancer, into words and phrases more familiar to the family. Such translation work helped family members cooperate as fully as possible with the medical team's recommendations.

Learning activities and reflections

1. Theories are used by social workers to achieve particular ends. Like tools, theories have a variety of functions. Each function can contribute to the processes of assessment, intervention, and evaluation. There are six common functions related to theory application.

    Theories provide explanations. Social workers often encounter puzzles requiring theoretical inquiry. Why is the client system experiencing this problem or challenge? What has happened to the helping process and relationship that is blocking cooperative action? In what ways, are different forces in the environment hindering or helping the client system's problem solving efforts? Why has the agency changed so that agency culture, policies, or procedures are undermining effective work with client systems?

    Practice the use of theorizing to generate causal explanations. First, ponder the question: what are the likely causes for the intergenerational transmission of poverty? You might consider biological–genetic causes. You might identify psychological causes. You might identify causes related to social, political, economic, cultural and other large-scale factors. You might prefer to combine causes and present a multiple cause explanation. Offer an explanatory summary of your thinking about this question. Summarize your causal explanation in a few sentences. What arguments and evidence could you use to support your explanation? What arguments and evidence could a critic use to challenge your explanation? With what theoretical tradition or school of thought is your explanation most clearly associated?

    Second, identify some theoretical puzzle that you have experienced in your family household, work setting, or school environment. Attempt to describe the puzzle clearly and in a comprehensive way. Then offer a tentative explanation of the puzzling phenomenon. Summarize your explanation, if possible, using scientific theory (or theories) and scientific concepts to do so.

2. Theorizing is often used to classify phenomena. Select a classification scheme used by social workers in a field such as mental health, health, correction, children and family services, gerontology, international aid, and so on. Identify some of the categories included in the scheme and describe each. Identify some of the principles or criteria used to place different instances into the classification categories. If possible, identify some studies or reviews from the scientific literature asserting the accuracy or inaccuracy of the classification process. What theoretical base, if any, guides the classifying process? What are some of the challenges associated with the classification process?

   Reflect also on a time in your life when a representative of an official organization classified you, your physical symptoms, your thinking style, your behavioral patterns, or your overall mental health. What did this experience mean to you?

3. Theorizing is also used to make predictions about the future. Theoretical knowledge about past and current events and their likely impact can be used to make tentative statements about future choices, events, careers, or trajectories. For example, attachment theorists predict that children who have certain types of negative attachment experiences early in life are more likely to experience later relationship difficulties than children who had secure attachments.

   Take out your glass "fortune-teller's ball," and practice the use of theorizing to predict. Be sure to consider both micro-level and macro-level variables when making your predictions. What information would help you predict the gender ideals (macho female or delicate male, for examples) that a young boy or girl will embrace later in life? Or a preteen's sexual orientation? Or, what variables could help you and other correctional social workers predict the post-prison choices of various adult offenders? How would you test the accuracy and the strength of your theory-based prediction?

4. Social workers might collect thousands of pieces of data about any person-in-environment-with-a-problem configuration. Theories can be used to guide the processes of information organization necessary to assessment, and the organization of such information as an assessment formulation.

   Pick a theory that you understand fairly well, for examples, the strengths perspective, Erikson's life stage model, family systems theory, or Piaget's cognitive development stage theory. List five to ten pieces of information that the theory directs the worker to collect. Summarize also a possible assessment conclusion that a practitioner using the theory might develop based on collected information and then share with his or her field instructor or supervisor. Reflect on how the theory might help you make sense of the vast amount of information associated with a confusing practice challenge.

5. Theories are critical to the helping process and to worker effectiveness. Theorizing can direct social workers in decision-making processes, and in the selection of and implementation of developmentally and ecologically sensitive intervention procedures.

   Work backwards and identify several interventions that you have learned in a social work class, in your field placement, or during volunteer service. For each intervention, identify the formal or informal theory that connected the intervention to expected outcomes. Search the literature or the web also to identify the theoretical sources for these interventions. Look in your search also for empirical evidence supporting any claims of the effectiveness of the theory-based interventions.

6. Theories are like languages and their fluent use can improve cooperation between members of a helping team; their clumsy use can lead to difficulties with colleagues and/or clients. Recall a visit to an organizational setting where a specialized professional or disciplinary language was used—a courtroom, a hospital, a church, a psychiatric ward, a state house, or a nursing home. Specify the speakers in the setting and the kind of language and even "dialect" spoken by each (for example, the hospital includes doctors and nurses. Each uses a biomedical language but probably with some noticeable differences in "dialect'). Identify how a person unfamiliar with the setting might first become aware of language differences (picking up a brochure, overhearing a specialist speak to a colleague, trying to read an official document) and how he or she might experience some confusion. How specifically might the differences between specialized theoretical language and the visitor's native language undermine cooperation in the setting? Finally, brainstorm ideas about how a skilled and knowledgeable social worker might serve as a translator and reduce the misunderstandings that undermine cooperation.

7. Conclude with reflections on these learning activities. What have you learned that will prepare you to utilize theoretical frameworks to guide the processes of assessment, intervention, and evaluation?

References

Buchanan, D. R. (1998). Beyond positivism: Humanist perspectives on theory and research in health education. *Health Education Research: Theory and Practice, 13* (1), 439–450.

Burr, W. R. (1995). Using theories in family science. In R. D. Day, K. R. Gilbert, B. H. Settles and W. R. Burr (Eds), *Research and theory in family science* (pp. 73–90). Pacific Grove, CA: Brooks/Cole.

Burton, D. L. and Meezan, W. (2004). Revisiting research on social learning theory as an etiological proposition for sexually abusive male adolescents. *Journal of Evidence-Based Social Work, 1* (1), 41–80.

Chafetz, J. S. (1978). *A primer on the construction and testing of theories in sociology.* Itasca, IL: F. E. Peacock.

Cummings, S. M., Bride, B. and Rawlins-Shaw, A. M. (2006). Alcohol abuse treatment for older adults: A review of recent empirical research. *Journal of Evidence-Based Social Work, 3* (1), 79–99.

Drumm, R. D., Pittman, S. and Perry, S. (2003). Social work interventions in refugee camps: An ecosystems approach. *Journal of Social Service Research, 30* (2), 67–92.

Forte, J. A. (2006). *Human behavior and the social environment: Models, metaphors, and maps for applying theoretical perspectives to practice.* Belmont, CA: Thomson Brooks/Cole.

Howe, D. (1997). Relating theory to practice. In M. Davies (Ed.), *The Blackwell companion to social work* (pp. 170–176). Oxford: Blackwell.

International Federation of Social Workers (2012). Introduction. Retrieved July 12, 2012, from http://ifsw.org/policies/definition-of-social-work.

Olson, D. H., McCubbin, H. I., Barnes, H., Larsen, A., Muxen, M. and Wilson, M. (1989). *Families: What makes them work* (2nd ed.). Los Angeles: Sage.

Reynolds, P. D. (1971). *A primer in theory construction.* Indianapolis: Bobbs-Merrill.

Rubenstein, E. (1991). An overview of adolescent development, behavior, and clinical intervention. *Families in Society, 72* (4): 220–225.

Smith-Osborne, A. (2005). Comparative theoretical perspectives on a social problem: Psychopathology and middle-class teen female shoplifters. *Journal of Evidence-Based Social Work, 2* (3/4), 73–84.

Stacy, P. D. (2006) Early childhood attachments as a protective factor comparing resilient and non-resilient siblings. *Journal of Evidence-Based Social Work, 3* (2), 49–65.

Turner, C. (2010). *Investigating social theory.* Los Angeles: Sage.

Turton, P., McGauley, G., Marin-Avellan, L. and Hughes, P. (2001). The adult attachment interview: Rating and classification problems posed by non-normative samples. *Attachment and Human Development, 3* (3), 284–303.

<table>
<tr><td>

5

</td><td>

Use a metatheory to guide selection of theoretical languages for helping

</td></tr>
</table>

(EP 2.1.3 Apply critical thinking; EP 2.1.7 Apply knowledge)

Educators have sought to develop a metatheory that would simultaneously explain human behavior at the intrapsychic, interactional, and sociocultural levels.

(De Hoyos, 1989, p. 131)

The tri-level model provides structure to the eclectic approach and reminds practitioners of the person-in-environment ... [it] helps workers maintain a dialogue with diverse practice theories while continuing to search for a framework that is unique to social work practice.

(De Hoyos, 1989, p. 138)

The professional toolbox of theories has become larger and larger over the last several decades. When a sloppy social worker looks into the toolbox to pick the tools needed for a particular task in a particular setting, he or she may feel overwhelmed by the number and the disorder of the tools collected. I have become a compulsive organizer, and in this lesson, I offer a way to organize theories for professional purposes so the toolbox will be orderly and the selection process will be manageable. The commentary in this lesson may seem very abstract and complex but it will serve the reader well in later lessons as we learn to use fourteen different theories to guide helping work during each phase of the planned change process.

Metatheorizing and metatheory: definitions

You have become familiar with the "person and environment" framework, a central and classic approach to organizing knowledge (Karls and O'Keefe (2008). It is one of the most common organizing frameworks for social work knowledge and is often referred to as the person-in-environment (PIE) perspective. James Karls, its key creator, received a distinguished award in 2008 from the National Association of Social Workers (NASW) Foundation for the development of a PIE assessment system (National Association of Social Workers, 2013), and the PIE approach was commended for increasing public appreciation of social work, distinguishing social work from other professions, and encouraging social work leadership in a wide range of fields. The NASW also chose "helping people in their environment" as a key theme in their public education campaign; the phrase is displayed, for instance, prominently in the 2013 brochure. Karls and O'Keefe (2008) have recently updated their 1994 PIE system for classifying problems in social functioning. Their assessment approach surpasses in comprehensiveness tools that only consider micro-level factors or macro-level factors. The approach helps practitioners identify and assess personal elements as they are connected with environmental elements. It also offers directives for creating holistic four-factor assessment formulations that guide intervention selection. The four factors are mental health, physical health, role functioning, and environmental resources.

You may have even read commentaries about this PIE framework and its strengths and limitations. It is less likely that you have read that the builders of the person and environment framework were engaging in metatheorizing or heard the framework called a metatheory. What is metatheorizing and what is a metatheory? *Metatheorizing* is a scientific activity that involves theorizing about theorizing. Ritzer (1991), a prominent expert on metatheorizing urged theory users to study "theories, theorists, and communities of theorists" (p. 6). Metatheorizing activities include the systematic study of the knowledge base of a discipline or profession. In the case of social worker, metatheorizing involves "*theoretical reflexivity*," the self-examination of the profession's theoretical development by the profession's members (Zhao 2001).

Ritzer (1991) identified three kinds of metatheorizing. First, he recommended that professionals work to deepen their understanding of the full range of relevant theories. He called this activity "*metatheorizing for understanding*." Human behavior educators in schools of social work often engage in this kind of theorizing activity. Social work scholars like Malcolm Payne and Francis Turner who write theory survey books do such metatheorizing.

The second type is called "*metatheorizing for the development of a new theory*." Currently, this is done by a small set of social work theorists and researchers who endeavor to add to the profession's knowledge base. We are beginning to see new theories about human behavior, for instance, inspired by advances in neuroscience and the study of the brain and the nervous system. Social work specialists like Rosemary Farmer (2008) are thinking about how to best organize and share this knowledge with educators and practitioners. Few social workers aim to become theory creation experts. However, I believe that every practitioner can and should create modest theories, or, at least, use current theories, revise these theories, and feed back their discoveries to theory specialists.

Ritzer (1991) called the third type of metatheorizing, "*metatheorizing for the creation of an overarching theoretical perspective.*" Such metatheorizing results in the creation of a *metatheory*, a theory about theories, or to return to my metaphor, a theory about how to organize a set of theoretical tools. The prefix "meta" means "above or "beyond" (Zhao, 2001). A metatheory goes above and beyond a specific theory. Metatheories are at a higher level of abstraction than behavioral theories or theories of specific client problems. A theory's subject matter is something about human behavior in the physical and social environment, for example, the problems experienced by children with insecure attachments. A metatheory's subject matter transcends a theory's content. The focus is the interrelation of a range of theories in a discipline or profession. A metatheory might present, for example, an elaborate statement "about what counts as knowledge (knowledge includes theory), which knowledge structures are important, and how to structure knowledge within the discipline" (Kramer, 1997, p. 51).

The empirical practice movement has alerted social workers to the importance of learning science. Metatheory or "metascience" is the "the science of sciences" because of its attention to "the methods, history, sociology, and language of sciences" (Morris, 1946, p. 510). Metatheories are important tools that help social workers to learn, select, and use scientific theories from a large knowledge base.

Illustrations of metatheory as ordering framework

Lister (1987) was one of the first social workers to develop a metatheory for organizing all social work knowledge. His metatheory made central use of systems theory and role theory, and conceptualized social work practice as the differential implementation of a set of roles to achieve varied system tasks. First, we enact roles for system development (the creation of new organizations, for example). Relevant roles are planner, policy developer and researcher. Second, we enact roles to maintain systems (the maintenance and enhancement of system resources, for example.) Relevant roles are administrator, supervisor, teacher, and team manager. Third, we enact roles for the purpose of system linkage (the connection of a client system to systems with resources, for example). Relevant roles include advocate, mediator, broker, and case manager. Finally, we enact roles for direct client intervention such as caseworker, group worker, or family counselor. Each professional role, according to Lister, has a distinctive knowledge base and distinctive processes, skills, and techniques. Lister followed the development of his metatheoretical framework with a report on his empirical study attempting to identify the theoretical knowledge associated with each role in educational curriculums. For example, behavioral and cognitive theories inform social workers' understanding and use of counselor roles.

Breunlin, Schwartz, and Kune-Karrer (1992) developed a "metaframework" to guide work with families. They proposed an integration of knowledge by the use of smaller conceptual frameworks built on a social systems theory foundation, supplemented by other major theories, and addressing six major domains. The internal member framework uses Bateson's ecological ideas and illuminates the mind and the multiple aspects of the self. The sequences framework modifies interactionist theories to illuminate patterns of interaction, routines, events that ebb and flow, and the generational transmission of dispositions. The organizational framework uses family structural theories to illuminate the structuring of family systems as hierarchies of power and control. The developmental framework uses family life cycle theories to illuminate the relation of human development to multiple levels of external social systems. The multicultural framework uses anthropological and cultural history perspectives to illuminate culture forces including ethnicity, race, and religion as these present opportunities and constraints to family members. The gender framework uses the feminist perspective to illuminate the range of possible gender-based arrangements in families from traditional to egalitarian. The metaframework, the interrelated set of these six frameworks, is recommended as a guide to family therapy and case illustrations are provided showing how practitioners might use the framework.

Metatheoretical social work and the PIE framework

I have developed a metatheoretical framework to guide your theory selection and theory use, and I am sharing it in this lesson (see Figure 5.1 opposite). My metatheorizing was influenced by Brooks-Harris (2008) and his approach to multi-theoretical psychotherapy but adapts his framework to the specifics of social work practice and to our profession's PIE guiding frame of reference especially our attention to multiple contexts.

Some basic principles guided my metatheorizing. First, human behavior and the social environment are conceptualized as five interrelated dimensions of the person transacting with seven environmental contexts. The framework requires holistic thinking by social workers: part-whole thinking and comprehensive assessment that explains how person-level dimensions are related to environmental contexts for each client.

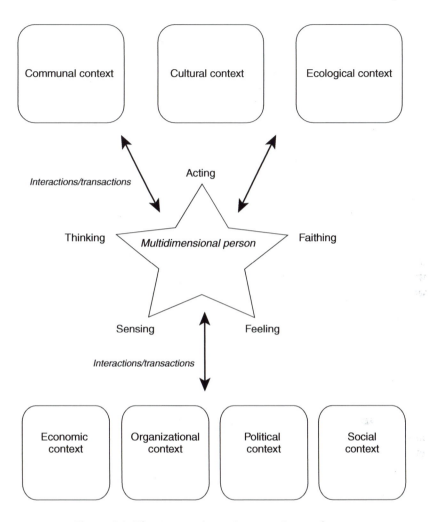

Figure 5.1 The "person-in-environment" metatheory

Second, fourteen major theoretical frameworks are integrated into the over-arching metatheoretical framework on the assumption that each theoretical framework has an explanatory strength in relation to the PIE configuration. Table 5.1 summarizes my judgments about which theoretical traditions best inform each aspect of this "multi-dimensional person transacting with vari-ous environmental contexts" metaframework.

I have chosen this particular set of frameworks for a variety of rea-sons. I picked theoretical traditions that have long been prominent in the social work literature, added the constructionist, economic, faith, and

Table 5.1 Multi-theoretical social work: a "person-in-environment" metatheory

The Person (multi-dimensional)

Dimension	Theory
Acting	Behavioral
Faithing	Interpretive anthropology
Feeling	Psychodynamic
Sensing	Evolutionary biology
Thinking	Cognitive

Interacting/transacting in

Process	Theory
Transaction*	Pragmatist symbolic interactionism

Physical environment contexts

Context	Theory
Community	Strengths–resilience
Cultural	Social constructionist
Economic	Exchange
Organizational	Role
Physical environment	Ecological
Political	Critical and feminist
Social	Systems

*Dewey: Problem-resolving transactions versus problem-sustaining transactions

strengths–resilience as relatively new but very important traditions, and I matched each tradition based on my understanding of its central focus and contribution to understanding human behavior and the environment. I aimed to create an assembly of theories suitable for a multi-dimensional, multi-contextual, and multi-theoretical approach to social work (Hutchison, 2012). There is some evidence that many of these theoretical traditions (behavioral, cognitive, ecological, psychodynamic, spirituality, strengths-resilience, and systems) are endorsed by social work practitioners (Forte, 2006; Forte and LaMade, 2011). There is also some evidence (Forte, 2009) that many are taught by social work human behavior educators as indicated in syllabi content (behavioral, cognitive, critical, ecological, psychodynamic especially attachment and Erikson's life stage theory, social constructionist, strengths-resilience, and systems) and as indicated in the table of contents for prominent "human behavior and the social environment" textbooks (behavioral especially social learning theory, cognitive development theory, ecological, feminist, psychodynamic, role, social constructionist, spirituality especially the faith development tradition, and symbolic interactionism). I was also guided in my selection by the accrediting body in the United States and their mandate regarding educational content, "Social workers apply theories and knowledge from the liberal arts to understand biological, social, cultural, psychological, and spiritual development" (Council on Social Work Education, 2008, p. 6). Finally, while evolutionary biology and economic exchange theoretical traditions don't appear to be preferred by practitioners, educators, or writers of major textbooks as documented in previous studies, these theoretical traditions have become increasingly relevant due to advances in biological sciences demonstrating the relevance of biological processes to human behavior and due to the profession's growing awareness of the importance of economic conditions and processes to clients' life chances. I reviewed the arguments for including these two theoretical traditions in an earlier book (Forte, 2006). Future social work metatheorists may offer alternative overarching conceptual systems.

Third, I designed this unifying framework as a metatheoretical tool to enhance the organization and purposeful selection of theoretical knowledge as it is needed in particular cases. For instance, practitioners might identify the most salient personal dimensions, environmental contexts, and interaction processes, and then select and use the relevant theories during assessment and intervention planning work.

The person

The person is conceptualized as a complex whole with five interrelated dimensions. Full understanding requires understanding of all dimensions and their interrelationship. The five critical dimensions are the active human processes of acting, feeling, faithing (my word—it refers to the process of developing and affirming spiritual or faith convictions), sensing, and thinking. Reducing human behavior to only one or two dimensions omits critical information. Like a diamond, the client has multiple facets or dimensions, and the skilled social worker uses theoretical knowledge to examine each of these dimensions during the information gathering and assessment processes. Many of the remaining commentaries in this part of the book will increase your familiarity with these five dimensions.

The environment

The environment is conceptualized as a set of interrelated contexts for human action and development. To interpret or accurately make sense of any PIE configuration, we must appreciate both the relevant context(s) and the position in this context of the acting and developing person. Human action is a flow of continually changing person-place-time configurations with influences and outcomes part of intricately connected activities. The social work practitioner must immerse herself or himself in the client's contexts, formulate meanings specific to this context, appraise the quality of the interconnectedness of client system, temporal factors, and contextual factors, and seek timely, culturally-sensitive and practical solutions to change problematic transactions. The seven major environmental contexts are the community context, the cultural context, the economic context, the organizational context, the physical ecological context, the political context, and the social context.

The interface of person and environment

This interface is conceptualized in transactional terms. The pragmatist philosophers Dewey and Bentley (1949) provided the basic transactional philosophy for conceptualizing the relationship between person and environment. These philosophers analyzed the major approaches to conceptualizing human action. *Self-action* refers to when humans (and other living organisms) are acting by means of their own powers. Subjects act in relative isolation from each other. Persons are capable of generating their own locomotive steam. Scientists analyze self-action by identifying the essential substances or qualities of the acting agent and the properties of these substances. The individual is the focal system. Choice is independent of specific contexts and the person's movements are not related theoretically to the surrounding environment. This approach doesn't fit with social work.

Inter-action assumes that human beings are independent and distinct organisms but that a related set of humans influence each other as causal agents. People are like marbles colliding and causing change in the trajectory of other marbles (Dewey and Bentley, 1949). Modern proponents of the inter-actional view (not the same as the symbolic interaction perspective) use "variable analysis" to identify the correlated variables that generate movement. Scientists analyze inter-action by focusing on the causal interconnections of fixed entities with identifiable attributes. The interrelated variables make up the focal system. Choice is influenced by external causes and a "thing is balanced against a thing in causal interconnection" (Dewey and Bentley, 1949, p. 108). This approach improves on the self-action approach. However, the inter-acting elements or relations are still conceptualized as independent of the environmental contexts for the inter-action.

The *trans-action* concept assumes that persons are inseparable from their environmental contexts. The Dewey and Bentley (1949) notion of trans-action is similar to the social work notion of interface or inter-action (Germain, 1981; Karls and O'Keefe, 2008). It is recommended for our use, and a way to ensure that the "I" in PIE can be maintained. The persons involved in a trans-action "derive their meaning, significance, and identity from the (changing) functional roles they play within the transaction" (Emirbayer, 1997, p. 287). Scientists analyze trans-actions by focusing on the dynamic and unfolding person–environment process as the focal system not by focusing only on the individual elements or the environmental contexts. Actors meet and change challenging environmental conditions and environments respond back dynamically to the actor's choices. The transactional credo asserts:

> Our position is simply that since man as an organism has evolved among all other organisms in an evolution called "natural," we are willing under hypothesis to treat all of his behavings, including his most advanced knowings, as activities not of himself alone, nor even as primarily his, but as processes of the full situation of organism-environment.
>
> (Dewey and Bentley, 1949, p. 104)

The living organism and the environment are phases of a single natural trans-actional process. Neither aspect of the organism–environment circuit can be specified and described fully apart from the other aspects or constituents. These philosophers discuss the organism-environment transaction using the following imagery: "living body and environing conditions cooperate as fiddle and player work together" (p. 286). Following Dewey and Bentley, 1949, we can also contrast transactions that resolve PIE problems from transactions that sustain PIE problems.

Matching theoretical frameworks to dimensions, interface, and contexts

First, we can match theoretical frameworks to the five basic dimensions. Acting is conceptualized well by the behavioral theory, faithing by the anthropological perspective on religion and spirituality, feeling by psychodynamic theory, sensing by evolutionary biology, and thinking by cognitive theory. Second, we can choose the theoretical perspective that best explains the interface of person and environment. Interaction or transaction is well addressed by the pragmatist/symbolic interactionism approach. Finally, different theoretical frameworks can be matched to environmental contexts:

the strengths-resilience approach to community context, the constructionist approach to diversity in the cultural context, the exchange theory to the economic context, role theory to the organizational context, empowerment theory (critical and feminist approaches) to the political context, ecological theory to the physical environment, and systems theory to the social context.

Matching PIE theories to cases

Thanks to participants in the Empirical Practice Movement (Reid, 1994) and advocates of evidence-based practice including the editors of and the contributors to two journals, *Journal of Evidence-Based Practice* and *Research on Social Work Practice*, practitioners have substantial help in selecting research-supported assessment tools and interventions suited to the particulars of a case. However, most of this literature is mute on theory and the theoretical foundations of assessment and intervention strategies. The profession hasn't made advances in providing guidelines and evidence for matching theory-informed inquiry approaches and theory-based interventions to client needs and preferences.

The following are a set of provisional guidelines for using the PIE metatheoretical framework and matching theory to helping circumstances when relevant research on theory application is unavailable (Hochbaum, Sorenson, and Lorig, 1992; Solomon, 2007; van Ryn and Heaney, 1992).

Case and problem characteristics

Theory can be chosen based on the size of the focal system (individual, group, or community/micro, mezzo, or macro, for examples). Cognitive theory suits assessment of persons and the micro level, role theory has a track record of explaining group process at mezzo levels, and social network theory is often useful for understanding community level and societal issues at mezzo and macro levels.

Theory can be chosen based on the temporal nature of the problem (one time or sporadic versus long lasting, for example). Crisis-oriented psychodynamic theory is often used for intense, one-time problems while the behavioral approach addresses chronic patterns and old habits.

Theory can be chosen by the degree of the organizational embeddedness of the focal concerns from highly private and personal concerns to very public concerns shared among members of a large collective. The psychodynamic approach addresses troubled dreams while critical theorists have theorized extensively about political-economic factors leading to inequality.

Client preferences

Theory can be chosen with consideration of client concerns. Which theory's central assumptions and values best correspond to the core beliefs and values of the client system? This client-directed approach (Duncan and Miller, 2000; Duncan, Sparks, and Miller, 2006) begins with the client. The worker doesn't start with his or her theory preferences, and then proceed to use them to help the client. Theoretical frameworks are selected in consultation with the client. The worker starts by translating potential theories into plain summaries and asking the client about his or her reactions to these tools for inquiry and action planning. This approach to theory selection and integration will be discussed more in Lesson 17.

Organizational and practitioner features

Theory can be chosen by considering issues of fit to the organizational context and to practitioner capabilities. In relation to the service setting, the practitioner might ask various relevant questions. What are the purposes and goals of an organization and its programs and which theories will best contribute to the realization of these ends? What are the resources needed for the use of available theories (minimal to great) and how does this compare to the availability of resources (time, staff, funding)?

Finally, the practitioner might consider personal factors. He or she might choose theories that fit with the worker's own assumptions and values. Of course, practitioners must consider the degree of specialized knowledge and skill needed for theory use compared to his or her capabilities, and only choose theories that he or she can use competently and responsibly.

Deciding wisely on the best set of theories for a particular case requires significant familiarity with the literature on many different theoretical frameworks and their strengths and limitations. Such a demand hopefully inspires social workers to work hard to master and stay current with theoretical knowledge. Practitioners should scan book listings and review sections, journals, and workshop announcements regularly to identify new evidence supporting or challenging theories and their elements. Priority should be given to theories with documented evidence of effectiveness in a setting, for a problem or challenge, and with a population similar to those of the helping circumstances. Additionally, because of limits to our knowledge in this area, effective professionals will need also to rely on practice wisdom, professional intuition, and expert consultation in selecting theories from the PIE metatheoretical framework for use with their clients.

Learning activities and reflections

1. Social workers theorize about many different aspects of human behavior and the environment: social injustice, developmental protective factors, marital communication, addictions, optimal homes, and so on. Social workers use theories to guide all phases of the planned change process. Some social workers even theorize about theories. This process is called metatheorizing. The result of such theorizing activity is a metatheory, a theoretical framework that integrates and synthesizes knowledge from multiple theories.

    The social work knowledge base is like a large library (or hardware store with many tools, if we extend the toolbox metaphor) with an ever-growing number of books and articles describing an ever-expanding number of theoretical frameworks. How do we find what we need in such a vast library? A metatheory is a way to bring order to this vast intellectual body of work. It might be compared to a blueprint and catalogue of the library identifying every location and the resources in each location.

    In this activity, I invite you to engage in some metatheorizing. We will use the PIE construct as our starting point. First, report on how you conceptualize the person? What theoretical knowledge helps you understand the person? Second, report on how you conceptualize the environment? What theoretical knowledge helps you understand the environment? Third, how do you conceptualize what happens between the person and environment? What theoretical knowledge helps you understand the "in," the interaction or interface component of the person-in-environment metatheory? How might you synthesize your preferred knowledge about person, interaction, and environment into an integrative framework or metatheory?

2. Think of a contemporary personal problem, a recent developmental problem, a family problem, or a client problem. Identify several relevant personal dimensions, several relevant environmental contexts, and several transactional issues associated with this problem. For each, begin to sketch out which theories might best guide your information gathering and interpretation. Finally, identify two or three ways that your small-scale metatheory of the "person interacting in an environment faced with a challenge" can guide your assessment formulation and intervention design.

3. Finally, conclude with reflections on these learning activities. What have you learned that will prepare you to utilize theoretical frameworks to guide the processes of assessment, intervention, and evaluation?

References

Breunlin, D. C., Schwartz, R. C. and Kune-Karrer, B. M. (1992). *Metaframeworks: Transcending the models of family therapy*. San Francisco: Jossey-Bass.

Brooks-Harris, J. E. (2008). *Integrative multitheoretical psychotherapy*. Boston: Lahaska Press /Houghton Mifflin.

Council on Social Work Education (2008). Educational policy and accreditation standards. Retrieved June 16, 2010, from www.cswe.org/Accreditation/Reaffirmation.aspx.

De Hoyos, G. (1989). Person-in-environment: A tri-level practice model. *Social Casework: The Journal of Contemporary Social Work, 70*, 131–138.

Dewey, J. and Bentley, A. F. (1949). *Knowing and the known*. Boston: Beacon Hill.

Duncan, B. L. and Miller, S. D. (2000). The client's theory of change: Consulting the client in the integrative process. *Journal of Psychotherapy Integration, 10* (2), 169–187.

Duncan, B. L., Sparks, J. A. and Miller, S. D. (2006). Client, not theory, directed: Integrating approaches one client at a time. In G. Stricker and J. Gold (Eds), *A casebook of psychotherapy integration* (pp. 225–240). Washington, DC: American Psychological Association.

Emirbayer, M. (1997). Manifesto for a relational sociology. *American Journal of Sociology, 2*, 281–317.

Farmer, R. L. (2008). *Neuroscience and social work practice: The missing link*. Los Angeles: Sage.

Forte, J. A. (2006). *Human behavior and the social environment: Models, metaphors, and maps for applying theoretical perspectives to practice*. Belmont, CA: Thomson Brooks/Cole.

Forte, J. A. (2009). Teaching human development: Current theoretical deficits and a theory-enriched 'Models, metaphors, and maps' remedy. *Journal of Human Behavior in the Social Environment, 19* (7), 932–954.

Forte, J. A. and LaMade, J. (2011). The center cannot hold: A survey of field instructors' theoretical preferences and propensities. *The Clinical Supervisor, 30* (1), 72–94.

Germain, C. B. (1981). The ecological approach to people-environment transactions. *Social Casework, 62* (6), 323–331.

Hochbaum, G. M., Sorenson, J. R. and Lorig, K. (1992). Theory in health education practice. *Health Education Quarterly, 19* (3), 295–313.

Hutchison, E. D. (and contributing authors) (2012). *Essentials of human behavior: Integrating person, environment, and the life course*. Thousand Oaks, CA: Sage.

Karls, J. M. and O'Keefe, M. E. (2008). *Person-in-environment system manual* (2nd ed.). Washington, DC: NASW Press.

Kramer, M. K. (1997). Terminology in theory: Definitions and comments. In I. M. King and J. Fawcett (Eds), *The language of nursing theory and metatheory* (pp. 51–61). Indianapolis, IN: Sigma Theta Tau International.

Lister, L. (1987). Contemporary direct practice roles. *Social Work*, 32 (5), 384–391.

Morris, C. (1946). The significance of the unity of science movement. *Philosophy and Phenomenological Research*, 6 (4), 508–515.

National Association of Social Workers (2013). Social workers honor James Karls with the International Rhoda G. Sarnat Award. Retrieved July 1, 2013 from www.naswfoundation.org/awards/2008/sarnat.asp.

Reid. W. J. (1994). The empirical practice movement. *Social Service Review*, 68 (2), 165–184.

Ritzer, G. (1991). *Metatheorizing in sociology*. Lexington, MA: Lexington Books.

Solomon, B. (2007). Taking "guilty knowledge" seriously: Theorizing, everyday inquiry, and action as "social caretaking." In S. L. Witkin and D. Saleeby (Eds). *Social work dialogues: Transforming the canon in inquiry, practice, and education* (pp. 94–112). Alexandria, VA: Council on Social Work Education.

van Ryn, M. and Heaney, C. A. (1992). What's the use of theory? *Health Education Quarterly*, 19 (3), 315–330.

Zhao, S. (2001). Metatheorizing in sociology. In G. Ritzer and B. Smart (Eds), *Handbook of social theory* (pp. 386–394). London: Sage.

Section 2

Multi-theoretical social work
and the planned change process

6 | Translate theories to guide the engagement process

(EPAS 2.1.7 Apply knowledge; EPAS 2.1.10 Engage, assess, intervene, and evaluate)

With an awareness of the varying theories and increased skill level in the use of techniques, students will be better prepared to provide services to clients. They will be guided by principles instead of good intentions, thus leading them to greater professionalism ... They will also be able to understand and adopt or adapt new techniques and models that arise in the future, as well as be able to test out various theories and techniques to determine those with which they are most comfortable.

(Boyle, Hull, Mather, Smith and Farley, 2009, p. 112).

Lesson 6 begins a new section. In this section, we will work on using fourteen different theories to guide the planned change process. Table 6.1 summarizes the specific questions that translated theories help us answer. The questions are organized by phases of the planned change process. In the lessons in this section, I will begin by a brief introduction to the multi-theoretical social work approach to the phase and the translation device or devices that transform theories for our practical use in that phase.

The engagement phase and translation by metaphors

The helping process begins as we engage our individual, group, community, societal, or international client. After preparing for a meeting with a

Table 6.1 Translating theories to answer questions at planned change phases

Phase	Question
Engagement	What theory-informed styles of engagement might we consider and translate for use, and which style or blend of styles fits with the case particulars?
Information gathering	According to our selected translated theory or combination of translated theories, which features of the PIE configuration should we focus on?
Assessment	Following theory translation, which theory-informed or multi-theory conceptualization best explains the PIE challenge?
Goal setting	What desired outcome(s) does the theoretical conceptualization (constructed following theory translation) suggest can be achieved?
Intervention	According to our chosen translated theory or integrated set of theories translated for use, how should the worker and client system act to progress toward targeted goals and objectives?
Evaluation	As recommended by the theory base that we have reconstructed from translated theories, what should we measure and how should we organize the evaluation of the effectiveness of the helping work?
Ending	When is the optimal time to end the helping service according to our translated-orienting theory or theories, and in what ways might the ending experience be optimized?

client or client system, the helping work begins. The client and worker have come into contact and the worker initiates the process of engagement. The Council on Social Work Education (2008) identifies several tasks necessary to engagement: substantively and affectively prepare for action with individuals, families, groups, organizations, and communities; use empathy and other interpersonal skills; and develop a mutually agreed-on focus of work and desired outcomes. The first two tasks involve worker actions like preliminary tuning into the client and client needs; conveying respect; demonstrating empathy through words, gestures and deeds; generating trust; and beginning to build a cooperative alliance or relationship. The third task will be covered more fully in Lesson 10. The engagement process, if successful, will create a foundation for the active involvement of the client or client system in the each of the phases of the planned change process.

Engagement is a critical phase of the planned change process. Successful helping requires that the worker engage the client or members of a client system. To engage help seekers, the worker uses a variety of helping procedures related to preparing the meeting space, greeting the client or client group in a respectful manner, conveying an intention to attend to client concerns with empathy, clarifying privacy protections, negotiating basic roles and rules, and removing any barriers to cooperative inquiry and problem solving work. Social workers have referred to this critical ingredient of the effective helping in a variety of ways: building a working alliance, creating a helping system, establishing rapport, joining with the client and so on.

There are many ways to approach the engagement process. *Multitheoretical engagement* involves the selective and purposeful use of diverse styles of relationship derived from fourteen theoretical traditions for conceptualizing engagement work and for reaching out to vulnerable populations and allies and in challenging villains. Each theoretical framework suggests a particular style or approach to engaging the client or the members of a client system (Brooks-Harris, 2008).

Each theoretical framework grows from a root metaphor. Any framework's preferences regarding engagement reflect the theory's "root metaphor" for conceptualizing the worker and the client. *Root metaphors* are basic comparisons that theorists use to make sense of an overall theoretical framework or a disciplinary stance toward human behavior and bio-psycho-social development (Pepper, 1942; Rigney, 2001). Practice theories related to the basic explanatory theoretical frameworks are also built on root metaphors (Martin and Sugarman, 1999; Neimeyer, 1999). The root metaphor influences the theory's conceptualizations of the client, the targets for change, the worker role and tasks, the engagement process, the change process, and the notion of optimal personal and system growth. For example, symbolic interactionists conceive of society as a conversation among different groups and within the minds of societal members. Applied symbolic interactionists conceive of the social worker as a communication expert who can master the languages of different membership groups, help groups learn each others' vocabulary, and use public and private conversations to organize problem solving work and solve problems. These metaphors shape the engagement processes informed by symbolic interactionism.

Conveyance metaphors are comparisons of more limited scope than root metaphors that theorists use to make sense of a selective aspect of human behavior and the environment or human development (MacCormac, 1985). Scholnik (2000) identified some familiar conveyance metaphors. Here, I will briefly discuss how these might be used for conceptualizing and orienting the engagement work. Kohlberg's conception of moral development makes many comparisons to learning by argument and dispute. Using this metaphor, the worker might approach a client as a debater and call into question premises and reasoning supporting immoral behavior. Piaget's cognitive developmental approach makes comparison of the developing person to a theoretician making a series of paradigm shifts toward personal theories of greater and greater complexity and rationality. From this starting point, the practitioner might approach the client as a fellow scientist and inquire about his or her thinking about and explanations for a troubling situation. Constructionist and narrative theorists compare human development to a series of stories. The social worker using a narrative conveyance metaphor might act as a listener of stories and invite the client to tell tales of early life triumphs, setbacks, and pivotal experiences.

Osborne (1995) also identified some conveyance metaphors used by developing theorists and argued that these metaphors should differentially influence the approach practitioners take toward practice with families. Humanistic theorists use images and ideas characterizing the developing person as naturally good and inclined to grow if validated. Here, the social worker engages the client like a loving parent who affirms the worth and the words of the growing child. Family systems theorists often use imagery characterizing the child as an element subject to multiple forces of energy and the parent to an electrician optimizing the flow of electric forces to the child. If we extend this metaphor to the engagement process, we might think of the social worker as an electrical inspector checking the range, adequacy, and quality of electrical connections between family members.

Fourteen approaches to the engagement phase

Multi-theoretical social work recommends the mastery of many theoretical frameworks and familiarity with each framework's metaphor-based conception of the helping role and engagement style. Such mastery increases the tools available for reaching out to, understanding, and forming a productive relationship with clients.

Although a worker's conception of the helping role and associated engagement style varies by theoretical framework, the current theoretical, research, and practice literature provides little guidance in identifying these variations. Practitioners will need to think carefully about which engagement style or styles will fit a particular helping situation. Table 6.2 summarizes my preliminary conception of fourteen different theory-directed engagement styles.

The following are summaries of a few illustrative theory-based engagement styles. Each is presented as a proposition linking the theoretical root metaphors for worker and client with the associated and expected helping actions during the engagement process.

Behavioral Theory: If the worker is like a lab scientist and the client like a participant in a study, the worker begins the helping process by carefully setting up the work setting and by using cues, rewards, punishments, and models to engage the full participation of the experimental subject.

Table 6.2 Translating theories to guide the engagement phase

PIE/theory	Conception of helper	Engagement tasks
Multi-dimensional person		
Acting (behavioral)	Laboratory scientist	Orient to procedures, begin scientific inquiry
Faithing (anthropological)	Reader, interpreter	Read and interpret sacred symbols and texts
Feeling (psychodynamic)	Analyst, deep listener	Identify, analyze psychic dynamics/emotions
Sensing (evolutionary biology)	Clinician, medical aid	Assist in study, diagnosis, treatment process
Thinking (cognitive)	Philosopher, logician	Question Socratically and judge ideas and logic
Interacting in		
Transact (interactionism)	Communication expert	Study clients' memberships and learn language
Environmental contexts		
Communal (strengths)	Coach, trainer	Find assets, appraise strengths, begin training
Cultural (constructionist)	Anthropologist, diplomat	Learn cultural practices, mediate differences
Economic (exchange)	Investment consultant	Appraise exchange patterns, advise prosperity
Organizational (role)	Playwright, director	Rehearse actor for performances
Physical environment (ecology)	Gardener, conservationist	Create ecological conditions for growth
Political (critical-feminist)	Critic, advocate, listener	Identify oppressed voices, fight for justice
Social (systems)	Choreographer, mechanic	Learn system parts and functions, rearrange, and fix

Biological Theory: If the worker is like a clinical health specialist promoting wellness and fighting illness and the client like a patient seeking expert consultation, then the worker begins by supporting behaviors that encourage healthful behavior (including the use of social work services, for instance) and promoting behaviors that reduce risky or harmful choices.

Conflict Theory: If the worker is like an advocate and a social critic and the client like an exploited factory worker, an oppressed minority member, or a silenced woman, then the worker begins the helping process by forming a partnership conveying a passion for championing the ally's cause, and learning the unjust arrangements contributing to the ally's misfortunes.

Role Theory: If the worker is like a theater coach and the client like a novice actor, then the worker begins the helping process by setting the stage, by contracting with the performer to commit to a part (agency client, for example) and by coaching, rehearsing, and trying out lines with the client for the new part.

Social Systems Theory: If the worker is like a mechanic and the client is like a part of a car or other machine, then the worker begins the helping process by learning about the whole of which the client is a part, by creating a new system with worker and helper as parts, and by exploring part-whole aspects of the client's problems.

Symbolic Interactionist Theory: If the worker is like a translator, an expert communicator in more than one language, and the client like a speaker of a different language, then the worker begins the helping process by learning the speaker's language, by translating the professional language of social work to the client, and by developing a mutual agreement to clarify all difficult words and gestures.

Matching theory-directed engagement style and helping circumstances

A social worker might tailor his or her engagement style to the particular features of the client's person-in-environment (PIE) configuration, or the social worker might start with one engagement style and switch to another engagement style as client and life space circumstances change. For example, the worker will engage a client differently depending on whether the client has chosen to seek help or has been mandated by a court or a social service department. The worker will engage the client differently depending on the dominant emotions that emerge in the first meetings: fear, anger, excitement, hope, regret, grief, and so on. The worker will adjust his or her engagement work to systems of different sizes: individual, family, or a community forum, for examples.

Walsh (1995) provided an example of matching a theory-informed engagement style to client characteristics and basic needs. He developed a profile of clients diagnosed with serious mental disorders but living in the community not in a psychiatric facility. Relevant client-situation features included limited social skills, vulnerability to social isolation, ambivalence about pursuing personal goals, unmet purpose-in-life or spiritual needs, interaction difficulties resulting from stigma, a hesitancy to trust professionals, and, most importantly, a partial breakdown in the ability to use and interpret conventional social symbols. Based on this profile, Walsh recommended the use of a symbolic interactionist approach to engagement strategies. Such an approach prioritizes communication and the co-creation of shared meanings, and offers theoretical resources for decoding the idiosyncratic or bizarre symbols used by these clients. Patient engagement and relationship building following interactionist guidelines can convey respect for the client's current meaning system, help the client regain use of conventional symbols, validate through word and deed the client's identity and worth, and initiate the necessary process of social reintegration.

In summary, the specific theory-informed framework and strategies for engagement chosen will vary by the purpose and goals of the helping work; client characteristics such as age, level of physical ability and health, cognitive capabilities, emotionality, openness to faith and spirituality explorations, cultural memberships, and so on; and by environmental characteristics such as the stability of the person's housing and work situations, the degree of social support, the ecological setting for the helping session, and community attitudes toward social work.

Learning activities and reflections

1. Each theoretical orientation toward practice suggests a distinctive conceptual emphasis on the helping role, and thus a distinctive style of engaging the client. Review Table 6.2 and the brief summaries of fourteen major theoretical frameworks, their conceptions of their helping role, and their characterization of engagement tasks. Multi-theoretical social work makes it possible for workers to select an engagement style compatible with your personal and professional convictions, and equally important suitable to the specific PIE configuration of each client.

   Reflect on your own ideas about the engagement phase. How do you characterize this phase and what are worker attitudes and activities that result in successful engagement. On what theoretical approach is your approach to engagement based?

2. Next, consider the alternative theory-directed engagement styles identified in Table 6.2. Which theory-based style or styles fits best with your own approach to social work helping? Identify the specific engagement attitudes and actions associated with your use of this style to begin to form a helping relationship with a possible client. How does the theoretical framework influence how you engage the client and what you do in the early phase of the helping

process? How will you communicate to the client your theoretical preference regarding an engagement style?

3. Social workers serve in many different settings with many different kinds of clients facing many different challenges. Multi-theoretical social work makes it possible to match your engagement style to your particular work circumstances. Reflect on some of the specific circumstances that you face now or may face as a social worker related to client characteristics like age, race, gender, religion, and other memberships; to client needs or problems; to client preferences; or to organizational constraints on service delivery like time limits, client mandates, and fee structures. Match a style of engagement to the specific helping circumstances providing details and examples, and justify your selection of this style.

4. Think about your work engaging desperate and needy persons in the following circumstances. How would you have engaged victims of Hurricane Katrina in New Orleans following its devastating impact in late August, 2005, or the 2012 victims of Super Storm Sandy in the northeastern United States? Which theoretical framework or frameworks would be most suitable under these circumstances? Imagine that you are doing crisis work in a very poor neighborhood. The majority of those you are helping are working class people and/or people of color with memories of discriminatory treatment from officials, police officers, and service providers. They have received no or minimal services from the local, state, or federal governments for six days after the disaster and flooding. Many lack the basic necessities: clean water, food, and safe shelter. Many have lost their homes, their possessions, their pets, and some of their loved ones. They are in shock and still grieving.

5. Finally, conclude with reflections on these learning activities. What have you learned that will prepare you to utilize theoretical frameworks to guide the processes of assessment, intervention, and evaluation?

References

Boyle, S. W., Hull, G. Jr., Mather, J. H., Smith, L. L. and Farley, O. W. (2009). *Direct practice in social work* (2nd ed.). Boston: Pearson Allyn and Bacon.

Brooks-Harris, J. E. (2008). *Integrative multitheoretical psychotherapy*. Boston: Lahaska Press/Houghton Mifflin.

Council on Social Work Education (2008). 2008 Educational policy and accreditation standards. Retrieved June 16, 2010, from www.cswe.org/Accreditation/Reaffirmation.aspx

MacCormac, E. R. (1985). *A cognitive theory of metaphor*. Cambridge, MA: MIT Press.

Martin, J. and Sugarman, J. (1999). *The psychology of human possibility and constraint*. Albany, NY: State University of New York Press.

Neimeyer, R. A. (1999). An invitation to constructivist psychotherapies. In R. A. Neimeyer and M. J. Mahoney (Eds), *Constructivism in psychotherapy* (pp. 1–10). Washington: DC: American Psychological Association.

Osborne, P. (1995). The parenting experts. In R. D. Day, K. R. Gilbert, B. H. Settles and W. R. Burr (Eds), *Research and theory in family science* (pp. 320–333). Pacific Grove, CA: Brooks/Cole.

Pepper, S. C. (1942). *World hypotheses: A study in evidence*. Berkeley: University of California Press.

Rigney, D. (2001). *The metaphorical society: An invitation to social theory*. Lanham, MD: Rowman and Littlefield.

Scholnik, E. K. (2000). Engendering development: Metaphors of change. In P. H. Miller and E. K. Scholnik (Eds), *Toward a feminist developmental psychology* (pp. 241–254). New York: Routledge.

Walsh, J. (1995). Clinical relatedness with persons having schizophrenia: A symbolic interactionist perspective. *Clinical Social Work Journal, 23* (1), 71–85.

7 | Translate theories to guide the information-gathering process

(EPAS 2.1.7 Apply knowledge; EPAS 2.1.10 Engage, assess, intervene, and evaluate)

All observations of the social world are shaped either consciously or unconsciously by social theory—such theory provides the framework that highlights or erases what might be observed.

(Kinchloe and Berry, 2004, p. 2)

The inquiry and assessment process is critical to effective social work. The Council on Social Work Education (2008) refers to this work as assessment and identifies assessment as a major phase of the planned change process. The Council's policy document states that to "collect, organize, and interpret data" are important worker assessment tasks. Related to this part of assessment, practitioner activities include focusing the information-gathering process, gathering information by using questions, and formulating an explanation of the focal problem or challenge. The commentary in this lesson will show how theories can be used to focus and guide the information-gathering process. Upcoming lessons will address other aspects of assessment.

Assessment: focusing information seeking

After engaging the client or members of the client system, the practitioner typically attempts to focus the information gathering and assessing processes. To begin the inquiry, each social worker must answer a very important question: what do I need to know to assess and help a client or client system? The answer then guides the information-gathering work. Theories help us answer this question.

The practitioner begins this assessment process by listening and observing carefully. The worker and client are attempting to transform a puzzling problematic situation, one in which relevant variables or themes have not been fully determined, into a situation that makes sense. Often this inquiry centers on the identification of problems and the causes, consequences, components, and careers of each of the problems (Hepworth et al., 2009). However, the concept "problem" is very broad, and the amount of information relevant to fully understanding the "person interacting in an environment facing a problem" is great. When using our guiding metaphor of a pie with five slices representating the basic dimensions of the person, seven slices representing the environmental contexts influencing human behavior, and one slice representing the transactions connecting person and environment, it is clear that the pie is incredibly big. Client system problems are complicated mixtures of personal elements, environmental elements, and processes of interaction between persons and environments. Moreover, the client challenges that are identified as target problems vary greatly by client characteristics and needs, by the environmental contexts, and by the helping setting's mission and policies. In one agency, we might focus on the family and economic factors contributing to domestic violence. In private practice, we may prioritize mental health concerns and their bio-psycho-social causes.

It is often difficult, therefore, to determine which features of the client system challenge or problem merit the greatest focus and attention. Specifically, the worker and the other members of the helping system need to decide which slices of the pie to learn about first and which slices, if any, may not be relevant in this case. The use of a theoretical framework or frameworks reduces the likelihood of amassing a random collection of facts and observations while the theories focus and streamline the information-gathering process (Beckett, 2006). A theory, then, offers a way to make sense of the bewildering amount of information about specific events, recurring problems, and system features that a client brings to the agency or clinic (Walt, 2005). Social learning theory (SLT), for instance, a highly regarded and empirically supported theoretical approach associated with the behavioral tradition, can neatly guide the worker's information-gathering work (van Ryn and Heaney, 1992). Specifically, SLT calls for the focused gathering of information on knowledge, skills, self-efficacy, and outcome expectations—the major factors theorized to contribute to a client's difficulty in implementing a change plan.

Let's return to our notion of theories and lenses. As perception structuring tools,

> the concepts and theories of social science afford the man of practical affairs alternative ways of viewing the world around him. Each set of concepts serves him, in effect, as a pair of spectacles, bringing into focus

a few selected aspects of his world which he would not have singled out for his attention otherwise.

(Campbell, Charters, and Gragg, 1960, p. 179)

For example, the practitioner sees and hears the client talk about a bad habit and adopts the behavioral lens to gather additional information. Then, the worker notices the client's frequent use of negative self-statements and supplements the inquiry with cognitive theory-based information-gathering strategies and tools (Brooks-Harris, 2008). As Campbell and his team note, "the practitioner in trying out the various concepts ... is regarding them as alternatives, each adding a different dimension to his own total view" (Campbell et al., 1960, p. 179).

Multi-theoretical assessment deepens information focusing, gathering, and understanding about person-interacting-in-environmental contexts by using polytheoretical inquiry focused on the array of processes facilitating and restraining individual and collective fulfillment. Our fourteen theoretical traditions can assist us to focus the assessment process if we translate them into their major terms. Using multiple theories increases the odds that we will focus on all relevant indicators of the client's personal dimensions, transactions with the environment, and environmental contexts.

Translating by major terms

To focus our perceptions about a person-in-environment (PIE) with a challenge configuration, we can use the major terms of a theory identified from our mapping its structure (major concepts, propositions, and linkages of propositions in an orderly way). We might also refer to glossaries identifying and defining major terms provided in books by theory experts. The collection of concepts for all the theories comprising a theoretical tradition provides us a rich vocabulary. Multi-theoretical social work consolidates these vocabularies as a comprehensive dictionary of theoretical terminology.

When studying a culture, linguists attempt to identify its *major terms*, also called key words. These are the words that "are particularly important and revealing in a given culture" (Wierzbicka, 1997, pp. 15–16). Key words are used frequently and serve often as the center of many clusters of phrases. For example, "freedom" is a very important concept in the United States. It is commonly used by politicians, by advertisers, and by citizens and it is associated with many common phrases like freedom of speech, freedom from hunger or poverty, and freedom to act. Key words can be studied as focal themes, Wierzbicka recommends, and such study increases our understanding of particular domains of a culture.

Like a culture, each theoretical framework has a set of key concepts or major terms. You are learning such vocabularies in your "human behavior and the environment" classes. Major terms in the interactionist tradition, for example, include: appraisals, mind, gesture, symbol, interaction, act, society, culture, role, role-taking, self, self-esteem, significant other, reflexivity, and definition of the situation. Some experts on theory use the term, "*construct*," to refer to a very abstract or general concept (Shoemaker, Tankard, and Lasorsa, 2004). For them, a list of a theory's major terms must include the central constructs of the theory. For example, family systems theorists consider "healthy family functioning" as a construct, one that includes more specific concepts such as optimal adaptability, cohesion, and communication. In employing the translation device of major terms, we can craft a focus for information-gathering questions using the construct or we could craft a set of focusing questions using the concepts constituting the construct—a question about family adaptability, a question about family cohesion, and a question about family communication.

Fourteen theoretical approaches to focusing information gathering

How might the worker bring some order to the information-gathering process? Explanatory theories can provide direction to inquiry and assessment. Each theoretical framework helps the worker and client identify the information that will bring clarity to particular elements of the whole pie. The theory suggests where to look, what to look for, and how to make sense of particular problematic or puzzling experiences of the client seeking help. The possession of multiple theories in our practice toolbox increases our ability to learn about and understand all relevant dimensions, transactions, and contexts.

According to Marsh (2004), "all theories highlight particular component parts, and can, in fact, be differentiated according to the components they emphasize" (p. 28). For practical theorizers, I argue that each theoretical framework provides a particular set of *major terms* or focus markers indicating its emphases. Table 7.1 summarizes the major components of the PIE metatheory, the theoretical tradition associated with each component, and some of the major terms for each theoretical tradition. Check one of your favorite theory survey books for definitions if these theoretical concepts seem unfamiliar to you.

Table 7.1 Translating theories to focus information gathering

PIE/theory	Information gathering by major terms/focus markers (illustrations)
Multi-dimensional person	*Major terms/focus markers*
Acting (behavioral)	antecedents–behavior–consequences (rewards, punishments) configuration behavior deficits, behavior excesses, behavior quality (frequency, duration, intensity), learning history, models
Faithing (anthropological)	faith convictions or doubts, faith development, religious beliefs, religious identification, religious–spiritual history, sacred symbols
Feeling (psychodynamic)	attachments, ego defenses, dreams and fantasies, emotional development, emotional patterns (anger, guilt, grief, shame, etc.), impulses, inner conflicts, level of insight into emotional processes, object relations, transference
Sensing (evolutionary biology)	abilities and disabilities, compliance with medical instructions, concerns about appearance or weight, genetic predispositions, health concerns, health practices, physical development, physical symptoms, stress, substance use
Thinking (cognitive)	attribution of blame, automatic thoughts, cognitive development, core beliefs or schemas (self, other, role, event), information processing skills, self-talk
Interacting/transacting	
Transact (interactionism)	communication patterns, interaction style, labels, meta-communication patterns, perspective-taking ability, relationship norms, reference groups, self, significant symbols (verbal, nonverbal, appearance), social worlds, socialization
Environmental context	
Communal (strengths)	environmental assets, flow, potentials, protective factors, risk factors, resilience, self actualization, signature strengths, strengths, vulnerabilities
Cultural (constructionist)	acculturation experiences; cultural heritage, cultural practices, discrimination, identities, majority–minority group, prejudice, racism, sexual orientation, traditions, values
Ecological (ecology)	crowding, design of built environment, ecology, hazards, nature, niche, population density, resources, space, territories, toxic substances, sustainability, weather patterns

PIE/theory	Information gathering by major terms/focus markers (illustrations)
Economic (exchange)	competition, consumption patterns, debt, economic cycle, economic development, exchange norms and patterns, exploitation, markets (health, housing, labor), poverty, regulations, supply and demand
Organizational (role)	career paths, careers, competence, impressions, positions, roles, role expectations, role problems (ambiguity, conflict, incompetence, etc.), role set, scripts, stages (backstage, front stage)
Political (critical-feminist)	alienation, coercion, conflict, consciousness, democracy, domination, elites, exploitation, ideology, injustice, oppression, power and status differences, patriarchy, power, privilege, rights, sexism, voice
Social (systems)	boundaries (clarity, permeability), energy state, hierarchies, linkages, multi-generational patterns, parts differentiation and integration, system state (equilibrium, disequilibrium), systems, structure, subsystems, whole system functioning

These major terms or focus markers are signs or clues to the information needed to assess in a comprehensive way each aspect of the PIE configuration. Remember, however, that clients rarely use the theoretical concepts common to the vocabulary preferred by professional social workers. Some translation work is required. The effective social worker watches and listens carefully for subtle or obvious clues and directs the investigation accordingly. A self–derogatory statement, "I am stupid," is a marker or clue according to the cognitive theoretical framework that self-concept and self-esteem issues are relevant to the client and should be explored further. A statement like "I was born into the wrong body and should be female not male" is a clue linked to the multi-cultural orientation and the queer theory orientation—two variants on the social constructionist approach to cultural difference covered in this book. This statement directs the investigation to biological sex, gender role expression, and sexual identity issues. Focus markers point to the clusters of PIE where particular theories might be helpful in directing further inquiry (Hochbaum, Sorenson and Lorig, 1992).

As the helping conversation proceeds, then, the worker can listen with eyes and ears wide open for cues or theory-based focus markers that suggest the aspects of the PIE configuration that are most salient to the particular case (Brooks-Harris, 2008). This increases our effectiveness. Reik (1948) used the image of listening with a third ear. He suggested that the effective helper cultivates sensitivity to the words of the client (first ear), the non-verbal and subtle communications of meanings in ways transcending words (second ear), and the deep meanings of the complete communication (third ear). In a sense, multi-theoretical social workers can learn to listen with a fourth ear, a theory ear.

While interacting with the client system, we learn to use our listening skills, our observational skills, our professional judgment, our research knowledge, and our empathic imagination to identify which aspects of the PIE configuration are most relevant to the helping circumstances. The theory-based major terms used as focus markers alert us to dimensions that require greater exploration. I will conclude this lesson with a few final examples. If a client dealing with the death of a loved one indicates that they are questioning their belief in God, the worker notes this marker and explores further faith and spirituality issues. If a group of members of a rural community report that they feel powerless as an international utility company begins to take over public lands and prepares to build a coal powered electric plant, then critical theories can be used to identify other relevant topics for exploration. With practice, we can discern the theoretical frameworks implied by a client's words, gestures, and deeds and we could learn to hear client stories in ways that allow us to recommend acceptable theoretical interpretations of these clues and in ways that guide further information-gathering work.

Learning activities and reflections

1. Information gathering is an important part of the assessment phase in the planned change process. Select an imaginary focal client system (individual, family, group, community, organization, society) and identify the basic information that you typically gather (or should gather) as you begin to provide service to that system.
2. Multi-theoretical social work directs us to use a multi-dimensional PIE framework for data gathering. Select two theoretical frameworks identified in Table 7.1 and for each theoretical framework translate several focus markers into the words, images, symbols, and metaphors that might be used by a client or members of a client system. Here are some examples. An adolescent girl complains:

"No one really listens to me." Translation suggests that she may be pointing to an issue identified by the feminist marker, voice. Or a family discussion may center on images of open versus closed doors in the household. This might be translated tentatively as a "boundary" concern and suggest the usefulness of systems theory markers.

3. Reflect on an effort to help a client or friend. Referring to Table 7.1, identify some of the markers that emerged during the helping conversations with the person, and how you might have used the markers to focus more fully and gather detailed information on particular aspects of the PIE configuration: person dimensions (acting, faithing, feeling, sensing, thinking), particular transactions between the client system and the environment, and particular environmental contexts relevant to the client system problem (communal, cultural, ecological, economic, organizational, political, or social). Identify a set of topics for exploration suggested by the focus markers. Comment also on the following question. In what ways, does the use of the PIE framework and the theory-based focus markers help you answer the question; what do I need to know to assess and help a particular client or client system?

4. Use a life course/human developmental multi-dimensional perspective and the focal markers identified in Table 7.1 for each dimension. Ask questions of an older acquaintance to identify some of the changes that occur in late adulthood related to some of the major dimensions such as: behavioral, biological, cognitive, emotional, or spiritual. Reflect on how a social worker might summarize his or her multi-dimensional understanding of the person in a theoretical synthesis. Reflect also on how the theory might guide the social worker as he or she tries to help the developing person in late adulthood maintain a reasonable degree of dignity, vitality, and engagement as they and significant others adapt to the changes associated with this developmental stage.

5. Finally, conclude with reflections on these learning activities. What have you learned that will prepare you to utilize theoretical frameworks to guide the processes of assessment, intervention, and evaluation?

References

Beckett, C. (2006). *Essential theory for social work practice*. London: Sage.

Brooks-Harris, J. E. (2008). *Integrative multitheoretical psychotherapy*. Boston: Lahaska Press/Houghton Mifflin.

Campbell, R. F., Charters, W. W. Jr. and Gragg, E. L. (1960). Improving administrative theory and practice: Three essential roles. In R. F. Campbell and J. M. Lipham (Eds), *Administrative theory as a guide to action* (pp. 171–189). Chicago: University of Chicago.

Council on Social Work Education (2008). 2008 Educational policy and accreditation standards. Retrieved June 16, 2010, from www.cswe.org/Accreditation/Reaffirmation.aspx.

Hepworth, D. H., Rooney, R. H., Larsen, J. A., Strom-Gottfried, K. and Rooney, G. D. (2009). *Direct social work practice: Theory and skills* (8th ed.). Belmont, CA: Brooks/Cole Cengage Learning.

Hochbaum, G. M., Sorenson, J. R. and Lorig, K. (1992). Theory in health education practice. *Health Education Quarterly*, 19 (3), 295–313.

Kinchloe, J. L. and Berry, K. (2004). *Rigour and complexity in educational research: Conceptualizing the bricolage*. Maidenhead: Open University Press/McGraw-Hill Educational.

Marsh, J. C. (2004). Theory-driven research versus theory-free research in empirical social work practice. In H. E. Briggs and T. L. Rzepnicki (Eds), *Using evidence in social work practice: Behavioral perspectives* (pp. 20–35). Chicago: Lyceum.

Reik, T. (1948). *Listening with the third ear: The inner experience of a psychoanalyst*. New York: Farrar Straus.

Shoemaker, P. J., Tankard, J. W., Jr. and Lasorsa, D. L. (2004). *How to build social science theories*. Thousand Oaks, CA: Sage.

van Ryn, M. and Heaney, C. A. (1992). What's the use of theory? *Health Education Quarterly*, 19 (3), 315–330.

Walt, S. M. (2005). The relationship between theory and policy in international relations. *Annual Review of Political Science*, 8, 23–48.

Wierzbicka, A. (1997). *Understanding cultures through their key words: English, Russian, Polish, German, and Japanese*. New York: Oxford University Press.

8 Translate theories to guide informational question formation

(EPAS 2.1.7 Apply knowledge; EPAS 2.1.10 Engage, assess, intervene, and evaluate)

To understand the place of theory in practice, it is essential to appreciate how professional questions are shaped by theory and in turn utilize it when directions needed to guide action are being recovered from memory.

(Lewis, 1982, p. 63)

Besides translating theory to focus the information-gathering process, social work practitioners use a variety of theory-informed strategies to collect, organize, and interpret information during the assessment phase. The information-gathering question is one of the most commonly used strategies for assembling the pieces necessary to solve a "person interacting in an environment" puzzle.

Theory-based information-gathering questions

Lesson 7 discussed the use of a metatheoretical framework to focus information gathering. Helen Harris Perlman (1957) created such an overarching perspective. She referred to the person-in-environment (PIE) configuration in terms of the four Ps: a *person* in a *place* with a *problem* that must be partialized (broken down into manageable pieces) while participating in a helping *process*. Social workers, she suggested, could gather detailed information about the case and the focal problem using questions stated in terms of the four parts of her approach. I have offered a somewhat similar PIE information-gathering metaframework for directing the formulation of questions for a comprehensive case investigation. This framework recommends inquiry into the dimensional aspects (a person with five interrelated dimensions), the interactional aspects (the transactional processes linking person and environment), and the environment aspects (like Perlman's notion of place but differentiated into seven distinct contexts) of the case and a focus on the problem, or from a strengths approach, the challenge faced by the person interacting with the environment.

Theoretical frameworks help us focus our inquiry and they also can be used to generate theory-based information-gathering questions useful in investigating all aspects of the case. When working with a client or family, the practitioner might be mandated by the agency to begin the information-gathering work by soliciting standard information. Questions about employment status, housing conditions, perceived needs or problems, prior use of services, social support, and specific reasons for seeking help are common. Such questions may not be aligned to a particular theoretical tradition. However, assessment also requires the creative use of questions to learn about the lived experiences, the troubles, and the joys of the client and about the client's situation in more depth. Theory-informed questions can be very useful in such circumstances.

Social workers often make use of two different types of questions to gather information. A *closed-ended question* is a question structured in a way that the respondent answers in a simple and narrow way: yes, no, or by a short piece of information like age. For example, a social worker might ask a client a non theory-oriented question at intake: Have you requested service from this agency before? Or, the worker might ask a closed-ended question suggested by feminist theory: had your husband been ignoring consistently your feelings and needs before this incident of abuse? An *open-ended question* is a question formulated so that it can't be answered with a one-word answer or very short statement. The question allows the respondent leeway in answering and he or she can provide extensive and detailed information or relevant stories. For example, the worker might use a cognitive approach and ask a client: In what ways do you hope your future schemas (ideas) of self and others will be different following your participation in this support group?

The game of twenty questions invites contestants to identify a mystery guest and his or her career by asking closed-ended, yes or no, questions. Playing this game, information gathering is slow and guesses about the guest's identity are often wrong. Multi-theoretical social work suggests that solving the "mystery guest" puzzle is easier when many kinds of information gathering closed-ended and open-ended questions and instruments are used. Theory-derived informational questions and measurement tools are especially useful for learning about client mysteries. Table 8.1 summarizes the multi-theoretical social work approach to question formation. The table provides two general questions per theoretical approach; one focused on PIE issues and the second focusing on person-developing-over time issues. These sample questions are stated in very technical and general terms. They would need to be translated and tailored to specific case circumstances to become useful.

For example, the Council on Social Work Education (2008) identifies "assess client strengths and limitations" as an assessment task, one well guided by the strengths theoretical perspective and strengths-oriented questions. Table 8.1 suggests two question templates for the strengths perspective: how are the client strengths and community assets related to the client's presenting concerns, and how are processes of self actualization relevant to the client's presenting concerns? The practitioner, for example, might transform the first broad question into a series of specific questions that pinpoint ways that the client has and might mobilize personal, family, and community strengths to support a father dying from cancer. The practitioner might also tailor the second strengths question into a bunch of developmental questions to learn how the client has and might transform the challenges of preparing the family for a death into opportunities for growth. The table provides similar templates for thirteen other theories.

Translating via major terms

Theory-based questions can be built from a theory's major terms after these are translated into words and phrases familiar to the client or members of the client system. For example, symbolic interactionism includes many concepts related to the self, such as the concept of self-esteem. Self-esteem is a concept characterizing one dimension of the self. It might be defined, dictionary style, as a person's evaluation of his or her worth with consideration of the opinions of significant others. You could use this concept, and incorporate it into an open-ended information-gathering question directed to a counselee: How are your dating difficulties related to your ideas and feelings about your own value as a person? The first part refers to the client's identification of a problem in his or her own terms. The second part rewords the theoretical concept into plainer English. Or the practitioner might ask a range of related questions associated with this theoretical term such as how has your self-esteem changed over the course of your relationship? What relationship experiences have enhanced your sense of worth and what experiences have lessened your sense of worth? Are you satisfied with your current evaluation of esteem?

Table 8.1 Translating theories to ask information-gathering questions

PIE/theory	Information-gathering questions (illustrations)
Multi-dimensional person	
Acting (behavioral)	How is the client's presenting concerns impacted by behavior patterns (behavior excesses or deficits) and specific contingencies related to antecedents, consequences, and models? How is the client's presenting concerns influenced by behavioral learning processes?
Faithing (anthropological)	How are spiritual practices and symbols related to the client's presenting concerns? How are faith development processes related to the client's presenting concerns?
Feeling (psychodynamic)	How are the client's feelings and his or her emotional processes (conscious, or semi-conscious) related to the presenting concerns? How are psychosocial development processes relevant to the client's presenting concerns?
Sensing (evolutionary biology)	How is the client's presenting concerns related to physical sensations or bodily processes? How are processes of physical maturation important to the client's presenting concerns?
Thinking (cognitive)	How are client's thoughts and his or her thinking processes related to the presenting concerns? How are cognitive development processes related to the client's presenting concerns?
Interacting/transacting	
Transact (Interactionism)	How are client's sense-making, communication, and interaction processes related to the presenting concerns? How is progress in self and language development related to the client's presenting concerns?
Environmental context	
Communal (strengths)	How are client strengths and community assets related to the client's presenting concerns? How are processes of self-actualization relevant to the client's presenting concerns?
Cultural (constructionist)	How are cultural heritage and cultural practices related to the client's presenting concerns? How are acculturation processes related to the client's presenting concerns?

PIE/theory	Information-gathering questions (illustrations)
Economic (exchange)	How are economic factors and exchange processes related to the client's presenting concerns? How are processes of economic/wealth development related to the client's presenting concerns?
Organization (role)	How are organizational role structures, expectations, and processes related to the client's presenting concerns? How are role sequences and career processes relevant to the client's presenting concerns?
Physical environment (ecology)	How are ecological patterns and processes related to the client's presenting concerns? How are ecological development processes related to the client's presenting concerns?
Political (critical-feminist)	How are patterns of privilege and processes of conflict related to the client's presenting concerns? How are processes of identity development in oppressive situations significant in relation to the client's presenting concerns?
Social (systems)	How are the client's presenting concerns related to system dynamics and to important social systems like the family? How are socialization and family life cycle processes related to the client's presenting concerns?

Translating via propositions culled from theory maps

Theoretical or formal analysis involves identifying the elements of a theory and the way that these elements are arranged as a coherent system. I have called this process "theory mapping," and defined theory mapping as the visual or verbal representation of a theory and its elements to guide assessment formulation and intervention planning. While concepts are essential ingredients of questions, social workers can also construct information-gathering questions by studying existing theory maps (as reported in books, journals, or slide presentations, for example) or by creating their own theory map and identifying salient theoretical propositions. Propositions link two theoretical concepts or major terms. A practice theory generally includes a set of interrelated propositions: statements of relationships or principles to guide key phases of the helping encounter. An especially useful proposition for practice theory, particularly if supported by research evidence, is the causal or conditional proposition. Such a proposition links an independent variable, the focus of intervention, and a desired outcome, the dependent variable. Behaviorists, for instance, assert that the provision of positive reinforcements following the desired behavior causes the focal behavior to become a lasting part of the client's set of behaviors.

Here's an extended example. Applied symbolic interactionists theorize often about the impact of the appraisals of significant others (a significant other is a mother, best friend, supervisor, or other person who influences our self and identity processes) on a person's self-esteem. Stated in propositional form, interactionists might suggest that a series of validating appraisals from a significant other (independent variable) raise the receiver's sense of worth (dependent variable or outcome). The practitioner might transform this proposition into theory-informed questions. The social worker might ask: what has been the impact of constantly negative verbalized appraisals from your father on your sense of self worth (after translating this into the vernacular spoken by the client, of course)? Or to what degree, do frequent statements of high praise and deep appreciation from your grandmother raise your sense of esteem? Later in the helping process, the practitioner might use the answers to these questions to design an intervention.

As you have already learned, we can also think of a theory as a collection of variables: concepts stated in measureable form, linked in sentences as propositions, and organized as a network of propositions. Depending on the circumstances, any variable from a theory might be viewed as an independent variable, a dependent variable, or a moderating variable. Ecological theory includes many concepts that can be operationalized as variables such as temperature, degree of climate stability, consumption of resources, biodiversity, population density, noise, attachment to place, residential segregation, toxicity, attractiveness of a building's design, sustainability, and person–environment fit. In formulating theory-based information-gathering questions, the social worker should decide how to best categorize the theoretical concept in the specific circumstances. The practitioner, for example, might decide that person–environment fit is the relevant dependent variable (starting with the client's concern or problem) and then identify place attachment as a relevant independent variable (a possible factor exacerbating or lessening the problem). Here are a few possible questions enriched by this ecological-attachment theory blend for information gathering use with a new resident complaining about life in a nursing home. How attached were you to your home? How attached were you to your neighborhood? To your possessions? To your yard? In what ways, were these attachments related to your sense of fitting in the old environment? How have your attachments changed following your move to a nursing facility? How would you characterize your attachment to this new environment? How are attachment issues influencing your sense of fitting in here? Answers to these questions will help the practitioner and client begin to formulate an assessment of the relationship between attachments and the perceived fit of the client with the new residential environment.

Theory-based assessment tools

Information-gathering questions are also available in the form of rapid-assessment instruments. *A rapid assessment tool* often includes a list of questions related to a problem or challenging condition. Respondents answer verbally or using pencil and paper by choosing a response to each item on a scale; responses may range from strongly agree to strongly disagree, or frequently to rarely.

Many rapid-assessment instruments have their origins in a specific theoretical framework, and are available thanks to the work of a theory user translating theoretical concepts or constructs into information-gathering questions. These tools can be used to supplement information-gathering questions during the assessment process. Or since the instruments include individual items often informed by the overall theory, some of these items can be converted to information-gathering questions. The social worker, for example, might use the multi-item self-report questionnaire developed by a symbolic interactionist expert on the self-concept and self-esteem, the Rosenberg Self Esteem Scale (Rosenberg, 1965). The questionnaire includes ten information-gathering closed-ended items to which respondents select one of the following responses: strongly agree, agree, disagree, or strongly disagree. One item is worded "I feel that I am a person of worth, at least on an equal plane with others," and another, "I wish I could have more respect for myself." Overall scores on this device would indicate whether a client has low, moderate, or high self-esteem. Each item or selected items could be rephrased too as an information-gathering question.

Other examples of theory-based information-gathering tools include the Beck Depression Inventory (Beck et al., 1961), a cognitive theory-guided measurement that asks 21 questions focused on respondents thoughts about the world, the future, and the self; and the FACTS instrument, the Functional Assessment Checklist for Teachers and Staff (March et al., 2000), a behavioral theory tool, used to guide an interview by providing questions about problem behaviors including problem characteristics, events triggering behavior, consequences maintaining behavior, and contextual factors (where, when, and with whom) associated with the problem behavior.

Learning activities and reflections

1. Information gathering is a critical element in the social work assessment process. Social workers often gather information about a client system and its problems and challenges by asking questions about the person (system)-in-environment (PIE) features. Different theoretical frameworks address different aspects of the PIE configuration, and accordingly suggest the formulation of different theory-specific questions. See Table 8.1 for a summary of information-gathering questions associated with fourteen different theoretical frameworks. (Remember that these questions are stated in theoretical language and need to be translated to the client's language for effective use).

   Let's expand our understanding of the range of information-gathering questions that might be asked during the assessment process. Reflect on and summarize your ideas about the basic questions that social workers ask when learning about a client or client system and problems. Identify five to ten samples of such basic questions.

2. Let's formulate some specific questions. Referring to Table 8.1, select two or three theoretical frameworks that will help you gather information about a particular client system, its dimensions, its contexts, and its challenges. For each start with the general question, and then develop a few specific closed- and open-ended questions appropriate to the helping circumstances. Compare your questions with those of another student.

3. Review some of the assessment tools that you have learned about and attempt to identify each tool's link to a theory. If this is difficult, conduct a search using a social work-oriented database or a web search engine for theory-based assessment tools, or take a look at a collection of rapid-assessment instruments (Corcoran and Fischer, 2007). Examine several information-gathering tools and the questions that are included. Summarize your ideas about how you might use these tools and their questions to enhance the information gathering and assessment processes.

4. Apply the social exchange theory, a sociological theory that examines how parties in a relationship engage in cost-benefit analysis, calculate the likely profit from a transaction, and negotiate to obtain the best possible gains. Think about your client's or friend's relationship with his or her spouse, lover, roommate, boss, or coworker, and pick one important area of the relationship:

decision-making about finances, holidays, or purchases; intimacy; division of labor; support; or relationship maintenance. Use the exchange theory and develop a set of information-gathering questions to ask the client. You might begin by translating the following questions into words and phrases familiar to the client or friend. How equitable are the exchanges in this area? Are you "over-benefited" or "under-benefited"? Are you economically dependent? How do the exchange patterns in this relationship compare to possible alternative relationships? How have the current exchange patterns developed over time? What changes would make the relationship more equitable? Develop some of your own economic-oriented questions too. Comment on the utility of the theory for gathering information about the strengths and weaknesses of this exchange relationship.

5. Finally, conclude with reflections on these learning activities. What have you learned that will prepare you to utilize theoretical frameworks to guide the processes of assessment, intervention, and evaluation?

References

Beck, A. T., Ward, C. H., Mendelson, M., Mock, J. and Erbaugh, J. (1961). An inventory for measuring depression. *Archives of General Psychiatry, 4*, 561–571.

Corcoran, K. and Fischer, J. (2007). *Measures for clinical practice and research: A sourcebook two-volume set* (4th ed.). New York: Oxford University Press.

Council on Social Work Education (2008). 2008 Educational policy and accreditation standards. Retrieved June 16, 2010, from www.cswe.org/Accreditation/Reaffirmation.aspx.

Lewis, H. (1982). *The intellectual base of social work practice: Tools for thought in a helping profession.* New York: The Haworth Press.

March, R. E., Horner, R. H., Lewis-Palmer, T., Brown, D., Crone, D., Todd, A.W., et al. (2000). *Functional assessment checklist: Teachers and staff.* Eugene, OR: Educational and Community Supports.

Perlman, H. H. (1957). *Social casework: A problem solving process.* Chicago: University of Chicago Press.

Rosenberg, M. (1965). *Society and the adolescent self-image.* Princeton, NJ: Princeton University Press.

9

Translate theories to guide the assessment formulation process

(EPAS 2.1.7 Apply knowledge; EPAS 2.1.10 Engage, assess, intervene, and evaluate)

If theory can be used to predict an outcome or can guide the sorting out of problem areas, its use is warranted.

(Munson, 1983, p. 155)

The Council on Social Work Education (2008) directs social work practitioners to complete a variety of tasks associated with the assessment formulation process. These include: collect, organize, and interpret client data; agree with the client or members of the client system about intervention goals; and select appropriate interventions. In the previous two lessons, we have discussed the use of theories to focus data collection and organization. The next lesson will provide a commentary on setting goals.

In this lesson, let's look at how the theory savvy practitioner can use fourteen theories to develop *explanatory hypotheses*, provisional interpretations of the problem or the challenge faced by the person/system interacting in environmental contexts. Additionally, we will examine how the practitioner can use these theories to develop *intervention hypotheses*, statements about what might change the problematic elements of a client situation. Mastery of this lesson will be an important step on the path to intervention selection and implementation.

Theory-based explanatory hypotheses

As the worker and client review the data about a focal problem that has been collected and organized, they begin to interpret or explain this data. Common questions for the process include the following. Why does this particular problem or challenge exist? How did it start? What specific factors are contributing to its continuance? What factors might decrease or eliminate the problem? How are the problem and relevant factors influenced by the ecological and historical context? To answer such questions, the practitioner begins to formulate hypotheses. Defined simply, a *hypothesis* is a statement of a predicted relationship between an independent variable and a dependent variable. For example, we might hypothesize that there is a relationship between participation in social media (Facebook, Twitter, etc.) and face-to-face service activities in the community: the greater the participation the less the time spent in service.

Scientific hypotheses are critical to knowledge accumulation. They merit systematic testing, and, thus, are stated in a form that lends itself to experimental studies generating data suggesting support or rejection for the hypothesized claim. Practitioners can formulate and test hypotheses in less rigorous ways, too, in the helping setting and with the participation of the client.

Many human behavior theories, human development theories and other social science theories offer explanations of assorted individual problems and undesirable environmental conditions or processes (National Cancer Institute, 2013). Practitioners can productively use these theories to answer assessment questions, identify additional information needed, and formulate interpretations or explanatory hypotheses, tentative predictions about the key factor or factors causing a focal problem (van Ryn and Heaney, 1992). A *theory-based working hypothesis* is one kind of explanatory hypothesis. It is a statement of relationship between two or more concepts derived from a theoretical framework that is used to structure data about a client in a way leading to explanatory, decision-making, and intervention choices (Ingram, 2006). For example, the cognitive practice theory offers some general ideas useful for formulating a theory-based working hypothesis: client's emotional difficulties are caused often by faulty information processing. Faulty information processing is one theoretical concept, the independent or causal variable in this sentence. Emotional difficulty is the second theoretical concept, postulated here to be the effect of the dependent variable. Of course, the worker and client would need to translate these variables into more precise definitions and specify how each could be measured. A second example: your doctor, versed in biomedical knowledge and research, offers you a tentative explanatory working hypothesis when she conjectures that your contact with a flea-ridden dog and bites from the fleas have caused your skin rash.

Multi-theoretical explanations

Each theory advances a different explanatory hypothesis regarding the primary source of a specific person-in-environment (PIE) difficulty. Berzoff, Flanagan, and Hertz (2008) illustrate this by suggesting how practitioners using different approaches within the psychodynamic tradition might begin to explain the same case. They discussed the example of a black Catholic Haitian man in the United States. He had been raised to meet high standards by his parents and teachers. While walking one day in a public place, he was arrested without cause. During a period of temporary incarceration, the man was assaulted and degraded by fellow prisoners in repeated and racially motivated attacks. After release, the man began constantly berating himself, and frequently he experienced painful feelings like guilt and shame associated with the irrational conviction that he deserved this punishment. This pattern became so severe and distressing that he finally sought therapeutic help.

Berzoff and company (2008) noted that his choice of a therapist would determine how his problem was interpreted and explained. A drive theorist beginning to explain the problem would hypothesize about issues regarding aggressive impulses, their discharge, and successful or failed attempts to control these impulses. An ego psychologist would consider issues regarding the inability of the ego defenses to manage annihilation anxiety as central to the problem's explanation. Object relations theorists would formulate interpretations of the case by focusing on factors regarding past self and object representations and the strain of trauma resulting in new representations of the self as worthless and representations of others as dangerous. The self-psychologist would hypothesize about the tremendous injury to the man's sense of self and how this psychic injury caused the troubling thoughts and feelings.

Translation tools for assessment formulation

To transform the relevant elements of a theory into an explanatory working hypothesis, we can use the theory translation device of *mapping theory*, a narrative or display summarizing the theory's structure, its major terms, its statements of relationships between these terms, and the linkage of these propositional statements into a network of statements. We want to give special attention to theory maps identifying propositions linking theory-suggested causes with client problems.

Middle-range theorizing is another translation device useful during this part of the assessment process. The practitioner can create a middle-range theory: a small-scale system of ideas explaining a particular individual or collective problem (Bartholomew, Parcel, Kok, Gottlieb, and Fernandez, 2011; Fawcett, 2005), or the busy practitioner can search the literature for a sound middle-range theory needed for the case and for the research studies validating the theory. My *Human behavior and the social environment* textbook (Forte, 2006) about a "Models, Metaphors, and Maps Approach" to theoretical knowledge summarizes more than ten middle-range theories. The theories covered include a behavioral approach to explaining substance abuse, a psychodynamic theory of grief and its differential management, a cognitive theory of child neglect and abuse, an interactionist model of chronic depression, an ecological theory of disputes about homelessness, a systems approach to explaining the dysfunction of some military families, and an economic-exchange middle-range theory about advocacy for a threatened social work program. The most useful theoretical traditions include accurate middle-range theories that organize explicit statements about some or all of the biological, psychological, and social processes, the transactions, and the contextual conditions most applicable to explaining a particular problem. Ideally, the commentary accompanying these middle-range theories specifies the relative importance of each causal process or factor influencing the challenging condition or the problem (Rothman, 2004).

Table 9.1 could help us develop explanatory hypotheses. The table identifies fourteen theoretical traditions, the theoretical focus of each, and the central explanatory constructs translated from the theoretical maps of fourteen human behavior and the environment theories and fourteen developmental theories. These are stated very generally but the practitioner could start with a focal concern and scan the table to determine possible causes. For example, the practitioner might start from the psychodynamic tradition and hypothesize that the ill person's defensive denial of the severity of a disease are undermining the family's requests for him to comply with the established treatment regime. In summary, these theories can guide our effort to characterize a client system problem and to identify the most relevant problem elements.

Additionally, Table 9.1 can help practitioners work to formulate a *multi-theoretical case conceptualization*, an integrative interpretation and description of relevant PIE causes and conditions that synthesizes ideas from complimentary theoretical frameworks to explain the salient problem or challenge identified in a particular case (Brooks-Harris, 2008). The practitioner might acknowledge the importance of psychic defenses, for example, but add factors related to family system dynamics and to medical staff role performances to explain a patient's non-compliance. Here are some brief expansions on the Table 9.1 content as relevant to the explanation of personal problems.

The behavioral framework directs us to focus on problems understood in terms of learning histories, conditioning, patterns of reward and punishment, and the use of inappropriate behavioral models.

Table 9.1 Translating theories to guide the assessment formulation of explanatory hypotheses

Theory/PIE	General	Human behavior and environment (explanatory emphasis)	Life course (explanatory emphasis)
Multidimensional person			
Behavioral	Actions	Behavior patterns, learning processes	Learning histories
Anthropology	Convictions	Sacred meanings, worship processes	Faith development
Psychodynamic	Feelings	Psychic dynamics, unconscious conflicts	Psychosocial development
Evolutionary biology	Sensations	Illness, biological processes	Growth and decay
Cognitive	Thoughts	Cognitions, information processing	Cognitive development
Interacting/transacting			
Interactionism	Interaction	Symbols, communication processes	Membership socialization
In context			
Strengths (community)	Assets/risks	Strengths use, creative processes	Self actualization
Construction (culture)	Constructions	Typifications, enculturation processes	Individualizing emancipation
Critical-fem (political)	Power order	Privilege patterns, political processes	Progressive democratization
Ecology (ecological)	Environment	Ecologies, ecological processes	Ecological cultivation
Economic (exchange)	Distribution	Markets and resources, exchange processes	Economic development
Systems (social)	Networks	Institutions, system processes	System
Role (organization)	Structure	Positions and roles, role processes	Career trajectories

The biological framework directs us to focus on problems interpreted in terms of illness or disease, minimal physical vitality, inadequate awareness of one's physical state and needs, and other disordered mind/body states.

The cognitive framework directs us to focus on problems explained in terms of irrational or unrealistic thoughts, faulty information processing, and emotional and behavioral patterns triggered by self-defeating thoughts or misinformation.

The psychodynamic framework directs us to conceptualize problems in terms of minimal awareness of impulses and psychic needs, inner conflicts, ego defenses, insecure attachments, and the unconscious influence of internalized harsh or rejecting parental figures.

The symbolic interactionist framework directs us to develop explanations in terms of misunderstandings stemming from failures to interpret correctly the meaning of others' words, gestures, facial expressions, appearance, or action.

The social role framework directs us to focus on problems understood in terms of ambiguous role expectations, inadequate socialization for a role, conflicts between the expectations of two or more roles, or role overload.

The critical framework directs us to understand client system problems in terms of internalized oppression or external oppression caused by discrimination, exploitation, domination, and structural inequities.

When explanations are combined from various theoretical traditions, we are engaging in multi-theoretical social work. I have used a multi-theoretical approach to data interpretation and explanation, for example, to understand a very strange and stressful family situation. After my siblings and I moved my 84-year-old and peaceful mother into a home near to me and recruited a roommate as an informal aid to help her with tasks of daily life, she began to act in strange ways. These involved wandering at odd times around the neighborhood in search of a daughter who lived hundreds of miles away, complaining often that the roommate (a very gentle person with much elder care experience) was "out to get me," and brandishing a kitchen knife as she strolled the short halls of her house. Varied theories helped me begin to identify possible explanatory factors. The biological approach emphasizes illness; her doctor and I decided to arrange tests for dementia. Erikson's life stage developmental theory prioritizes key events in life and their influence on ego strengths and vulnerabilities. I began to consider how my mother's childhood abandonment by her father and mother had left her with little trust and much fear of others. Interactionist theory identifies communication processes as major contributors to adjustment issues. Perhaps there had been specific talk and interaction between my mother and the new house resident that evoked fear, fight, and flight reactions. The ecological perspective considers features of the ecology as central to human functioning. My mother had lived alone for the past thirty years with total control over her life spaces, and her new house was small. Perhaps the new tenant seemed invasive and evoked territorial protection reactions. The multi-theoretical social work approach helped me realize that all these theory-suggested factors, and perhaps others, might be relevant to my search for a set of explanatory hypotheses synthesizing the varied possible interpretations of my mom's difficulties.

Theory-based intervention hypotheses

There is no sharp and fine dividing line between the phases of the helping process. Inquiry during the assessment process blurs into the intervention phase and the identification, selection, and implementation of an intervention work. Developing a theory-informed explanation of the nature of a problem is closely associated with the process of developing a theory of what needs to be changed. Both types of theory can contribute to practitioner reasoning about the best intervention (Moen and Coltrane, 2005). We will conclude this lesson with a discussion of a useful tool for using the "theory of the problem" to craft a "theory of change." This is the theory-based intervention hypothesis. The next lessons will further our examination of the tasks associated with intervention phase.

Let's first review the idea of a hypothesis about intervention. Bloom, Fischer, and Orme (2006) commented on the notion of intervention hypothesis. An *intervention hypothesis* is a statement of predicted relationship between independent variable (intervention) and dependent variable (target problem or challenge). Evidence-oriented social workers state hypotheses in testable form with benchmarks for successful achievement included. The hypotheses are recognized as tentative but reasonable predictions, and they are ideally supported by research evidence documenting the causal linkage of the selected interventions with the desired outcomes in similar circumstances with similar clients with comparable problems. For example, your doctor might hypothesize that your intake of a prescribed medication every day for two weeks will eliminate completely the skin rash. You closely monitor the skin's condition and call back at the end of the second week to report success. For another example of an intervention hypothesis, we might predict that a group member who participates in an anger management group for eight weeks will reduce angry outbursts from an average of six a day to no daily outbursts. A single-system design could be implemented to evaluate the predicted changes in the member. Social workers should develop hypotheses about the likely causes of the focal problem or problems and about the likely outcome following the implementation of a specified intervention.

Scientific social workers like Bloom and his colleagues also discuss two versions of an intervention hypothesis. The *null hypothesis* predicts that the intervention, the independent variable or X, will have no impact on the target problem, the dependent variable or Y. Generally, the *alternative hypothesis* predicts that the intervention will have a positive and measurable effect on the problem. I won't elaborate on these concepts here but they will be useful when you begin to think about practice evaluation.

Creators of a *theory-based intervention hypothesis,* a theory-informed linkage of helping action and likely consequence, derive their ideas about what intervention will achieve a desired outcome from a theoretical tradition. Here are several examples. Involvement by fifty at-risk students in a behavioral intervention program training members in conflict resolution skills will reduce the number of conflicts at their school to less than three per month. The use of a progressive relaxation procedure based on biological stress theory will reduce the anxiety associated with a medical procedure for a patient to below the cutting point on a standardized anxiety scale. Participation in an interactionist theory-informed bereavement group providing information, sense-making experiences, social support, and emotional comfort will reduce grief-related symptoms for the ten members who have recently suffered the death of a loved one to a level defined by each member as acceptable.

Translating theories into if–then propositions and intervention hypotheses

Intervention hypotheses can be derived from theory-based if–then propositions. These are the important elements of a theory map that we have discussed earlier. There is a standard if–then form to these statements: if there is a change in the causal variable, X (the worker, client, or collateral actions, the client transactions, or the environmental conditions expected to activate change processes), then there will be a change in the PIE processes sustaining or resolving the focal problem, and this change will contribute to progress toward the desired outcome, Y (that PIE aspect which the worker and client want to improve).

Table 9.2 lists basic if–then propositions related to human behavior in the environment and to human development for fourteen different theoretical frameworks. These are stated in very general terms. For use in practice circumstances, the worker and client must translate the propositions into more concrete and precise intervention hypotheses. The intervention hypothesis becomes the specific and testable statement of the predicted effect of a particular intervention with a particular client working to resolve a particular problem. For example, symbolic interactionists offer the if–then proposition: If there are changes in symbolic interaction processes, then there will be changes in problem-sustaining (or problem-resolving) transactions. A marital counselor might specify this as a theory-based intervention hypothesis for a particular couple—if there is an increase in accurate reciprocal perspective-taking ability (each person more accurately listens to and interprets the partner's verbal and nonverbal symbolic communication as measured by a reliable and valid assessment tool), then there will be a seventy percent reduction in misunderstandings (as recorded by each partner on a daily log) at the end of four weeks.

Table 9.2 Translating theories to guide the assessment formulation of intervention hypotheses

PIE/theory	Theory-based if–then propositions (brief illustrations) (HBSE and Life Course versions)
Multi-dimensional person	
Acting (behavioral)	If there are changes in antecedent-behavior-consequences configurations, then there will be changes in problem-sustaining (or problem-resolving) transactions.
	If there are changes in behavioral learning histories, then there will be changes in problem-sustaining (or problem-resolving) transactions.
Faithing (anthropological)	If there are changes in the person's use of spiritual resources, then there will be changes in problem-sustaining (or problem-resolving) transactions.
	If there are changes in the faith development process, then there will be changes in problem-sustaining (or problem-resolving) transactions.
Feeling (psychodynamic)	If there are changes in psychic dynamics especially unconscious emotional dynamics, then there will be changes in problem-sustaining (or problem-resolving) transactions.
	If there are changes in psychosocial development, then there will be changes in problem-sustaining (or problem-resolving) transactions.
Sensing (evolutionary biology)	If there are changes in biological processes, then there will be changes in problem-sustaining (or problem-resolving) transactions.
	If there are changes in physical maturation, then there will be changes in problem-sustaining (or problem-resolving) transactions.
Thinking (cognitive)	If there are changes in cognitive processes, then there will be changes in problem-sustaining (or problem-resolving) transactions.
	If there are changes in cognitive development, then there will be changes in problem-sustaining (or problem-resolving) transactions.

PIE/theory	Theory-based if–then propositions (brief illustrations) (HBSE and Life Course versions)
Interacting/transacting	
Transact (interactionism)	If there are changes in symbolic interaction processes, then there will be changes in problem-sustaining (or problem-resolving) transactions.
	If there are changes in socialization processes, then there will be changes in problem-sustaining (or problem-resolving) transactions.
In context	
Communal (strengths)	If there are changes in the person's acceptance of freedom and responsibility, then there will be changes in problem-sustaining (or problem-resolving) transactions.
	If there are changes in the identification and mobilization of strengths, then there will be changes in problem-sustaining (or problem-resolving) transactions.
	If there are changes in self-actualization processes, then there will be changes in problem-sustaining (or problem-resolving) transactions.
Cultural (constructionist)	If there are changes in the person's cultural sensitivity and competence, then there will be changes in problem-sustaining (or problem-resolving) transactions.
	If there are changes in the enculturation process, then there will be changes in problem-sustaining (or problem-resolving) transactions.
Ecological (ecology)	If there are changes in ecological conditions and processes, then there will be changes in problem-sustaining (or problem-resolving) transactions
	If there are changes in cultivation of the ecology/ecological development, then there will be changes in problem-sustaining (or problem-resolving) transactions.
Economic (exchange)	If there are changes in exchange patterns and opportunities, then there will be changes in problem-sustaining (or problem-resolving) transactions.
	If there are changes in economic development, then there will be changes in problem-sustaining (or problem-resolving) transactions.
Organization (role)	If there are changes in role definitions or structures, then there will be changes in problem-sustaining (or problem-resolving) transactions.

Continued

PIE/theory	Theory-based if–then propositions (brief illustrations) (HBSE and Life Course versions)
	If there are changes in career opportunities or constraints, then there will be changes in problem-sustaining (or problem-resolving) transactions.
Political (critical-feminist)	If there are changes in the distribution of power and privilege, then there will be changes in problem-sustaining (or problem-resolving) transactions.
	If there are changes in processes of liberation, then there will be changes in problem-sustaining (or problem-resolving) transactions.
Social (systems)	If there are changes in system adaptability (or integration), then there will be changes in problem-sustaining (or problem-resolving) transactions.
	If there are changes in systems differentiation (or integration), then there will be changes in problem-sustaining (or problem-resolving) transactions.

The following translates four other theories into if-then propositions summarizing central causal factors and expected changes. Practitioners could start with each to develop a series of theory-based intervention hypotheses—perhaps, separating out each causal factor into a distinct hypothesis. First, let's translate critical theory. Directing our intervention thinking, critical theory provides the resulting proposition: If there are changes in speech situations, public discourses, and critical consciousness (processes of liberation), there will be changes in problem-resolving transactions related to inequality and power imbalances. Exchange theory proposes that if there are changes in sympathy markets, sympathy margins for vulnerable groups, and exchange patterns, then there will be changes in problem-resolving transactions related to basic needs and economic development. Feminist theory proposes that if there are changes in the listening practices of relevant others, the articulation of silenced voices, and the awareness of the effects of gender socialization that has been sexist, then there will be changes in problem-resolving transactions related to realization of developmental potentials.

Multi-theoretical intervention hypothesis formulation

Multi-theoretical social workers formulate intervention plans that are based on more than one intervention hypothesis. With a toolbox of different theories, we can work to combine complimentary intervention hypotheses and to create an integrative, multi-theoretical intervention plan (Ingram, 2006). This plan can be tailored to the preferences of the client and the client system while addressing the focal or relevant aspects of the PIE configuration. Following the information collecting, organizing, and interpreting work, a community center worker counseling an adolescent gang member, for example, might decide to develop intervention hypotheses related to behaving, feeling, and thinking dimensions, to social interaction processes, and to economic and organizational contexts. The worker might plan also to integrate these hypotheses into a multi-pronged intervention plan to help the adolescent sever gang affiliations and establish bonds with pro-social, law-abiding peers.

Learning activities and reflections

1. Assessment is a complex and challenging part of the helping process. The assessment phase as all phases of the helping process requires careful and thoughtful theorizing.

   Identify one client system that you are helping (or a friend or family member that you have helped in the past) and select one problem to analyze. Use a theoretical framework to develop an explanatory formulation of this focal problem. First, review the typical elements of a problem as identified by the theory. Then, select the elements relevant in this case. Report on your formulation including the identification of the relevant theoretical framework, a theory-based summary of the key elements or factors that explain the problem, a brief description of the empirical indicators for each element, and your preliminary one to two sentence theory-based explanatory statement synthesizing your understanding of the problem and its elements.

2. In this book, we will focus specifically on the development of hypotheses about the client's difficulties, needs, or problems. When practitioners theorize about the likely relation between their helping actions and desired outcomes, they are formulating hypotheses. Briefly summarize your understanding of the term, "hypothesis" and comment also on how hypotheses are used by social workers. Brainstorm a few hypotheses related to efforts to explain some personal or collective problem. Brainstorm a few hypotheses related to efforts to change the same personal or collective problem.

3. An explanatory hypothesis is a theoretical statement identifying tentatively and in a testable fashion the likely relationship between

variables constituting the client's focal problem or challenge. For example, when assessing a young man's belligerent behavior from an interactionist perspective, the practitioner might begin to hypothesize by forming a proposition: when the man perceives the self as under attack, defines the best defense as aggression, tells himself that aggression is morally justifiable, and lacks the disposition or motivation to take the other's perspective, he resorts to verbal or physical aggression. This complex proposition can be broken into specific propositions and, then, hypotheses and checked against data collected from the client.

Table 9.1 provides human behavior and life course causal factors associated with each of fourteen different theoretical perspectives. The factors are stated at a general level but can be adapted for use in forming working explanatory hypotheses with a particular client with a particular challenge in a particular context. Select two or three theoretical frameworks from the table. Identify a client or client system problem. Then, formulate an explanatory hypothesis summarizing your assessment of the focal problem.

4. An intervention hypothesis is a theoretical statement identifying tentatively and in a testable way the likely relationship between interventions and desired outcomes. Returning to the young man discussed in activity three, a worker might begin to develop such a hypothesis by speculating the following sequence. If the young man can invite others to challenge him more carefully and if he can more accurately interpret "threatening" interaction with others, take the others role, ask for feedback about his interpretations, develop empathic dispositions that serve as a brake on aggressive impulses, then the young man's acts of verbal and physical aggression will decrease.

Use Table 9.2, and select two or three theoretical frameworks that might help you develop an action plan with a person that you know. Formulate a specific intervention hypothesis based on each chosen framework's if-then propositions. Comment too on how you might test these hypotheses during the helping process.

5. Applied developmental science is an interdisciplinary and holistic orientation to the integration of life course and human developmental theory and research with programs and policy initiatives to promote the development and enhance the life chances of client systems. Reflect on how you might use theories and research about the life span and the life course to help a client system explain and manage puberty and the associated stressors. Answer each of the following questions. What specific life span or life course issues,

problems, or challenges are they facing in puberty? What specific theoretical, research, and practice knowledge would better enable you to understand this individual and their stage-specific challenges? What theory-informed explanatory hypotheses might you suggest for consideration? What theory-informed intervention hypotheses might you propose?

6. Since human beings have multiple dimensions and interact with persons, groups, and organizations in many different environmental contexts, one hypothesis may not adequately address the necessary interventions. Reflect on a client or a friend that you know well. Formulate an integrated set of intervention hypotheses. Attempt in this multi-theoretical intervention plan to address more than one dimension of the person (acting, faithing, feeling, sensing, thinking), to change the symbolic interaction between person and the environment, and to influence positively two or more contexts (communal, cultural, ecological, organizational, economic, political, social). Discuss why you think that this set of intervention hypotheses best fits the details of the case.

7. Finally, conclude with reflections on these learning activities. What have you learned that will prepare you to utilize theoretical frameworks to guide the processes of assessment, intervention, and evaluation?

References

Bartholomew, L. K., Parcel, G. S., Kok, G., Gottlieb, N. H. and Fernandez, M. E. (2011). *Planning health promotion programs: An intervention mapping approach* (3rd ed.). San Francisco: Jossey-Bass.

Berzoff, J., Flanagan, L. M. and Hertz, P. (2008). From theory to practice. In J. Berzoff, L. M. Flanagan and P. Hertz (Eds), *Inside out and outside in: Psychodynamic clinical theory and psychopathology in contemporary multicultural contexts* (pp. 271–280). Lanham, MD: Jason Aronson.

Bloom, M., Fischer, J. and Orme, J. G. (2006). *Evaluating practice: Guidelines for the accountable professional* (5th ed.). Englewood Cliffs, NJ: Prentice-Hall.

Brooks-Harris, J. E. (2008). *Integrative multitheoretical psychotherapy*. Boston: Lahaska Press/Houghton Mifflin.

Council on Social Work Education (2008). 2008 Educational policy and accreditation standards. Retrieved June 16, 2010, from www.cswe.org/Accreditation/Reaffirmation.aspx.

Fawcett, J. (2005). Middle-range nursing theories are necessary for the advancement of the discipline. *Aquichan*, 5 (1), 32–43.

Forte, J. A. (2006). *Human behavior and the social environment: Models, metaphors, and maps for applying theoretical perspectives to practice*. Belmont, CA: Thomson Brooks/Cole.

Ingram, B. L. (2006). *Clinical case formulations: Matching the integrative treatment plan to the client*. Hoboken, NJ: John Wiley and Sons.

Moen, P. and Coltrane, S. (2005). Families, theories, and social policy. In V. L. Bengtson, A. C. Acock, K. R. Allen, P. Dilworth-Anderson and D. M. Klein (Eds), *Sourcebook of family theory and research* (pp. 543–565). Thousand Oaks, CA: Sage.

Munson, C. E. (1983). *An introduction to clinical social work supervision*. New York: Haworth.

National Cancer Institute (2013). Theory at a glance: A guide for health promotion practice (2nd ed.). Retrieved February 21, 2013 from www.cancer.gov/cancertopics/cancerlibrary/theory.pdf.

Rothman, A. J. (2004). Is there nothing more practical than a good theory? Why innovations and advances in health behavior change will arise if interventions are used to test and refine theory. *The International Journal of Behavioral Nutrition and Physical Activity, 1* (11), 1–11.

van Ryn, M. and Heaney, C. A. (1992). What's the use of theory? *Health Education Quarterly, 19* (3), 315–330.

10 Translate theories to guide the goal setting process

(EPAS 2.1.7 Apply knowledge; EPAS 2.1.10 Engage, assess, intervene, and evaluate)

The establishment of a theory-based treatment plan includes theory-specific (a) goals and (b) interventions. The goals, sometimes referred to as objectives, should immediately address (a) the client's problem issues and (b) the therapist's theoretical perspective. Because they address these two issues goals are the critical bridge between theory and practice.

(Gehart and Tuttle, 2003, p. 6)

Social workers attempt to make helping goals explicit. Goals provide a direction to the helping work, increase worker and client accountability, facilitate productive discussions between trainees and supervisors, and make possible the evaluation of effectiveness. Goal and objective setting should be parts of a mutual process so the client or client system are involved in every aspect of identifying and deciding on desired outcomes. The Council on Social Work Education (2008) refers to the goal setting component of a contract or agreement with a client or members of a client system. CSWE places goal setting in the assessment phase and calls on social workers to become competent at the task of developing mutually agreed-on intervention goals and objectives.

While discussion and negotiation about the elements of a working agreement such as goals and objectives first occurs in the beginning sessions, the agreement may be revisited at any point. Goals and objectives serve as a view in the beginning phase of the planned for end of the helping work. Goals and objectives guide the efforts of worker and client in the middle or work phase toward this end. At the concluding phase of a helping process, practice evaluation and termination activities involve judging the degree to which the goals and the planned for end has been realized.

Translating theory-based eco-maps to set goals

Theoretical frameworks typically provide a vision of the ideal. One way to translate theories into visions useful to goal setting work involves the construction of two theory-informed eco-maps—an eco-map of the current person- or system- in-environment configuration and an eco-map of the ideal configuration. This ideal might include the display of new systems that the client would like to add to their environment such as a workplace or a gym, the characterization of connections between client and focal system (the client's family, for example) under optimal circumstances such as a positive connection replacing a stressful or tenuous connection, and the addition of resources obtained from external systems such as money or emotional support and offered to other systems such as volunteer service to one's place of worship. Forte (2006) provides discussions and displays of ten theory-informed eco-maps and a summary of what the ideal eco-map would look like for each of these ten theoretical frameworks.

Each theoretical framework offers a distinctive conceptualization of the optimal "person interacting in environmental contexts" configuration or ideal PIE. Social workers who make use of a theory-informed eco-map as an assessment and goal formulation tool, for example, might create with the client a contemporary behavioral-theory eco-map but also generate an ideal eco-map using behavioral theory. These practitioners could translate the theoretical framework into the language and imagery of an eco-map and depict the client's notions (as linked to the translated theory) about ideal connections, ideal systems included in their environment, systems ideally excluded from the operative environment, resources that were ideally available from surrounding systems, and so on. The comparison between the actual eco-map and the ideal eco-map forms a solid foundation for *theory-based goal setting*: the specification of planned outcomes conceptualized from the helper's theoretical framework(s) that address client needs and problems and make sense to the client (Gehart and Tuttle, 2003).

Let's talk a bit more about the basics of this theory-informed goal setting process. Theory creators conceptualize the ideal PIE in terms of the relevant theoretical assumptions, concepts, and propositions. For example, role theorists conceive of the person or focal system as a role performer (Forte, 2006). The person's environment includes a variety of social systems characterized as formal or informal organizations with identifiable structures of positions and associated roles. Optimally, the person enacts roles effectively, responsibly, and satisfyingly. These are criteria for judging the quality of connections to organizations. Positive transactions between the role actor and the organizational structure of position-based roles involve creative yet sensitive performances, and such transactions contribute to the achievement of actor and organizational needs. The organizational context for role performances provides clear expectations for the roles associated with each position, protection from conflicts between the expectations associated with different roles, and manageable demands relative to the actors' capabilities to avoid role overload. These are some of the resources that the person acquires in exchanges with organizations. In return, the person enacts roles as part of a division of labor that enables organizations and their teams to accomplish their purposes. Such role enactment and the role-performer's knowledge, skill, and dispositions such as loyalty are resources offered to environmental organizations. Using this role theoretical characterization of the ideal PIE configuration, the practitioner and the client might aim to transform current eco-map conditions and set goals related to role competence, organizational role patterns, and the person's performances within central role structures.

David Gil (1994, 1998, 2002, 2004), a distinguished social work theorist, has drawn on empowerment theories (critical and feminist approaches, for instances) to develop another vivid conception of the ideal PIE configuration. In brief, he imagines the person as an active citizen with a critical consciousness and a capacity for dialogue with others. Transactions are I–Thou exchanges with each person treated as an equal, autonomous, authentic subject with the same rights and responsibilities as any other person. The ideal environment for Gil is a just society, one free from coercion, exploitation, and oppression and one characterized by wise stewardship of resources, member participation in workplace decision making, and the fair and balanced distribution of goods and service. In the ideal and just society, all can meet their basic needs, governance is democratic and nonhierarchical, and there are opportunities for each person to develop his or her human potentials. The practitioner might take this justice-oriented depiction of the ideal eco-map, compare it to the current eco-map of a client and formulate with the client a set of goals and objectives to realize better connections, resource exchanges, system processes, and even, societal patterns.

Theory-based goals and objectives

Theory-based goals are general statements informed by a theory about the aims of the collaborative helping activities. Theories point to targets of intervention and thus help with goal setting. A practitioner using social learning theory, for example, would collect information about client knowledge, skills, self-efficacy, and outcome expectations as possible factors contributing to a client's difficulty in acquiring a desired behavioral pattern. The worker and client using this theory can set goals to improve the specific areas that need improvement (van Ryn and Heaney, 1992). Theoretical knowledge and its application can also influence the choice of goals, the discussion of the desirability of various goals, and the feasibility of attaining particular goals (Walt, 2005).

A set of theory-based goals for a client might be considered a flexible vision of the ideal future state (or eco-map configuration), and goals specify this ideal or optimal condition in relation to the person or focal system, the transaction patterns, or the relevant environment contexts. Using our metaphorical imagination, we can say that the goal identifies the destination at the conclusion of the helping journey. At the personal level, a client agrees with the worker recommending a role theory approach to endeavor to perform better his role as husband, for instance. Focusing on interaction from the symbolic interactionist framework, the husband agrees with his wife and the social worker to reduce weekly arguments. Addressing the physical environment using the ecological perspective, the husband agrees to redesign the home (with his wife's input) so it includes a room for shared leisure time activities that don't include televisions, computers, sports, or snacks.

From the perspective of evidence-based practice, let's note a difference between theory-based goals which focus on desired future outcomes, the end of the helping process, and intervention methods, the means to achieve the end. Sometimes workers specify *process goals*, statements of the nature and quantity of interventions that should occur during the helping work. A plan to engage the husband for five counseling sessions involving role play activities and role rehearsal tools focuses on the method not the outcome. Or the correctional social worker using control theory negotiates with the non-violent offender to build relationship bonds with five conventional law-abiding citizens (Glaser, 1980). The ultimate goal is a crime-free life style; the relationship bonds are a means or process to this end.

A theory might also provide the worker and client direction in identifying a chain of goals such as immediate, intermediate, and ultimate goals (Hoogerwerf, 1990). We might refer to such plans as including goals and objectives related to intervention but for evaluation purposes, we should ensure that the plan includes theory-based objectives specifying outcomes to be achieved by the end of the helping work. *Theory-based objectives* are the specifications of a theory-based goal statement in ways that identify planned for outcomes in a form that is clear, measurable, achievable, time-limited, and anchored in a benchmark of success. For example, the practitioner suggests starting from the symbolic interactionist framework and the husband agrees to increase his communication of empathy towards his wife as indicated by a ten-point improvement on a valid and reliable empathy scale, The Davis Empathy Scale (Davis, 1983) before the end of ten weeks of counseling.

Illustrations of theory-based goals and multi-theory goal setting

Setting goals with clients and client systems can be usefully informed by theory. Each framework suggests a different approach to goal formulation.

Table 10.1 Translating theories to guide the goal setting process

PIE/theory	Helping goals (illustrations)	
	(Actions)	(Possible theory-based targets)
Multi-dimensional person		
Acting (behavioral)	decrease, extinguish, increase, learn, modify,	behavior
Faithing (anthropological)	access, develop, use, deepen	faith
Feeling (psychodynamic)	develop, increase	insight
Sensing (evolutionary biology)	activate, heal, support	biological processes
Thinking (cognitive)	challenge, dispute, learn, modify, restructure	cognitions
Interacting/transacting		
Transact (interactionism)	increase, deepen, improve	understanding
In context		
Communal (strengths)	facilitate, identify, increase, mobilize	assets, strengths
Cultural (constructionist)	increase	respect, tolerance
Ecological (ecology)	enhance, improve, sustain	quality of fit
Economic (exchange)	increase	prosperity
Organization (role)	deepen, increase	role competence
Political (critical-feminist)	expand, increase	power, life chances
Social (systems)	balance, change, improve, unbalance	system functioning

Theory-based goals, then, are derived from the theoretical framework or frameworks that the worker and client system agree will guide the helping process. Table 10.1 specifies possible goal-related action terms and targets identified in fourteen theories. Together, these can be used to create theory-based goals and objectives.

Our basic formulations for a theory-based goal are

> *Theory-based goal = to reduce specific undesirable thoughts, feelings, actions, interactions, events, conditions, or contextual features,*

or

> *Theory-based goal = to increase specific desirable thoughts, feelings, actions, interactions, events, conditions, or contextual features*

These formulations could be adapted to incorporate the actions and targets of any preferred theory, and these formulations could be modified slightly for use in setting objectives related to ultimate outcomes. Sample theory-based goals include the following. Applying behavioral theory, the worker and mother agree to attempt to reduce a child's inappropriate hitting behaviors. Using cognitive theory, the worker, husband and wife agree to aim to transform the irrational beliefs about sex that are inhibiting the couple's attempts to become physically and emotionally intimate. Adopting family systems theory, the practitioner and the family agree to strengthen a wife/mother's boundaries in relationship to her demanding husband and children. Applying social role theory, the worker and the leaders of an organizational department decide to change the role expectations (now characterized by ambiguity) and relationship norms (now emphasizing competition) that contribute to workplace conflict. Using symbolic interactionst theory, the group leader and the members agree to help all in the group to develop new, explicit, and usable interpretations of the meaning of chronic depression. Each of these theory-based goals could be fruitfully made more specific and transformed into a theory-based objective as discussed earlier.

A worker and client might also take a multi-theoretical approach to goal setting. *Multi-theoretical goal setting* uses the major theoretical languages to generate and state images and verbal descriptions of ideal and desired outcomes for members and communities. Using a variety of theoretical frameworks, the worker might assemble and propose an interrelated set of goals and objectives in response to the range of concerns or challenges identified by the client.

Learning activities and reflections

1. Theoretical frameworks typically provide a vision of the ideal world. In social work terms, the perspective offers a distinctive conceptualization of the optimal "person interacting in environmental contexts" configurations or PIE. This vision of the better, optimal, possible, preferred, or ideal configuration can serve many practical uses. For example, practitioners can use diverse theoretical frameworks as sources for the construction of the helping plan including the helping goals and objectives for a particular case.

   Identify a person that you have helped (or reflect on your own resolution of a life difficulty) and summarize your initial thoughts during the planned change process about the preferred future or better scenario. How did this conception specify each aspect of the person interacting in environmental contexts: optimal personal qualities, optimal transactions between the person and his or her environmental contexts, and optimal features of the environment?

2. Identify your understanding of the concepts: goal and objective, and your understanding of the goal formulation process in social work. Specify also several illustrative goals and objectives related to your experiences as a helper or related to your experiences with a personal change project.

3. A goal is founded on a formal or informal conception of how things might be better. Table 10.1 summarizes some of the targets for change identified by various theoretical frameworks. Each theoretical framework considers many other possible change targets. These are only illustrations. The table also lists some of the theory-based action terms that might be incorporated into a goal statement. We can make use of a general formula to translate each theory into a theory-based goal. A theory-based goal = the "theory-based action term" as the process leading to change in the "theory-based target" at the specified focal level "person, transaction, environmental context, or multiple levels."

   Reflect on a set of possible and preferred changes that you can imagine for yourself or a client. Then, select two or three theoretical frameworks and generate goal statements derived from each framework. For several of these goals, transform the goal statement into one or more specific objectives. Justify your choice of theoretical bases for the formulation of your goals and objectives.

4. Finally, conclude with reflections on these learning activities. What have you learned that will prepare you to utilize theoretical frameworks to guide the processes of assessment, intervention, and evaluation?

References

Council on Social Work Education (2008). 2008 Educational policy and accreditation standards. Retrieved June 16, 2010, from www.cswe.org/Accreditation/Reaffirmation.aspx

Davis, M. (1983). Measuring individual differences in empathy: Evidence for a multidimensional approach. *Journal of Personality and Social Psychology*, 44 (1), 113–126.

Forte, J. A. (2006). *Human behavior and the social environment: Models, metaphors, and maps for applying theoretical perspectives to practice*. Belmont, CA: Thomson Brooks/Cole.

Gehart, D. R. and Tuttle, A. R. (2003). *Theory-based treatment planning for marriage and family therapists: Integrating theory and practice.* Pacific Grove, CA: Brooks/Cole-Thomson.

Gil, D. G. (1994). Confronting social injustice and oppression. In F. C. Reamer (Ed.), *The foundations of social work knowledge* (pp. 231–263). New York: Columbia University Press.

Gil, D. G. (1998). *Confronting injustice and oppression: Concepts and strategies for social workers.* New York: Columbia University Press.

Gil, D. G. (2002). Challenging justice and oppression. In M. O' Melia and K. K. Miley (Eds), *Pathways to power: Readings in contextual social work practice* (pp. 35–54). Boston: Allyn and Bacon.

Gil, D. G. (2004). Perspectives on social justice. *Reflections, 10* (4), 32–39.

Glaser, D. (1980). The interplay of theory, issues, policy, and data. In M. W. Klein and K. S. Teilman (Eds), *Handbook of criminal justice evaluation* (pp. 123–142). Beverly Hills, CA: Sage.

Hoogerwerf, A. (1990). Reconstructing policy theory. *Evaluation and Program Planning, 13* (3), 285–291.

van Ryn, M. and Heaney, C. A. (1992). What's the use of theory? *Health Education Quarterly, 19* (3), 315–330.

Walt, S. M. (2005). The relationship between theory and policy in international relations. *Annual Review of Political Science, 8,* 23–48.

11 Translate theoretical frameworks to guide the specification of change theory and logic model

(EPAS 2.1.7 Apply knowledge; EPAS 2.1.10 Engage, assess, intervene, and evaluate)

A theory of change is the articulation of the underlying beliefs and assumptions that guide a service delivery strategy and are believed to be critical for producing change and improvement in children and families ... Theories of change create meaningful associations between the context of service delivery, the children and families being served, the strategies or activities that are being implemented, and the desired outcomes.
(Hernandez and Hodges, 2003, p. 4)

Over time novice social workers decide on and adopt preferred theories of change. The diligent practitioner builds his or her integrative and multi-theoretical theory of change by incorporating suitable theoretical frameworks, relevant research findings, lessons from practice, and educational experiences in professional social work programs. Additionally, the practitioner works to monitor the testing and improving of the change theories in the larger scientific community and in the specific field of practice.

Unfortunately, the Council on Social Work Education's (2008) recent *Educational policy and accreditation standards* document is silent about worker tasks related to articulating and using theories of change. However, this is an important topic and one relevant to the CSWE Standard EPAS 2.1.10 and specific planned change tasks including the assessment task of agreeing on intervention goals and the intervention task of helping clients resolve problems.

Theoretical frameworks and theories of change

Each theoretical framework offers a conceptualization of the process of change. This *theory of change* or change theory is a summary account including, ideally, a statement of the theoretical assumptions related to individual and/or collective change, the identification of the mechanisms (why change will occur) or processes (how the change occurs) by which the changes lead to desired outcomes, and the core components of the associated change plan translated into intervention strategies or social programs (National Cancer Institute, 2013; Schneider, 2006).

The theory of change helps the practitioner answer various questions important to accurate assessment and effective intervention (Louie and Guthrie, 2007; van Ryn and Heaney, 1992). How can the focal problem be best conceptualized to support change? What will the change process look like? What will be different if the change process is successful? What specific activities will the practitioner need to initiate to make this difference and contribute to the achievement of specific desired outcomes? What factors might accelerate or inhibit progress toward these outcomes?

The theory of change can serve as a road map guiding the worker and client during the intervention phase of the helping process. The theory of change is also an important part of the process of developing a *theory-based treatment plan*: a systematic guide to efforts to elicit changes in the "person-interacting in an environment" (PIE) configuration to resolve the presenting problem(s), a plan anchored in the practitioner's theoretical orientation (Gehart and Tuttle, 2003). When the plan or guide is a good one, expected changes and a resolution of the problem should follow. If the intervention strategies and actions derived from the theory of change don't work as expected, the worker and client need to question and revise this theory of change or reconsider their implementation strategies.

Illustrative theories of change

The idea of "theory of change" is fairly new, and not commonly discussed in the social work literature. Therefore, I will provide two detailed illustrations. Each includes many but not all of the elements identified above.

A role theory of change

Kiecolt (1994) provides an instructive and somewhat complex "role theory of self-change." She organizes her model in variable clusters: A, B, C, and D. The A cluster refers to variables stimulating the urge to change. These include stressors like chronic role strain or challenging life events; perceptions of unfavorable appraisals by others, of decreases in competence, and of unfavorable comparisons with others; troubling reductions in self-esteem, self-efficacy, or authenticity; and psychological distress. The B cluster refers to variables that condition the likelihood of intentional change: the identity relevance of the stressor, the attribution of responsibility to self for the stressor, the access to support for change, the belief that change is possible, and the calculation that change benefits outweigh the costs. The C refers to the critical event or turning point triggering change, and D is the decision to change oneself. Kiecolt's change model characterizes change as an interrelated group of processes. In the A set of variables, stressors lead to changed perceptions, new perceptions lead to reductions in self-judgments, and these self processes leads to psychological distress. Changes in A variables lead to changes of B variables. These changes moderate the degree of motivation to change and, in some cases, may stop the movement toward intentional change. If the process continues, B contributes to the power of influences supporting personal change leading to a turning point (C) and finally the decision to change oneself (D). Kiecolt's theory of change directs workers to look to changes in role-related stressors and changes in self-conceptions (role identities and traits) as keys to motivating personal change.

A critical theory of change

Fay (1977), a critical theorist, offers a different theory of change. His theory focuses on both micro and macro levels of the social environment. How is the focal problem conceptualized? Working class members of capitalistic societies often lack an understanding of their true needs, and tend to pursue false needs and self-destructive relationships and ways of living that frustrate their efforts to meet true needs. This results in suffering and the perpetuation of their victimization.

What are the specific origins of this problem? Upper class elite leaders cleverly and systematically indoctrinate working class people and gain their allegiance to maintaining the repressive social order. Continual and effective indoctrination creates a "false consciousness," systematic self and social misunderstandings with interrelated illusions about human needs, about the nature of happiness, about what is good and of value, about how to act with others to realize authentic needs, and about the good life. Additionally, indoctrination and oppressive socialization practices also result in the "internalization of oppression," that is, the working class people come to accept as their own the values, norms, and beliefs promoted by oppressors. They fail to see the degree to which they are exploited and oppressed, and they unwittingly collude with oppressors by participating in actions that maintain oppressive social conditions and practices and contribute to the misfortunes of the entire working class. Fay (1977) offers an example. Many working class persons yield to the persuasive power of advertisers. They organize and direct much of their energy, time, and talents in the quest for more and fancier consumer goods. Their daydreams and fantasies involve scenarios about winning the lottery and the resultant opportunities to buy things. Competition for bargains, for example, on Black Friday, the sales day in the United States after Thanksgiving, becomes more important than cooperation with others. Despite all the consumption, life still seems empty. New purchases don't bring meaningful social relationships or personal fulfillment. Additionally, opportunities for social action related to survival needs, improved salaries, work conditions, housing, and health care are missed.

According to Fay's critical theory of change, what are the sources of change? First, social movement leaders must engage the members of the working class in the critique of political "ideology." This historical critique demonstrates that the basic categories and associated evaluations (eager shopper, worthless poor, upwardly mobile worker) that people use to think about their identities are incoherent and inadequate. Adopting these ideas benefits the upper class oppressors, not the working class, and the category/belief systems were created at particular points in history as tools to sustain the privileges of the few. Second, critical social theorists and leaders must organize "consciousness raising groups." In these small circles supporting the free and non-coerced exchange of ideas between equals without any fear of punishment, working class people can identify the causal processes (ideologies and political-economic structures) that victimize people. As group members argue, debate, analyze, persuade, criticize, and educate together they achieve a new consciousness about how their participation in their own oppression contributes to unhappiness and powerlessness. They develop ideas, identities, social practices, and vocabularies radically different than those promoted by the rulers. They begin to free themselves from domination—rejecting the messages of advertisers and changing their habits of compulsive consumption, for instance. Third, citizens with self and social awareness develop action plans to create fulfilling ways of living and external conditions supporting such fulfillment, and then they implement these action plans. Fay (1977) points to the participants in women's consciousness raising groups and their advocacy for policies and programs attacking sexist and discriminatory patterns as exemplars.

What factors might inhibit the change process? Fay (1977) notes that privileged members of a society do not give up their advantages without a fight. To the degree that the privileged and dominating groups can restrict access to critical theories, to critical theorists, to a language of emancipation, and to forums for consciousness raising interaction, the likelihood of successful personal and collective change will decrease.

Translating theoretical content related to a theory of change

Understanding and articulating the underlying theoretical logic to the change process enables practitioners to work with clients to select and implement appropriate and effective interventions. Your human behavior classes, your practice classes, your meetings with your field instructor, and your reflections on your helping encounters are opportunities to learn different theories of change. For example, you may have taken an "Introduction to Sociology" class. Perhaps you learned how ancient sociological theories of change offered relatively simplistic notions of policy change processes (Coleman, 1978). Consider this outdated proposition—if the policy advocates simply expose the evil, exploitive, or oppressive conditions contributing to poverty (the initial policy intervention), then community leaders and other members will take actions to correct the negative condition. Hopefully, you have also learned some newer relevant and valid theories of change.

The effective practitioner can search for and select a science-based conceptualization of change, a *middle-range theory* from a theoretical tradition. A middle-range theory identifies precisely the relationships between a set of variables, and includes a set of propositions indicating how variables influence each other (Fawcett, 2005). This translation device is useful for converting theoretical content into explanations of client problems. Here we are focusing on middle-range theories that address how particular patterns or processes are changed. This kind of middle-range theory—when developed as a comprehensive theory of change—characterizes the focal problem or challenge, the causes or processes maintaining the problem at various levels, the factors that can be changed, the points of intervention for individual and system change efforts, the worker role as a catalyst for change, and the specific change actions (helper, client, and collaterals) including programs, interventions, and techniques shown to activate desired changes (Burdine and McLeroy, 1992).

The concepts in a theory of change can also be translated into directives for helping work, and the theory also offers a framework for practice evaluation. Since the members of a client system bring their own theories of change to the helping situation, the practitioner should discuss any similarities and differences in the worker's and clients' understanding of change and seek a consensus with the clients on the change theory that will guide the intervention phase. Practitioners who have a clear, scientific understanding of the planned change process, a theory of change (TOC), and obtain client consent to use the suitable TOC tend to engage in better practice than those with no theory of change (Nelson and Prior, 2003).

Multi-theoretical social work and theories of change

Theoretical frameworks vary in their conception or theory of change. Some identify external events as the major triggers of change. Some identify internal events or processes as the major triggers. Some assume that change is constant and natural. Others assume that stability is the norm, and human beings resist change. For certain theorists, change becomes possible when a person has exhausted all options and is desperate; rock bottom has been hit. Other theorists believe that a person can choose to change under many different circumstances. Some conceptions of change are fairly simple and some are complex and involve multiple variables, processes, or phases.

Each theory of change provides different guidelines for activating change in line with its conception of the nature of change. For example, symbolic interactionists suggest that symbol-using capacities are enhanced when communicators are supported in dealing with hard-to-interpret life challenges. A theory of change might also indicate conditions that must be met before change processes can begin. For critical theorists, persons with few privileges must first develop a critical consciousness, the awareness that the major sources of their problems are in unjust political, social, and economic arrangements not in personal failures. Then, the social worker is more likely to successfully invite the under privileged to mobilize and fight for a fair share of communal resources.

Let's consider another example. Social workers are committed to the alleviation of poverty. Different HBSE (human behavior and the social environment) theories offer different conceptions of the problem and needed changes and, thus, different suggestions for change targets (Moen and Coltrane, 2005). Some economic theories argue that the male breadwinner's lack of economic viability contributes significantly to family poverty; poverty programs should train men with knowledge, skills, and dispositions necessary to obtain employment in a information-oriented society. Stress theory suggests a primary focus on the consequences of role overload and role conflict for parents; poverty programs should provide child-rearing services and other supports to free parents, especially parents in single-parent households, from some of their multiple role obligations and allow them to devote more time to the work role. Feminist theory emphasizes the disadvantaged position of women especially mothers in labor markets: policies that ensure equal pay and penalize gender discriminatory practices are needed.

Table 11.1 Translating theories to specify a theory of change for intervention

PIE/Theories	Theory of change (illustration)
Multi-dimensional person	Change occurs because of:
Acting (behavioral)	different stimuli and consequences (rewards, punishments) related to behavior
Faithing (anthropological)	enhanced contact with and relation to the sacred (God, divine spirits, relics)
Feeling (psychodynamic)	more insight into emotions, ego defenses, and developmental patterns
Sensing (evolutionary biology)	healing damaged cells and other body parts and processes by medication
Thinking (cognitive)	increased knowledge, greater rationality and restructuring of beliefs
Interacting/transacting	
Transact (interactionism)	improved symbol using and symbol creating dispositions and abilities
In environmental contexts	
Communal (strengths)	mobilization of personal strengths and community assets
Cultural (constructionist)	cultural sensitivity and competence building in cooperative situations
Physical environment (ecology)	transformation of resource use and resource sustainability practices
Organizational (role)	preparation (role training, role rehearsal, role play) for performances
Economic (exchange)	smarter negotiation of exchanges reducing costs and increasing benefits
Political (critical-feminist)	use of persuasion, power, force compelling redistribution of privileges
Social (systems)	reorganization of parts and of rules governing system operations and supports

Table 11.1 summarizes in very brief form the core notion for theories of change derived from fourteen theoretical frameworks. Each theory is linked to a particular aspect of our PIE metatheory—personal dimensions, interaction, and environmental contexts. The summary stem derived from each tradition's middle-range theory of change begins with the phrase "change occurs because of," and this stem is completed for each theory with the essential conceptualization of the target and the mechanism. For example,

a biological theory of change focuses on the body and its systems as targets for change and includes the proposition that healing by means of medication can change disease states.

Social work is committed to the promotion of social justice. Change theories can assist our work in this realm. I have translated four theories from Table 11.1 to capture their approach to theorizing change towards greater justice. Focusing on the interactionist aspect of the PIE, symbolic interactionists theorize that the personal and collective exploration of and reconstruction of the symbols and their meanings sustaining injustice can lead to the new understandings and capabilities among members necessary for changing the larger symbolic order. Focusing on the economic context, exchange theorists propose that brokering more empathy for vulnerable populations by advocates can change exchange norms (give to affirm your beneficence or give to meet needs instead of give with the expectation of return, for examples) and this will modify exchange patterns between resource-rich and resource-poor groups to the benefit of poor and vulnerable partners in the marketplace. Focusing on the political context, critical theorists conceptualize change in the following way: democratic dialogue among oppressed peers facilitated by astute social critics can increase critical consciousness, and consciousness changes lead to persuasive social action resulting in successful fights for a fairer share of society's power and privilege. Feminists also focus on the political context, and they theorize that social workers who create groups and communities where women listen to each other and allow the emergence of silenced voices will increase the members' awareness of common lived experiences, shared standpoints, and similar instances of oppression in a sexist society. Such changes stimulate forceful and effective resistance to patriarchs. I believe that these four theories of change could be usefully integrated into an overall empowerment framework for practice.

I have summarized the essence of many different theories of change. Practitioners will need to do more reading or talking about the fourteen theories of change to obtain complete, detailed theoretical statements of the approach of each to personal and collective change.

A logic model for change

Besides identifying and selecting a theory of change, effective social workers should also try to answer a related question: How can I best display and discuss the theoretical logic and principles underlying the change process or sequences with a specific client in a specific setting? The answer often provides the information necessary for the construction of a logic model. A logic model (LM) typically identifies the context of helping services, the helping goals and objectives, the ingredients of the helping work (mechanisms or processes) leading to desired changes, and the expected client system short- and long-term outcomes (Hernandez and Hodges, 2003). Each component is like a link in the chain of service. This tool helps the worker and client translate theoretical ideas into action.

Unlike a theory of change, an abstract conceptualization of human and systems change that is a theory that must be translated for practical use, a logic model is a specification of the observable and concrete logical features of the change process for a particular helping team, program, or agency. A logic model is often presented as a visual display and the graphic representation shows the relationships and sequencing of the components of the model. Figure 11.1 identifies elements commonly included in a logic model.

A logic model might be developed without reference to any theory or it might incorporate or build on an explicit theory of change. A *theory-informed logic model* uses the perspective and language of a theory to specify the problem, context, objectives, intervention strategies, and desired outcomes relevant to a specific case. For example, a logic model derived from systems theory uses the systems language of input, throughput (intervention or program activities), output (immediate and long term outcomes), and feedback loop to organize the elements of a change sequence.

The practitioner often supplements the visual display of change logic by materials presented in narrative form. This narrative expands on the theoretical assumptions, concepts, propositions, and middle-range theory used by the worker, program team, or agency to describe and detail the characterization of client problems and the rationale for and principles of preferred interventions. The practitioner might develop and share the logic model display and written summary with the client, review and improve the model with a supervisor or colleague, and hopefully, use the logic model to guide the design and execution of an evaluation of effectiveness (Bartholomew, Parcel, Kok, Gottlieb, and Fernandez, 2011).

In the multi-theoretical social work approach, the practitioner assembles systematically multiple theories of change and creates an integrative logic model informed by these theories. Although adding complexity to the treatment plan, this approach enhances attention to several focal problems and challenges and responds to the social work emphasis on addressing multiple aspects of the relevant PIE configuration.

Client with Problem → Helping Context → Goals and Objectives → Change Strategies → Outcomes

---

Figure 11.1 A generic logic model

Learning activities and reflections

1. Change is a critical feature of life. A theory of change presents a distinctive perspective on the why and the how of the change process. Briefly describe your assumptions and beliefs about change. Comment also on your views of the major causes of change, the way positive changes are maintained, and the methods for preventing undesired change. In your view does change operate differently for individuals, families, and larger social systems like communities or organizations?

2. Contemporary practitioners may select from many different theories of change or even integrate multiple theories of change into a personal practice model. Table 11.1 summarizes the essential conception of change for fourteen different theoretical approaches. Select a human behavior or human development theory from Table 11.1 that you consider useful and expand on your understanding of how the theory could guide your design of a change plan with a friend or client.

3. Think through and report on how you might use the cognitive/ rational emotive practice theory of change to guide the intervention process. Identify a troubling personal, interpersonal, or organizational situation. Use the activating event–belief–consequence (feelings or actions)–dispute (A-B-C-D) formula developed by Albert Ellis (1979) to assess and change the situation. What is the activating event (A)? What beliefs (B) are associated with this event? What are the undesirable consequences (C) of the event-belief sequence? Try disputing (D) your irrational beliefs. Develop a change plan using this theory of change. How has this cognitive theory of the change process facilitated your understanding and improvement of the situation? What was useful and what was difficult about this theory application effort?

4. Visit the Harlem Children's Zone Project (www.hcz.org/index. php). Read through the website and focus on their helping efforts. Describe programs and interventions that they offer to children at two or three different stages of development. Comment briefly on the theory of developmental change that these programs and interventions seem to follow. Identify specifically what phrases, metaphors, presented concepts, stated assumptions or other materials led you to your conclusions about the theory of change. Discuss how well this project's logic succeeds or fails to incorporate the contemporary lessons from life course/human developmental science as you understand it.

5. We have discussed a tool used to describe important aspects of the change process, the logic model (LM). Select several social work programs (or programs in allied professions like education or nursing) with which you are familiar. Compare and contrast the logic for each program. What are the elements and sequences for each logic model? Based on your analysis, what do you view as the strengths and limitations of each program's logic?

   Imagine a case that you might deal with as a social worker and create a theory-informed logic model. Identify the theoretical foundation. Specify a particular client problem, the conceptualization of the change process, and the anticipated outcome for the case. Create a simple display depicting your logic model. Elaborate on the theoretical assumptions, concepts, propositions, and models that contribute to your approach to the client problem and the change process.

6. Finally, conclude with reflections on these learning activities. What have you learned that will prepare you to utilize theoretical frameworks to guide the processes of assessment, intervention, and evaluation?

References

Bartholomew, L. K., Parcel, G. S., Kok, G., Gottlieb, N. H. and Fernandez, M. E. (2011). *Planning health promotion programs: An intervention mapping approach* (3rd ed.). San Francisco: Jossey-Bass.

Burdine, J. N. and McLeroy, K. R. (1992). Practitioners' use of theory: Examples from a workgroup. *Health Education Quarterly*, 19 (3), 331–340.

Coleman, J. (1978). Sociological analysis and social policy. In T. Bottomore and R. Nisbet (Eds), *A history of sociological analysis* (pp. 677–703). New York: Basic Books.

Council on Social Work Education (2008). 2008 Educational policy and accreditation standards. Retrieved June 16, 2010, from www.cswe.org/Accreditation/Reaffirmation.aspx.

Ellis, A. (1979). The theory of rational-emotive therapy. In A. Ellis and J. M. Whiteley (Eds), *Theoretical and empirical foundations of rational-emotive therapy* (pp. 33–60). Monterey, CA: Brooks/Cole Publishing Company.

Fawcett, J. (2005). Middle-range nursing theories are necessary for the advancement of the discipline. *Aquichan*, 5 (1), 32–43.

Fay, B. (1977). How people change themselves: The relationship between critical theory and its audience. In T. Ball (Ed.), *Political theory and praxis: New perspectives* (pp. 200–233). Minneapolis: University of Minnesota Press.

Gehart, D. R. and Tuttle, A. R. (2003). *Theory-based treatment planning for marriage and family therapists: Integrating theory and practice*. Pacific Grove, CA: Brooks/Cole-Thomson.

Hernandez, M. and Hodges, S. (2003). Crafting logic models for systems of care: Ideas into action. (Making children's mental health services successful series, Volume 1). Tampa, FL: University of South Florida, The Louis de la Parte Florida Mental Health Institute, Department of Child & Family Studies. Retrieved August 22, 2011, from http://rtckids.fmhi.usf.edu/rtcpubs/CMHseries/IdeasintoAction.html.

Kiecolt, K. J. (1994). Stress and the decision to change oneself: A theoretical model. *Social Psychology Quarterly, 57* (1), 49–63.

Louie, J. and Guthrie, K. (2007). Strategies for assessing policy change efforts: A prospectus approach. *The Evaluation Exchange: A Periodical on Emerging Strategies in Evaluation, XIII* (1), 5.

Moen, P. and Coltrane, S. (2005). Families, theories, and social policy. In V. L. Bengtson, A. C. Acock, K. R. Allen, P. Dilworth-Anderson and D. M. Klein (Eds), *Sourcebook of family theory and research* (pp. 543–565). Thousand Oaks, CA: Sage.

National Cancer Institute (2013). Theory at a glance: A guide for health promotion practice (2nd ed.). Retrieved February 21, 2013, from www.cancer.gov/cancertopics/cancerlibrary/theory.pdf.

Nelson, T. S. and Prior, D. (2003). Theory of change projects in MFT programs. *Contemporary Family Therapy, 25* (2), 133–151.

Schneider, M. A. (2006). *The theory primer: A sociological guide*. Lanham, MD: Rowman and Littlefield.

van Ryn, M. and Heaney, C. A. (1992). What's the use of theory? *Health Education Quarterly, 19* (3), 315–330.

12 | Translate theories to guide the identification, selection, and implementation of interventions

(EPAS 2.1.7 Apply knowledge; EPAS 2.1.10 Engage, assess, intervene, and evaluate)

It is important to emphasize that theories and intervention techniques are not the same thing. Theories are abstract and include concepts that suggest to the social worker which intervention strategies may be effective with clients. Intervention strategies are the concrete actions taken by social workers to help clients achieve their goals. There should be consistency, however, between a practitioner's working theory and interventions.

(Walsh, 2010, p. 4)

Effective social workers ponder over the question: how can the desired change best be achieved? Theoretical frameworks can guide the engagement, information gathering, and assessment work necessary to professional social work. Theoretical frameworks can also guide the identification, selection, and implementation of intervention strategies. In the Council on Social Work Education (2008) statement of competencies and related practice behaviors, the Council indicates for EPAS 2.1.10 that assessment includes the worker task: develop mutually agreed-on intervention goals and objectives. We have discussed the multi-theoretical social work approach to this task in previous lessons. The Council also identifies the following tasks of the intervention phase: initiate actions to achieve organizational goals;

implement prevention interventions that enhance client capacities; help clients resolve problems; and negotiate, mediate, and advocate for clients. We will not examine each of these tasks in this lesson, but the general tasks of selecting and implementing interventions that resolve client problems.

Theory-informed intervention: an overview

Let's review some basic ideas about social work interventions. A *theory-informed intervention* is the specification of what theory-derived actions will be taken by the helper and/or client to achieve a theory-based goal (Gehart and Tuttle, 2003). The intervention is chosen from the range of possible theoretical sources following a comprehensive information collecting, organizing, and interpreting process. The theory and related empirical research provide a rationale with supporting evidence for decisions about what needs to be done to change a focal aspect of the PIE configuration. The practitioner organizes, operationalizes, and implements the helping actions to fit with the helping setting, the client population, the system level, the anticipated intensity and duration of the focal problem, and so on (Bartholomew, Parcel, Kok, Gottlieb, and Fernandez, 2011).

Plans for theory-informed interventions are like the designs of experienced architects. These designs organize a set of theoretical ideas in a way that provides the specifications of the actions to be taken by builders (carpenters, plumbers, electricians, and so on) often in a specified sequence to achieve an intended consequence during a building construction process (Argyris, 2003). At the job site, the carpenter adds his or her skill, craft wisdom, aesthetic sensibilities, and intuition to actions that actualize the architectural plan. In the realm of professional social work, social learning theory, for example, might suggest the basic architectural plan or design for a group forum intervention. The group worker will encourage low-income food purchasers to share testimonials about how they have incorporated frugal and healthy food buying practices into their shopping habits (to model for and influence new members in the budgeting group). During the actual group meeting, the social worker creatively adjusts and revises this intervention plan as the group members interact with each other.

There are several sources for interventions. First, interventions can be derived directly from existing explanatory theories, or practice frameworks and their change theories. If based faithfully on existing theoretical knowledge, the social worker judges whether the knowledge has been specified in a way lending itself to implementation. The worker might also ask questions. Does a theory suggest an intervention that can be used immediately, effectively, and feasibly in light of resources and constraints? Will the theory-informed intervention complement the practitioners' training, experience, skill repertoire, knowledge, and creativity (Hochbaum, Sorenson, and Lorig, 1992)? Under what specific condition, will the theory-informed intervention most likely result in helping success? Second, the intervention can be drawn from existing theoretical knowledge but use this knowledge in imaginative ways (Bryant, 1991). The novel use of existing theoretical traditions and their theoretical frameworks, generalizations, concepts, propositions, models can open up possible fields of helping action not previously perceived by the social worker or client. Additionally, the worker may modify the knowledge in creative and, sometimes, extensive adjustments using his or her practice wisdom to fill the gap between the theory and the concrete situation. For example, the worker tries to detect and correct errors during field uses of biologically oriented interventions until effective action is produced. Third, the practitioner may use the research literature to suggest interventions with proven effectiveness for particular clients with particular problems. These interventions may be linked to a theoretical base or offered as an atheoretical helping action. Finally, the worker and the client may create interventions based on their own life experiences, insights, and grounded theorizing about actions and their likely consequences.

Interventions can be categorized on a continuum from simple to complex (Bloom, Fischer, and Orme, 2006). A *theory-informed intervention technique* is a distinct helping action. Paraphrasing, the open-ended question, and the reflection of feelings are techniques commonly used by social workers during an interview. Often, these techniques have been conceptualized in line with the humanistic, client-centered theory developed by Carl Rogers and his followers. Giddens (1979, p. 248) suggested that the explanation of a theoretical concept can be considered an intervention technique:

> There is a two-way relation involved between lay language and the language of social science, because any of the concepts introduced by sociological observers can in principle be appropriated by lay actors themselves, and applied as part of "ordinary language" discourse.

Helping an abused woman, for instance, understand that she is an unwilling partner in a "inequitable exchange pattern" and that she can find "alternative relationships" that will be less costly provides new ways for her to think about the domestic situation.

A *theory-informed intervention package* is a limited set of interventions derived from a theory or a set of theories and assembled in a systematic way. A social worker using the behavioral perspective might conduct a parent skill training session using simulations combining the following intervention actions: demonstrations, modeling, coaching, prompts, and reinforcement. Or the practitioner might follow the guidance of Glanz and Bishop (2010), experts on the effectiveness of theory-guided practice, who believe that "the strongest interventions may be built from multiple theories" (p. 12). This practitioner creates a package or intervention model that combines several theory-informed interventions.

A theory-informed intervention program is a complex set of interventions derived from relevant theories and organized in a planned sequence and delivered over an extended period of time. Human service workers, for example, have made use of cognitive-behavioral anger management programs and of stress reduction programs integrating biological, cognitive, and behavioral approaches.

Whatever the level of complexity (technique, package, or program), scientific practitioners should specify their theory-informed intervention strategies in great and clear detail. This helps in implementing the strategy, appraising the effectiveness of helping work, and in communicating with clients, colleagues, and collaterals (Bloom et al., 2006). It also increases the possibility that other social workers can learn from and replicate the intervention as it was reported in an evaluation or case study. A thorough intervention description will specify details related to who is involved, what exactly is being done, where is the intervention offered, how often does the intervention occur, when is the best time to intervene, what is the duration of the intervention, what are the conditions necessary for success, and so on (Walt, 2005).

Theory-based intervention strategies: illustrations

Social workers can generate new interventions in consultation with client system members, colleagues, researchers, supervisors, and others. Often, however, practitioners turn to the theoretical frameworks and practice theories that they have learned during their professional socialization and select established theory-based intervention strategies from these resources.

Each theory provides a distinctive set of interventions with each intervention anchored in the metaphors, the assumptions, the logic of change, the if-then propositions, and the supportive research for the theory. For example, many behaviorist social workers embrace a metaphorical stance of laboratory scientist. They assume that behaviors are maintained by reinforcing or punishing consequences. Changing consequences will change focal behaviors. Thus, *behavior modification*, the systematic and planned changing of consequences to change a target behavior, is promoted as an intervention technique, and the *token economy*, the use of a set of tokens or symbols exchangeable for desired events, experiences, or goods to reinforce appropriate behaviors, has been established as an intervention program.

Table 12.1 provides a summary of basic intervention actions or techniques for fourteen theories. Practitioners who decide that interactionist interventions are appropriate might consider asking for reciprocal perspective

Table 12.1 Translating theories to guide the selection of intervention strategies

PIE /theory	Intervention strategies/actions (illustrations)
Multi-dimensional person	
Acting (behavioral)	assigning homework, behavioral contracting, coaching, controlling stimulus, desensitizing to fearful situations, establishing schedules of reinforcement, initiating a token economy, rehearsing new behaviors, shaping behavior patterns, training in skills
Faithing (anthropological)	accessing spiritual support, chanting, faith-based service, meditating, participating in sacred rituals, praying, reading sacred texts
Feeling (psychodynamic)	analyzing dreams, encouraging free association, facilitating emotional catharsis and expression, interpreting development and relationship patterns, managing loss, managing resistance, monitoring therapeutic relationship, working through inner conflicts
Sensing (evolutionary biology)	encouraging compliance, fostering bodily awareness, promoting wellness, reducing substance use, referring for medical intervention or medication, teaching relaxation methods
Thinking (cognitive)	appraising evidence and logic, brainstorming alternative solutions, disputing irrational thoughts, fostering mindfulness, monitoring self talk and thoughts, providing information, restructuring beliefs, thought stopping
Interacting/transacting	
Transact (interactionism)	asking for reciprocal perspective taking, facilitating support, framing messages, making new roles, reconstructing personal or social meanings, teaching communication skills, telling life stories
In environmental contexts	
Communal (strengths)	active listening, communicating empathy and positive regard, confronting, focusing attention, fostering here and now awareness, promoting freedom and responsibility, enhancing creativity, encouraging use of resources and strengths, identifying exceptions to weakness-orientation

Continued

PIE /theory	Intervention strategies/actions (illustrations)
Cultural (constructionist)	affirming diversity, cultural competence training, cultural sensitivity training, educating about a culture, facilitating identity development, promoting civil rights, reducing bias and stereotyping
Economic (exchange)	advocating for economic resources, budgeting, calculating costs and benefits, creating community cooperatives or credit unions, promoting fair exchanges or trades
Organization (role)	finding mentors, observing role models, rehearsing role performances, reversing roles, role bargaining, role playing, setting the stage for role performances, writing new scripts
Physical environment (ecology)	changing lifestyles, leaving the environment, mapping geographical regions, modifying the environment, referring to nature, milieu, or wilderness therapy, removing hazards or toxic substances
Political (critical-feminist)	advocating for policy change, challenging privilege, demanding ideal speech situations, fostering collective action, highlighting oppression, liberating social systems, organizing social movements, raising consciousness
Social (systems)	detecting repetitive patterns, interrupting destructive generational transmissions, linking to supportive systems, reshaping system hierarchies, resolve crises causing disequilibrium, strengthening boundaries

taking, facilitating support for difficult interactions, making new roles, reconstructing personal and social meanings, fostering self conversations, teaching communication skills, and telling life stories. Practitioners committed to critical theory as part of their orientation to a case would identify and select from interventions such as advocating for policy change, challenging privilege, demanding ideal speech situations, fostering collective action, highlighting oppression, organizing social movements, and raising critical consciousness. Exchange theory-oriented practitioners might use helping actions associated with advocating for economic resources, budgeting, calculating costs and benefits, creating community cooperatives or credit unions, and promoting fair exchanges or trades. A similar table that identifies intervention programs associated with each theoretical perspective could be developed.

A useful theoretical framework also can also guide macro practice and thinking about policy advocacy and intervention by providing predictions about the likely outcomes of different policy interventions. Sabatier (1999), for example, recommends the use of theory within the economic tradition, "institutional rational choice theory," for policy work. This framework is associated with exchange theory and directs policy advocates to focus on the leaders with decision-making authority in critical institutions, to assume that these leaders are acting to advance their interests (income, power, or status), and to intervene in ways that recognize that these leaders often make rational choices among policy alternatives to maximize their material interests. In contrast, pragmatists prefer policy interventions that invite all community stakeholders to weigh evidence related to the solution of public problems in publicly transparent and democratic ways and in ways that reconcile conflicting social values (Shapiro and Schroeder, 2008).

Translating theories for intervention

While theories are valuable resources for practitioners, they must be translated for specific uses. Such translation requires an understanding of the theory and its rationale for helping activities, an appreciation of theoretical features that may limit theory application, and insight into ways to tailor a theory-informed intervention for a particular application in specific settings and with typical and new populations. There are several relevant translation devices.

Mapping

Intervention mapping is a planning framework for the development of the best possible theory-based and evidence-based strategies for counseling, education, and other human service work. The term and the procedure were developed by health educators dedicated to the creation of effective intervention techniques, packages, and programs (Bartholomew, Parcel, and Kok, 1998; Bartholomew, Parcel, Kok, Gottlieb, and Fernandez, 2011). Intervention mapping is similar to the "mapping theoretical structure" device introduced in the preface. Using the theory as a foundation for intervention, the cartographer identifies the key determinants (personal, interactional, environmental causes) of the target problem, the theoretical conceptualization of the determinants that need to be changed, the theory-guided characterization of the actions that will accomplish desired changes, the change plan, and the evaluation plan. Like a logic model, the mapmaker depicts the path from problem or need recognition through intervention development to testing effectiveness of the attempted solution. Glanz and

Bishop (2010) reviewed some of the theoretical sources preferred by intervention experts mapping theories preferred in the health promotion field. These included the health belief theoretical model, the transtheoretical model of stages of change, the theory of reasoned action, social cognitive theory, and the social ecological model. Target problems have included diet, mammography promotion, sexually risky behavior, alcohol use, smoking, and HIV prevention, Their research review shows that interventions mapped from such relevant theories were generally more effective than interventions lacking a theoretical base in ameliorating health problems.

Middle-range theorizing

As you recall, middle-range theories fall between grand theories and simple empirical generalizations. They are small-scale theories of particular human behavior issues, aspects of the environment, or developmental challenges. Middle-range theorizing is a translation device that can contribute much to the identification of effective interventions (Baranowski, Lin, Wetter, Resnicow, and Hearn, 1997). Baranowksi and his team, for example, recommend that researchers and practitioners cooperate in projects to develop theoretically sound and empirically supported understandings of the mechanisms and processes that produce change. Although they don't use the term, they are encouraging practitioners to use middle-range theories specifying interventions (independent variables), mechanisms of change (mediating variables), and change targets (dependent variables) for particular personal and public problems. They are partial to middle-range theories translated from the language of the theory of reasoned action, a theory asserting the importance of changing behavioral intentions and subjective norms (perceived opinions and preferences of one's significant others) as a prelude to changing a target cognition, emotion, or action. They show how this theory could guide the selection of interventions to improve clients' choices. For example, they specify a middle-range theory guiding intervention with adolescent smokers. The target was the smoking patterns of high school students. The intervention was a school-level media campaign designed using their theoretical principles. The theory indicated that the program would influence in desired ways a set of relevant mechanisms or mediating variables: perceived expectations of adults, perceived expectations of peers, attitudes regarding smoking, knowledge of the prevalence of smoking among school members, knowledge of the immediate health consequences of smoking, and perceptions of the overall social acceptability of smoking in the school environment. Activation of these mechanisms, in turn, would reduce smoking.

Calderon and Varnes (2001) recommend middle-range theorizing within the social learning theoretical tradition and specify some of the common mediating variables related to acquiring new behavior patterns. These include perceptions of past experience with behavior (positive and negative experiences); self efficacy, belief in ability to perform a behavior to achieve desired outcome; social support, support received from others for particular behaviors; perceived norms, beliefs about what others think the actor should do; and motivation to comply with these expectations. Theory-informed interventions such as education, modeling, peer support, and efficacy strategies should be tailored to influence these mediating variables. The result will be greater success rates in changing the focal behavior patterns.

Many interventions, these theorizing practitioners argue, are not achieving the desired results because current theories inadequately predict bio-psycho-social change (often because the theory was not developed in a change-oriented practice context), and because current interventions are not substantially effecting change in the moderating variables (environmental factors, biological factors, cognitive processes, and so on) that must be influenced to foster progress toward the mutually agreed upon outcome variables. These practitioners conclude that this pattern suggests "the vital importance of theory in the behavior change process and the necessity to invest substantially more effort into the further development and refinement of theories" (Baranowski et al., 1997, p. S92).

Model profiling

Model profiling is the characterizing and imitating of exemplary theorists with reference to their contributions to helping work especially to assessment and intervention processes. Table 12.2 uses the PIE metatheory guiding our theory translation efforts and identifies a useful theorist associated with each aspect of the metatheory. The table focuses on recommended interventions. Based on my study of each theorist, his or her writings, and his or her life including service experiences, I have attempted to answer repeatedly the WWTD question—what would the theorist do? For example, what would Erving Goffman, a premier role theorist, recommend to the social worker providing a range of services to persons recently discharged from state mental hospitals or other mental health institutions? His general advice might be "Orient the person to the rights and obligations associated with the competent and responsible performance of the social roles necessary for success in the community—worker, tenant, friend, citizen, and so on." He might further suggest the use of role-play techniques to rehearse optimal performances in safe settings before the person encounters difficult role situations in natural settings.

Table 12.2 Translating theorists' profiles to guide the selection of intervention strategies

PIE/theoretical perspective	Theorists	Recommendation (WWTD— what would theorist do?)
The person (dimensions)		
Acting (behavioral)	Albert Bandura	Provide incentives to observe and imitate pro-social models
Faithing (anthropological)	Clifford Geertz	Encourage engagement in meaning-restoring sacred rituals and practices
Feeling (psychodynamic)	John Bowlby	Increase caregiver's ability to provide secure and sensitive attachments
Sensing (evolutionary biology)	Charles Darwin	Promote adaptive strategies suitable to environment and beneficial to progeny
Thinking (cognitive)	Aaron Beck	Challenge automatic thoughts and thinking distortions contributing to life difficulties
Interacting/transacting		
Interacting (interactionist)	Jane Addams	Foster respectful perspective taking and communication among interacting community members
In environmental contexts		
Community (strengths)	Dennis Saleeby	Shift focus to positive and mobilize strengths, positive experiences, positive emotions
Cultural (constructionist)	Peter Berger	Deconstruct racist beliefs and classification systems that sustain discriminatory actions and inequality
Economic (exchange)	Peter Blau	Consult to change exchange patterns in ways that increase profits and reduce costs
Organization (role)	Erving Goffman	Orient to rights and obligations associated with the competent performance of a social role
Physical (ecological)	Carel Germain	Enhance coping measures to obtain a favorable fit between person and environmental setting

PIE/theoretical perspective	Theorists	Recommendation (WWTD—what would theorist do?)
Political (critical-feminist)	Carol Gilligan	Listen so females can reclaim their voice and voice their identities, needs and standpoints confidently
Social (systems)	Talcott Parsons	Identify boundary issues and disrupt dysfunctional system patterns causing member/family problems

To use this translation device for intervention planning, familiarize yourself with the life work and life histories of your favorite exemplary theorists and theorizing practitioners. Develop a profile (or read those created by theorist specialists), specifically, of their thinking about intervention and their preferred intervention strategies. Follow up and learn more about each strategy. Continuing with role theory, for instance, I would recommend the use of profiles of Jacob Moreno, a key contributor to role theory and to role theory helping approaches such as pyschodrama and sociodrama, and Helen Harris Perlman, a social worker who translated role theory for use by practitioners. Each profile will offer much practical guidance in identifying and implementing interventions.

Multi-theoretical social work and intervention strategies

I am arguing for a multi-theoretical approach to intervention identification, selection, and implementation. Baranowski's team (Baranowski et al., 1997, p. S92), called this approach "*polytheoretical practice*," and recommended the incorporation of variables from a range of theories to enhance the practitioner's thinking about change actions, mediators, and targets and the consequent development of multiple interventions for each case. When using multiple theory-based interventions, the worker and client must consider which intervention strategies to select and how to best organize the implementation of the set of interventions (Ingram, 2006). For examples of the theory-guided selection of intervention strategies from the range of possible interventions, see chapters in books providing collections of theory-informed practice reports (Corcoran and Keeper, 1992; Thyer, 2001; Van den Bergh, 1992).

Regarding the organization and sequencing of a set of theory-informed interventions, there are many possible options. The worker might use *intervention adding*. In this approach, the worker identifies the focus of intervention (relationship difficulties between husband and wife, for example) and adds successively the chosen intervention. Rank and LeCroy (1983) provide an example of successful practice based on intervention adding. They offer a framework for assessing intimacy problems reported by a husband and wife by considering the quality of communication (the interactionist perspective), the equity of the social exchanges (the economic perspective), and the degree of relationship conflict or oppression (the critical theory perspective). Their multidimensional assessment suggests a set of interventions derived from these theories one added to another: empathy building activities, followed by bargaining for new exchange patterns, followed by conflict mediation work.

The worker might use the following *intervention sequencing* approach. Theory users can review the assessment formulation with the client and then decide together on the best sequence for introducing or using different theory-based interventions. For example, the issue of stigma and stigma management lends itself to intervention sequencing. Many social work clients are stigmatized because of their HIV infection, mental disorder, state of homelessness, or criminal record. Gramling (1990) argues that client-worker partners might tackle this problem in an orderly fashion. The team might first use the exchange perspective to appraise the personal gains and costs of the stigmatized condition and to plan how to bargain with others for tolerance. Then, the team might use the interactionist perspective and help the client choose and implement a preferred strategy for interacting with others: deny the condition, conceal the condition, or excuse the stigma. Finally, the team might try a critical perspective that challenges the community norms oppressive to stigmatized groups and begin a fight for a social order insuring respectful public encounters between citizens and those grappling with health or mental health difficulties.

Intervention sequencing can be tied to practice evaluation. Weerasekera (1996) recommends that a worker select a set of particular practice theory-informed interventions and implement them in sequence in relationship to "process markers" indicating progress toward outcomes. These are predetermined behavioral, cognitive, emotional, or system indicators of the readiness to shift from one theoretical framework to the next framework. For example, the worker might first use a behavioral intervention with a client struggling with anxiety disorders until "worrying behaviors" begin to decrease. Soon after the client begins to discuss underlying developmental issues. The social worker follows the behavioral work with a psychodynamic ego psychology intervention and begins the use of life review processes to foster insight into the sources of the disorder.

Differential *intervention assembling* is another approach to sequencing. Here, the practitioner assembles a range of interventions informed by different theories and integrates them according to some clear rationale. For example, the social worker might involve varied-size social systems in a helping project and consider a cognitive–behavioral orientation for work with the student struggling in school, a family systems approach to the student's family, and a strengths-oriented approach in collaborating with school officials and representatives. Or the client system might agree with the worker to pursue multiple objectives (a faith-based objective, a communication-oriented objective, and a financial objective tailored to market conditions), and the worker and client might assemble theories differentially suited for achieving each objective into a multi-component action plan.

In conclusion, theorizing practitioners should engage with academic knowledge and use theoretical insights into "challenges of living" to improve intervention planning and implementation (Cornelissen, 2000). With some translation work, general scientific theories can be translated into information providing practical and effective intervention solutions to problems identified in many different concrete cases.

Learning activities and reflections

1. An intervention is a strategic action or set of actions by a social worker and client expected to bring about a desired personal or collective change. Social workers helping micro and mezzo level systems use direct interventions to address the targeted problem or challenge and to meet needs. A social group worker, for example, might use "role rehearsal" to assist a developmentally challenged adult prepare for a new part time job. Social workers helping large social systems like neighborhoods, organizations, or policy arenas use indirect interventions to change conditions or processes in ways that will eventually benefit people. A community-oriented social worker might engage in legislative advocacy to change state laws regarding the punishment of sex offenders to better protect vulnerable children.

    Briefly summarize your understanding of the concept, intervention. Identify and describe some interventions that you have learned as a novice social worker. If possible, trace the source of the intervention strategy to a theoretical framework or practice theory.

2. Social work interventions are selected following the information gathering and assessment phases. Optimal interventions are appropriate, culturally sensitive, and evidence-based responses to client preferences, and to the specific person-in-environment (PIE) configuration profiled by the worker and the client or client system. From each theoretical framework, a set of intervention

strategies can be generated. These theory-based intervention strategies translate theory into action statements and guidelines that can be used by practitioners in line with the theoretical metaphors, assumptions, theory of change, and if-then propositions of the particular theory. Table 12.1 summarizes my thinking about the key intervention strategies associated with fourteen different theoretical frameworks.

Select two or three interventions from several different theoretical frameworks. Justify your choice in terms of the intervention strategies' suitability for work with a particular client. Identify the details of how you might implement each theory-informed intervention with this client.

3. Social workers practice in many different settings, with many different size social systems, and with many different kinds of personal and public problems. We need a large pool of potential intervention strategies. The multi-theoretical approach to social work equips practitioners with many different possible intervention tools. We can select the set of interventions that best match the specific features of a particular case, and that address the multiple aspects of any helping situation: person dimensions, interaction processes, and environmental contexts.

Reflect on a familiar individual, group, family, or community that you might help and a challenge faced by this system. Formulate a set of interventions, a multi-theoretical intervention plan, that best addresses the complexity of the challenge. Provide a justification for your selection and assembly of these interventions. Offer details in the plan for how you might integrate and sequence the different interventions into a coherent plan of action for the intervention phase of the helping process.

4. Finally, conclude with reflections on these learning activities. What have you learned that will prepare you to utilize theoretical frameworks to guide the processes of assessment, intervention, and evaluation?

References

Argyris, C. (1996). Actionable knowledge: Design causality in the service of consequentialist theory. *The Journal of Applied Behavioral Science, 32* (4), 390–406.

Argyris, C. (2003). Actionable knowledge. In H. Tsoukas and C. Knudsen (Eds), *The Oxford handbook of organization theory* (pp. 423–452). Oxford: Oxford University Press.

Baranowski, T., Lin, L., Wetter, D. W., Resnicow, K. and Hearn, M. D. (1997). Theory as mediating variables: Why aren't community interventions working as desired? *Annals of Epidemiology, 7* (S7), S89–S95.

Bartholomew, L. K., Parcel, G. S. and Kok, G. (1998). Intervention mapping: A process for developing theory and evidence-based health education programs. *Health Education & Behavior, 25*, 545–563.

Bartholomew, L. K., Parcel, G. S., Kok, G., Gottlieb, N. H. and Fernandez, M. E. (2011). *Planning health promotion programs: An intervention mapping approach* (3rd ed.). San Francisco: Jossey-Bass.

Bloom, M., Fischer, J. and Orme, J. G. (2006). *Evaluating practice: Guidelines for the accountable professional* (5th ed.). Englewood Cliffs, NJ: Prentice-Hall.

Bryant, C. G. A. (1991). The dialogical model of applied sociology. In C. G. A. Bryant and D. Jary (Eds), *Gidden's theory of structuration: A critical appreciation* (pp. 176–200). London: Routledge.

Calderon, K. S. and Varnes, J. W. (2001) Taking a step back: Developing interventions within a mediating-variable framework. *American Journal of Health Studies, 17* (3), 129–139.

Council on Social Work Education (2008). 2008 Educational policy and accreditation standards. Retrieved June 16, 2010, from www.cswe.org/Accreditation/Reaffirmation.aspx.

Corcoran, K. and Keeper, C. (1992). Psychodynamic treatment for persons with borderline personalities. In K. Corcoran (Ed.), *Structuring change: Effective practice for common client problems* (pp. 255–271). Chicago: Lyceum.

Cornelissen, J. p. (2000). Toward an understanding of the use of academic theories in public relations practice. *Public Relations Review, 26* (3), 315–326.

Gehart, D. R. and Tuttle, A. R. (2003). *Theory-based treatment planning for marriage and family therapists: Integrating theory and practice*. Pacific Grove, CA: Brooks/Cole-Thomson.

Giddens, A. (1979). *Central problems in social theory: Action, structure and contradiction in social analysis*. London: Macmillan.

Glanz, K. and Bishop, D. B. (2010). The role of behavioral science theory in the development and implementation of public health interventions. *Annual Review of Public Health, 31*, 399–418.

Gramling, R. (1990). A multiple perspective approach to using micro theory. *Sociological Inquiry, 60* (1), 87–96.

Hochbaum, G. M., Sorenson, J. R. and Lorig, K. (1992). Theory in health education practice. *Health Education Quarterly, 19* (3), 295–313.

Ingram, B. L. (2006). *Clinical case formulations: Matching the integrative treatment plan to the client*. Hoboken, NJ: John Wiley and Sons.

Rank, M. R. and LeCroy, C. W. (1983). Toward a multiple perspective in family theory and practice: The case of social exchange theory, symbolic interactionism, and conflict theory. *Family Relations, 32,* 441–448.

Sabatier, P. (1999). The need for better theories. In P. Sabatier (Ed.), *Theories of the policy process* (pp. 3–17). Boulder, CO: Westview Press.

Shapiro, S. A. and Schroeder, C. H. (2008). Beyond cost-benefit analysis: A pragmatic reorientation. *Harvard Environmental Law Review, 32* (2), 433–502.

Thyer, B. A. (2001). Behavior analysis and therapy for persons with phobias. In H. E. Briggs and K. Corcoran (Eds), *Social work practice: Treating common client problems* (2nd ed., pp. 148–168). Chicago, IL: Lyceum.

Van den Bergh, N. (1992). Feminist treatment for people with depression. In K. Corcoran (Ed.), *Structuring change: Effective practice for common client problems* (pp. 95–110). Chicago: Lyceum.

Walsh, J. (2010). *Theories for direct social work practice* (2nd ed.). Belmont, CA: Wadsworth Cengage Learning.

Walt, S. M. (2005). The relationship between theory and policy in international relations. *Annual Review of Political Science, 8,* 23–48.

Weerasekera, P. (1996). *Multiperspective case formulation: A step towards treatment integration.* Malabar, FL: Krieger.

13 Translate theories to guide the evaluation process

(EPAS 2.1.3 Apply critical thinking; EPAS 2.1.6
Engage in research-informed practice; EPAS 2.1.7
Apply knowledge; EPAS 2.1.10 Engage, assess,
intervene, and evaluate)

We must find a theory that will work; and that means something extremely difficult; for our theory must mediate between previous truths and certain new experiences.

(James, 1907/1955, p. 142)

How should a practitioner conceptualize and organize the appraisal of his or her effectiveness with a particular client system? Social work competency includes proficiency in the evaluation of the effectiveness of practice. Effective social workers can monitor the effects of interventions and evaluate their overall impact on clients and client systems. Specifically, the Council on Social Work Education (2008) identifies three tasks as essential to the evaluation phase of the planned change process: critical analysis of interventions, monitoring of interventions, and evaluation of interventions. In this lesson, I will show how theoretical knowledge can usefully guide practitioners in the competent achievement of these and other evaluation tasks. Let's first review some basic ideas about social work evaluation.

Social work practice evaluation: an overview

Practice evaluation is the systematic, ongoing, and evidence-based determination of whether social workers are achieving the goals and objectives of service that have been established with our clients (Bloom, Fischer, and Orme, 2006). Practice evaluators ask various evaluation questions. Has the intervention or the program produced the desired outcome? Have the positive changes persisted over time or faded soon after the conclusion of services? Was the expenditure of time, effort, and energy efficient in relation to the use of the intervention to achieve desired outcomes and larger impacts?

Social workers evaluate the effectiveness of their direct work with an individual, group, family, or other social system. They often use a single system design (SSD) for this purpose. Social workers also participate in the evaluation of programs. In addition to single system approaches, various scientific approaches including quasi-experimental and true experimental designs are available for such evaluation work. In each case, however, a somewhat predictable process of inquiry is followed. Steps include the identification of target problems, the establishment of goals and objectives with benchmarks for success, the creation or selection of measurement tools for appraising changes in target problems, the creation or selection of interventions (helping techniques, packages, or programs), the construction of a research design such as an ABA single system design (involving a no-intervention baseline phase, an intervention phase, and no-intervention withdrawal phase) specifying the details and sequencing of the evaluation process (sampling, measurement points, data gathering procedures, ethical safeguards, etc.), the collection of data during a monitoring process—generally at repeated points in time for SSDs, the analysis of data regarding progress toward benchmarks, and the decision about the effectiveness of the intervention, intervention package, or program.

Theory-based practice evaluation

Theoretical knowledge is relevant in many different ways to practice evaluation. First, let's consider how evaluation experts note that there are several ways of thinking about theoretical knowledge and practice evaluation. The *theory of evaluation practice* refers to the rules, principles and guiding conceptual frameworks that are adopted for a particular evaluation project (Donaldson and Lipsey, 2006). Such a theory tells the evaluation's stakeholders about the characteristics of a proper evaluation and the steps for conducting such an evaluation.

An *evidence-based social science theory* is a theory about the person and environment such as one derived from an HBSE framework, the social exchange approach or the structural functional perspective, or one derived from a human development framework like attachment theory or the life course perspective. This kind of theory is relevant to practice evaluation when it increases understanding about aspects of PIE related to the public problems and the client problems addressed by social work agencies and practitioners. If chosen for use, such a theory should be supported by empirical evidence, and used to help the evaluator identify the causes of focal problems, the environmental context relevant to focal problems, and the actions that change undesirable conditions or processes (Donaldson and Lipsey, 2006).

Finally practice evaluators identify program theory as important (White, 2009). A *middle-range theory of a program,* or a case evaluation plan, summarizes the theoretical assumptions associated with a logical chain from program intentions and inputs, through the program's processes of intervention implementation and change facilitation to the program's outcomes and impact for clients and related stakeholders. The program theory is like the logic model discussed in Lesson 11. It helps users articulate the rationale and justification for the program's structure, activities, and expectations of making a positive difference. Direct practitioners committed to evaluation of their practice may not use the term, program theory, but they generally formalize the theoretical logic model guiding their helping work. The purposeful employment of these three forms of theory—theory of evaluation, social science theory, and program theory is called theory-based or *theory-driven evaluation science* (Donaldson and Lipsey, 2006).

Variations in theory-based evaluation

There are identifiable differences between some of the major theoretical frameworks in preferences regarding evaluation design and implementation. Since the literature on this subject is scarce, practitioners might need to take three steps.

First, familiarize yourself with Neuman's typology. Neuman (2006) identifies three distinct scientific paradigms and their philosophical stances regarding inquiry and evaluation. Each paradigm includes a different approach to evaluation. The *positivist approach* prefers precise observations, a detached and objective practitioner, carefully controlled experiments in laboratory settings, and the search for causal patterns. The *interpretive approach* or constructionist approach prefers immersion in the symbolic world of the study participants, an engaged and empathic practitioner, naturalistic methods that capture real life conduct, and the search for meanings. The *critical approach* prefers the critical investigation of myths that support inequality, an activist practitioner determined to fight for justice, methods of structural analysis and critique, and the generation of empowering, liberating knowledge.

Second, review some of the foundational statements or overviews of each of the major theoretical frameworks regarding scientific inquiry and attempt to place them in one of the three paradigms. For example, my reading of the founders of symbolic interactionism would lead me to categorize it as an interpretive approach. Likewise, I would categorize behaviorism as a positivist approach.

Third, tailor the elements of your evaluation design in line with the philosophical assumptions of the approach to scientific inquiry that best fits the helping circumstances. Use the approach (positivist, interpretive, or critical) to customize your overall evaluation strategy, the role of the evaluator, the specific method of evaluation, the characterization of the evaluation product, and so on.

Theory-based evaluation, translation, and single system design steps

The Council on Social Work Education (2008) also expects social workers to demonstrate a critical thinking competency. This includes the ability to analyze models of evaluation. Unfortunately, in contrast to our discussion of theory-based approaches to other phases of the helping process—engagement, information gathering, intervention selection, and so on—I can't create a neat table specifying the distinctive approach of each of fourteen different theoretical frameworks to evaluation. The literature on applied theories doesn't support such a categorization yet.

However, our previous lessons and learning activities provide a foundation for practice evaluation. Past lessons have identified key points in helping work when evaluation is relevant and many components necessary for theory-based practice evaluation. I will summarize key points of these discussions, and make a few other points.

Early in the practice evaluation process, the worker makes a decision about the appropriate sample. For the single system evaluation approach, the focus will be on one unit: an individual client, group, family, or community, for examples. Experimental designs use more complex sampling processes. For interpretive evaluation, *theory-focused sampling* can help the practitioner match the characteristics of the sample members with the guiding theory (Glaser, 1980). For example, Glaser's differential control theory merges symbolic interactionist and behavioral assumptions and concepts. Glaser theorizes that young persons commit to pro-social definitions and behaviors following interaction with law-abiding peers and family members, and incorporate behavioral controls associated with the bonds forged in these relationships. A practitioner or group of practitioners choosing this theory would do well to include in the evaluation sample those who are young with limited criminal records, minimal progress in criminal careers, and no or few pro crime definitions. A program guided by differential control theory is expected to have the greatest positive impact on these types of clients.

We have discussed *theory-based information gathering* during the assessment process. Evaluation experts knowledgeable about diverse theories can recommend the use of appropriate, culturally sensitive, valid, and reliable measurement instruments to gather information and monitor changes in the target problems. Each theory suggests certain measurement strategies: the practitioner committed to the biological approach might use scales for weight or medical tests; behavioral theorists supply numerous observational checklists; cognitive theorists would be associated with self-report surveys, journals, and other introspective tools; interactionist theorists recommend participation observation in natural settings and life histories; users of economic approaches consider budgeting and cost-benefit analysis tools, and ecological theorists supports measures using records and traces of action obtained in the ecology.

We have discussed *theory-based problem formulation*. Evidence-oriented evaluation challenges the worker and client to examine the theoretical and research literature for alternative explanatory hypotheses about the problem and to select the empirically supported formulation that most logically fits the person-in-environment-with-problem facts. A theory can guide the worker and client in identifying and elaborating on the most relevant PIE factors explaining the problematic or challenging situation (van Ryn and Heaney, 1992).

We have discussed *theory-based goal and objective setting*. Scientific evaluation emphasizes formulating precise and realistic objectives with clear timetables for achievement and benchmarks for success. A theory can help specify these targets for change. For example, the social learning theory approach to new behavior acquisition suggests that the evaluation plan should appraise advances in skill level, increases in perceived self-efficacy at performing behaviors, the addition of beliefs about usefulness of behavior in achieved expected outcomes, and the accumulation of internal and external rewards for the performance of the behavior (van Ryn and Heaney, 1992). Table 13.1 translates fourteen theories using the "major term" device for theory translation. Major term interpreting is a translation process of identifying the major terms or key words of a theoretical language and rendering them into other words from the theory into Standard English terms or into the idiomatic language preferred by the client. A key term or word is identified for each theory's targeted outcome. This could be a starting point for developing theory-specific goals and objectives with benchmarks and timetables.

Table 13.1 Translating theories to specify targets and change criteria for evaluation

PIE/Theory	Evaluation planning by target specification and change criteria (illustrations)		
	Outcome target	Evaluation criteria	
		Problem solving	Problem sustaining
Multi-dimensional person			
Acting (behavioral)	behaviors	appropriate desirable	inappropriate unwanted
Faithing (anthropological)	convictions	ethical meaningful	unethical meaningless
Feeling (psychodynamic)	insight	self-realizing harmony creating	conflict-ridden self-deceiving
Sensing (evolutionary biology)	life processes	adaptive healthy	maladaptive unhealthy
Thinking (cognitive)	cognitions	rational accurate mindful	irrational distorted mindless
Interacting/transacting			
Transact (interactionism)	understanding	accurate coherent deep	inaccurate incoherent shallow
In environmental context			
Communal (strengths)	experiences	asset-based flow	risk-based divide attention/ interest
Cultural (constructionist)	constructions	individualized respectful	stereotypical disrespectful
Ecological (ecology)	person-setting fit	good fit favorable	bad fit unfavorable
Economic (exchange)	exchanges	efficient equitable prosperous	inefficient inequitable impoverished
Organizational (role)	performances	valued consensual sincere	disvalued divergent insincere
Physical environment (ecology)	person-setting fit	good fit favorable	bad fit unfavorable
Political (critical-feminist)	privilege sharing	just democratic	unjust non-democratic
Social (systems)	system dynamics	functional steady state	dysfunctional disequilibrium

An HBSE or policy theory can also help the worker and client set realistic benchmarks for success (Walt, 2005). Table 13.1 offers a set of descriptors associated with each theory's major terms. These include descriptors of positive outcomes, those that resolve problems or challenges and descriptors of negative outcomes, those that sustain or increase a problem in relation to duration, severity, or other unwanted attributes. Using the biological approach, for instance, we might work with a high school student with an eating disorder and set objectives related to life processes of eating such as weight, and agree with a client to reduce pounds to a healthier weight (180 pounds for a six foot man). We might also agree that a measured weight after an eight-week intervention of 200 pounds or greater would be unhealthy and indicate the need for more aggressive interventions.

We have discussed *theory-based change logic*. Scientific practitioners work hard to summarize in narrative report and display in visual form the elements and the sequencing of elements that serve as a logical base for the direct service or program's claim to achieve desired changes. Middle-range theorizing has already been discussed as a translation tool for specifying the change theory and logic for a particular theoretical tradition. A theory-based change logic can help social work practitioners link logically their explanatory hypotheses with their intervention hypotheses (identified change activities), and then relate both set of hypotheses to intermediate and ultimate outcomes.

We have also discussed *theory-based interventions* and principles for intervention selection. High quality practice evaluation requires specification of the intervention hypotheses following careful consideration of the research evidence documenting the effectiveness of alternative interventions in similar circumstances with similar clients, and, then, the selection of empirically sound interventions. Linder and Peters (1984) suggest some criteria for judging and selecting alternatives. These include reproducibility (has there been a record of success using the intervention in similar helping situations?), tractability (can the intervention be used easily by the worker), accessibility (can the intervention be used in a way that effects are readily monitored?), flexibility (can the intervention be adjusted as helping circumstances change?), credibility (is the intervention one that the worker and client believe will be effective?), and efficiency (are the costs of using the intervention reasonable?). We might also use the translation device, marking excellence, to judge the relative value of an intervention. *Marking excellence* involves the critical reflection on theories and theory-based interventions by referring to standards including the standards of science such as empirical support; practical standards like relevance and ease of use; and professional standards such as the affirmation of difference, the promotion of justice, and an emphasis on strengths.

We haven't yet discussed *theory-informed monitoring* but this is another important step in the practice evaluation process. The effective and accountable practitioner monitors continuously whether an intervention is working.

Theory-based assessment questions and measurement instruments are useful here. Also, a theory can help the worker make judgments about the fit of the intervention with the case (van Ryn and Heaney, 1992). At signs of trouble, the worker can revisit the theory and check whether the conditions theorized as necessary for success have changed or whether there has been a break in the theorized causal chain relating problem factors, intervention actions, and expected outcomes. Returning to differential control theory, for instance, the worker and rehabilitation organization planned that program activities would produce intimate relationship bonds between offenders and staff thus augmenting anti-criminal definitions and pro-social behavioral inclinations (Glaser, 1980). However, the alert and curious practitioner discovered that many program members had been secretly communicating with criminally acculturated and manipulative ex-prisoners undermining the program's positive impact.

Theory-informed decision-making processes encourage the practitioner to interpret the results of an intervention using a theoretical lens for this inquiry (Glaser, 1980). Let's focus on the interpretation of a failed intervention. Was there a problem in matching the theory to the case in relation to why, where, when, and for whom the intervention should work? Did the intervention meet the assumptions and include the ingredients called for by the guiding theory? Were the contextual conditions and service delivery processes necessary for effective implementation as specified by the theory met? Were there unintended consequences following intervention use that the theory failed to predict? After answering such questions, the social worker and client might consider varied conclusions: the theory-based intervention isn't effective and needs improvement; the theory-based intervention was not applied correctly or consistently; or the theory-based intervention doesn't work for this kind of population, problem, or place.

Finally, practice evaluation involves the distribution of results. The social work practitioner can report lessons from a theory-informed evaluation project and contribute to the profession's accumulation of sound knowledge (Rothman, 2004). For example, the worker can feed back evaluation lessons about the usefulness of particular human behavior and practice theories and their principles to theorists and researchers. This way the theory tested in practice (or its tested elements) can be revised, refined, or rejected. Additionally, sharing evaluation lessons can add information about the specific and best uses of theory by population, problem, place, practitioner type, or other specific features of the helping work.

Theory-based evaluation: illustrations

The Fishers and their colleagues (Fisher, 1997; Fisher, Fisher, Bryan, and Misovich, 2002) provide an exemplary report on the use of theory as a framework for evaluation of STD and HIV prevention programs geared toward inner city minority adolescents. Their strategy would be most compatible with the positivist approach.

First, Fisher identifies the social science theories that can help practitioners identify the likely causes of risky behavior. Their integrative approach has roots in the behavioral and cognitive theoretical traditions: traditions often subsumed under the positivist approach. The information–motivation–behavioral skills theory (IMB model) suggests that persons who engage in unsafe sexual practices are characterized by three factors: inadequate information about how to easily practice preventive behavior, insufficient motivation and social support to practice prevention, and inadequate behavioral skills for effective prevention actions. Social network theory explains how individuals participate in social networks and how these networks and the network's opinion leaders establish norms and enforce normative behavior related to sexual intercourse. The theory of reasoned action points to the relevance of three factors for condom use. These are positive attitudes about abstaining from unsafe sex, social support for preventive behaviors from reference groups, and the personal conviction that the youth can effectively carry out preventive actions.

Second, Fisher (1997) shows how the social science theories direct the construction of assessment and intervention plans. Let's focus on assessments and interventions based on the IMB model. Cognitive–behavioral needs assessment determines the assets and deficits of a program's population in regard to safe-sex information, motivation, skills, and behavior. Empirically targeted interventions include classroom interventions such as STD/HIV prevention information, motivation building, and skills development; peer interventions using popular students who interact with friends and associates outside the classroom to reduce IMB deficits and to change social norms regarding risky behavior; and a combined classroom and peer-based intervention package (classroom intervention for five successive classes with simultaneous peer interventions in the classroom).

Third, Fisher (1997) provides a narrative and display summarizing the program theory recommended for use in high schools and other settings serving at-risk youth. This shows the flow from the assessment of program members in terms of pre-intervention levels of factors theorized to influence preventive behavior, the design and implementation of targeted interventions to change the factors theorized to influence preventive behaviors, and the evaluation of the impact of program interventions on these theorized factors.

Finally, the Fisher team (Fisher et al., 2002) reported on their theory-driven approach to evaluation of the IMB model. They used a quasi-experimental controlled trial design in four urban high schools in Connecticut with 1,532 mostly ninth grade participants. The classroom-based intervention resulted in sustained changes in HIV prevention orientations including greater knowledge of sexually transmitted diseases, greater knowledge of prevention behavior such as condom storage and proper use of condoms, favorable attitudes toward prevention, and abstinence from intercourse and condom use. Regarding negative findings, the team theorized about the relatively low impact of peer interventions and hypothesized that in these kinds of schools influential peers often leave the school for various reasons and undermine their credibility as role models when they are perceived as engaging in risky behaviors. Future interventions should take this lesson into account.

Multi-theoretical evaluation offers the resources of fourteen theories to the practitioner for designing a plan to evaluate effectiveness, efficiency, or satisfaction. The work of Fisher and his team illustrates the usefulness of integrating a set of theories when designing a program, implementing the program, and carrying out an evaluation of program effectiveness.

Learning activities and reflections

1. Evaluation is a very important component of contemporary social work. Evaluation helps us establish our accountability as a professional and evaluation helps us make informed and good decisions at key points in the helping process. Briefly summarize your understanding of practice evaluation, its purposes, its value, and its methods.

2. Reread the commentary above for this lesson. Reflect on an experience helping a client or friend. Assume that you will engage the person in a new and extended helping process. Develop a theory-based evaluation plan for how you might judge your effectiveness. Include ideas about all relevant aspects of a single system design: problem formulation enhanced by social science theories, theory-based objectives, theory-oriented information-gathering strategies, a logical theory of change, theory-based interventions with empirical support, theory-guided monitoring of progress, and so on. Discuss also how you will tailor your evaluation design in line with the paradigm (positivist, interpretive, critical) that best fits with the client needs and your theoretical or multi-theoretical framework. If possible, connect each step of the evaluation plan to your preferred theory.

3. Finally, conclude with reflections on these learning activities. What have you learned that will prepare you to utilize theoretical frameworks to guide the processes of assessment, intervention, and evaluation?

References

Bloom, M., Fischer, J. and Orme, J. G. (2006). *Evaluating practice: Guidelines for the accountable professional* (5th ed.). Englewood Cliffs, NJ: Prentice-Hall.

Council on Social Work Education (2008). 2008 Educational policy and accreditation standards. Retrieved June 16, 2010, from www.cswe.org/Accreditation/Reaffirmation.aspx.

Donaldson, S.I. and Lipsey, M.W. (2006). Roles for theory in contemporary evaluation practice: Developing practical knowledge. In I. Shaw, J. C. Greene and M. M. Mark (Eds), *The handbook of evaluation: Policies, programs, and practices* (pp. 56–75). London: Sage.

Fisher, W. (1997). A theory-based framework for intervention and evaluation in STD/HIV prevention. *The Canadian Journal of Human Sexuality*, 6 (2), 105–111.

Fisher, J. D., Fisher, W. A., Bryan, A. D. and Misovich, S. J. (2002). Information-motivation-behavioral skills model–based HIV risk behavior change intervention for inner-city high school youth. *Health Psychology*, 21 (2), 177–186.

Glaser, D. (1980). The interplay of theory, issues, policy, and data. In M. W. Klein and K. S. Teilman (Eds), *Handbook of criminal justice evaluation* (pp. 123–142). Beverly Hills, CA: Sage.

James, W. (1907/1955). *Pragmatism and four essays from "The Meaning of Truth."* New York: Meridian.

Linder, S. H. and Peters, B. G. (1984). From social theory to policy design. *Journal of Public Policy*, 4 (3), 237–259.

Neuman, W. L. (2006). *Social research methods: Qualitative and quantitative approaches* (6th ed.). Boston: Pearson.

Rothman, A. J. (2004). Is there nothing more practical than a good theory? Why innovations and advances in health behavior change will arise if interventions are used to test and refine theory. *The International Journal of Behavioral Nutrition and Physical Activity*, 1 (11), 1–11.

van Ryn, M. and Heaney, C. A. (1992). What's the use of theory? *Health Education Quarterly*, 19 (3), 315–330.

Walt, S. M. (2005). The relationship between theory and policy in international relations. *Annual Review of Political Science*, 8, 23–48.

White, H. (2009). Theory-based impact evaluation: Principles and practice. Retrieved September 29, 2013, from www.publicpolicyadvocacy.info/biblioteca/MVI_114.pdf.

14 Translate theories to guide the ending process

(EPAS 2.1.7 Apply knowledge; EPAS 2.1.10 Engage, assess, intervene, and evaluate)

Many students and other practitioners who have a firm grasp of practice theory and intervention techniques seem to feel less assured when it is time for them to end their work with clients.

(Walsh, 2007, p. xvii)

The termination phase is the last phase in the planned change process that we will discuss. In the educational policies developed by the Council on Social Work Education (2008), the Council identifies ending work as part of competency EPAS 2.1.10c, intervention. I consider it a distinct and final phase of the helping process although discussion and consideration of ending issues should occur also in the beginning and middle phases. The CSWE does identify the specific tasks of "facilitating transitions" and "facilitating endings" as critical to competent social work.

Social work practice and ending: overview

Let's review some basic ideas about social work endings. The social work ending phase is also called the termination phase. To terminate evokes vivid and unpleasant associations to *Terminator* movies and drone attacks, so we will use the more neutral terms, end and ending. Ideally, the ending process is planned with the client or members of the client system. It is often discussed in the first few helping sessions and included in the working contract. A worker and client may agree then, for example, about the helping objectives and the specific benchmarks for determining readiness for ending. The worker and client may also agree to set the optimal number of helping sessions. The choice about duration of service, however, is constrained by agency or reimbursement policies.

Unfortunately, some clients end their use of services without any discussion with the worker. They must relocate. They have been incarcerated. They are troubled by thoughts and feelings that emerge during helping work. They dislike the worker or the other members of a helping group. They can't afford the fees. They stop participating in services without offering any justification or apology. Explanatory theories of human behavior may contribute to the worker's efforts to understand such abrupt departures. For example, psychodynamic theory points to the client's use of defensive processes like avoidance to manage the painful emergence of repressed memories and impulses. Family system theorists suggest that other family members may notice client actions that begin to change the family equilibrium and pressure the client to cease growing. In the case of unplanned endings, the worker may be able to arrange one final meeting or phone call to do some ending work.

In addition to CSWE leaders, social work experts have identified some specific tasks that are common to the helping work of facilitating transitions and ending (Walsh and Meyersohn, 2001; Walsh, 2007). These include dealing with the bonds formed between the worker and the client and the bonds between clients in helping groups; validating and working through the positive and negative emotions that clients experience at the ending phase; reviewing and reflecting on the significant moments in the helping process; evaluating the degree to which objectives have been achieved and appraising satisfaction with the services; and planning to meet future needs by referral or a strategy to generalize gains to new settings. Many social workers use some type of ritual or program activity to accomplish ending tasks and to mark and celebrate progress to the ending point.

Theory-based ending approaches and translation by metaphor

Each theoretical framework provides a conceptualization of the ending phase, a vision of the optimal state or processes indicating readiness for ending, and insight into particular issues and opportunities that may emerge during the ending phase. Table 14.1 summarizes briefly my understanding of the approach of fourteen theoretical traditions to the ending phase. For each, I started from the tradition's root metaphors. Recall a root metaphor is a foundation to a theory specifying a comparison between an abstract theoretical conceptualization of person, environment, interaction between the person and environment and an everyday character, event, object, or process. After identifying the root metaphor, I used the translation device of metaphorical imagination to identify likely theoretical conceptualizations of the ending phase. Take the faith-based tradition. The person is like a seeker on a quest for religious or spiritual meaning, often, following a threat to meaningfulness (events that he or she can't make sense of, like death, disaster, or dreams; suffering and the challenge of enduring lengthy distress; or evil occurrences overwhelming our moral judgment). Ending is the conclusion of the quest and the achievement of a new harmony of meanings. I also suggest positive and negative issues identified by each theory that might inform the worker's approach to the ending process. For example, despite extensive pastoral counseling, following the murder of a cherished loved one the client might still experience doubts about God's mercy, the afterlife, and the possibility of forgiveness.

Table 14.1 Translating theories to guide the ending process

PIE/theory	Metaphorical conceptualization of ending/illustrative issues
Multi-dimensional person	
Acting (behavioral)	Ending is like the assumption of sole responsibility for a behavior management program;
	Generalization and maintenance (supports) of behavioral changes/problems with completion of behavioral homework
Faithing (anthropological)	Ending is like the fulfillment of a quest;
	Achievement of a degree of spiritual peace or harmony/existential doubts
Feeling (psychodynamic)	Ending is like the death of a relationship;
	Progress in resolving unconscious conflicts and ending symptoms/eEmotional reactions to severing of attachment to helper
Sensing (evolutionary biology)	Ending is like discharge from a hospital or health center;
	Revitalization of body and commitment to healthful practices/anticipated threats to health, sobriety, mortality
Thinking (cognitive)	Ending is like the final switch from an old computer operating system to a new system;
	Restructuring of cognitive patterns and processes/Irrational thoughts regarding ending (self-efficacy, possible selves, future dangers)
Interacting/transacting	
Transact (interactionism)	Ending is like a meaning-rich event in the community;
	Co-construction of new self, symbols, patterns of symbolic interaction/managing symbolic meaning of ending

PIE/theory	Metaphorical conceptualization of ending/illustrative issues
In environmental contexts	
Communal (strengths)	Ending is like the completion of a strengths training program;
	Shift to language of possibilities and powers/Capacity to commit to decisions and live with consequences
Cultural (constructionist)	Ending is the conclusion of a deconstruction and rebuilding project;
	Creating culturally appropriate ending rituals/ Remnants of "isms" (racism, sexism, heterosexism, classism, and so on)
Ecological (ecology)	Ending is like uprooting and relocating in new ground;
	Adaptation to requirements of ecological setting and adoption of sustainable life styles/Stressors associated with new person–ecology fit
Economic (exchange)	Ending is like dissolving a financial partnership;
	Calculation that desired service has been received at acceptable price/financial considerations associated with continuance
Organizational (role)	Ending is like the finish of a theatrical performance;
	Capability and readiness to perform challenging organizational roles/lack of support for role identities and role performances
Physical environment (ecology)	Ending is like uprooting and relocating in new ground;
	Adaptation to requirements of ecological setting and adoption of sustainable life styles / Stressors associated with new person–ecology fit
Political (critical-feminist)	Ending is like cessation of struggle between foes;
	Victory (or loss) in advocacy or political action campaign/apprehension about retaliation from oppressors and likelihood of new battles
Social (systems)	Ending is like the reconstitution of family system after departure of key member (social worker);
	Shared understanding and improvement in system dynamics (cohesion and adaptability)/inadequate differentiation of self from system

Social workers can select the framework most suitable to the needs of the client system and the agency mission. For instance, in one of my first social work jobs at the Daily Planet Community and Counseling Center (Forte, 1988), we used role theory to understand and guide the planned change process including the ending phase. The majority of our clients had spent decades or longer in state mental institutions. After discharge, they needed our agency's support as they relearned how to perform community roles in effective, responsible, and vital ways. Role theory helped us appreciate that successful re-socialization after a lengthy stay in a mental hospital would take much time. Therefore, the agency set no arbitrary cut off point on services. The center's members could use our counseling, group activity, work training, and meal programs as long as they wanted. Role theory, however, also helped us make judgments with members about their readiness to reduce the use of agency support. We conferred with them on their confidence and capabilities related to roles central to community reintegration: the tenant role, the worker role, the friend role, and the citizen role. We used on-site observations of members' role performance and self-reports from members and their associates to assess readiness. We also used behavioral role-plays. Many members successfully shifted to successful community life and reduced contact with the agency, but returned occasionally for supplemental role coaching and support as needed. Some members experienced severe emotional difficulties and interpersonal disturbances that undermined attempts at independent role performance, and they continued to live in sheltered ways and to use many agency and community supports.

Bowen's approach to family systems theory (Bartle-Haring, Glebova, and Meyer, 2007) provides another illustration of theory-based ending. According to this approach, recipients of family therapy services are ready for the ending phase when they have achieved a high degree of differentiation of self from their marriage and/or family system. This differentiation includes freedom from automatic emotional reactions to family events and a significant reduction in negative emotional responses to family provocations including responses such as self-defense, counter attack, or withdrawal. Differentiated family members show an ability to make choices regarding their own behavior that are not compelled by the other system member. In their study, Bartle-Haring's team also identified an important Bowenian issue associated with ending. Husbands, wives, and other family members in systems characterized by the low differentiation of selves and by high emotional reactivity to family events were likely to find the ending phase very troubling and often terminated the helping process prematurely.

In facilitating transitions and ending, the advanced practitioner might engage in multi-theoretical social work. *Multi-theoretical ending* requires the identification of possible opportunities and complications related to the termination process from multiple theoretical perspectives and skilled pluralistic guidance in resolving these issues, ceasing the helping process, and preparing the client system for the future. Thus, the worker and client would assemble theoretical resources from several relevant frameworks and use these to accomplish ending tasks.

Matching theory-based ending approaches to helping circumstances

To my knowledge, there isn't any research that social work practitioners can use in judging the relative strengths and limitations of each theoretical approach to ending or in deciding which helping circumstances dictate the selection of a particular approach. This knowledge gap needs to be reduced.

There are some general non-theoretical factors that workers consider as they tailor the ending process to the client system. These include the overall degree of change achieved, the client's satisfaction with the helping process, the client's previous experiences with endings, the range of supports available to the client after the service ends, the degree of bonding between the client and worker or helping group, and the rules regarding insurance reimbursement (Walsh and Meyersohn, 2001).

In matching a theory-based ending approach to specific circumstances, practitioners may need to rely for now on case studies and practice wisdom. There are a few illustrations of common sense matching choices. In my own work in community-based corrections (Forte, 1989), I began to notice that some of our non-violent offenders were running away from the residential program before completing their court-ordered rehabilitation contract. We were hearing reports of many difficulties that they experienced after escape. I theorized that these residents were not engaging in careful and systematic cost–benefit analyses of the unauthorized departures. Economic exchange theory seemed relevant. The agency began to include in the weekly group counseling sessions a review time. This challenged members to focus on the perceived benefits of unauthorized exit: freedom from onerous rules and regulations, escape from confining quarters and forced contact with disagreeable peers, more choice about food and leisure-time activities, unmonitored intimate relationships, and so on. However, we also highlighted the very likely costs of such departures: community life with continual fear of contact with police and probation officers, obstacles to legitimate employment, re-arrest, extended sentences in prison rather than in community facilities, and death following risky gang involvement, for examples. We called on group members be more business-like and to make new and systematic cost–benefit calculations, and to continue through program completion to maximize their benefits and minimize their costs.

Frey (1994) discusses the selection of the symbolic interactionist theoretical framework to guide a resident program group dealing with the death of HIV infected members. His rationale for this matching decision seems reasonable. Symbolic meanings were central to the support group experience.

Each death was like a mini-ending for the entire group and one rich in symbolic value. Whenever a member died, the group participants wrote final goodbye messages articulating what the deceased member meant to them, and attached these farewell statements by strings to colored balloons. The balloons were let loose in unison representing the member's soul freed from the earthly shackles of disease and stigma. This kind of symbol-laden ritual, Frey says, "affirms the resident's life and acknowledges his or her release from the struggle with AIDS and symbolizes a letting go for the bereaved in a joyous way" (Frey, 1994, p. 569). The ritual and its symbols also helped the members and leader remember the lost participant while they began the process of reconstituting the group as a surviving collective.

Learning activities and reflections

1. Effective social work requires careful and sensitive helping action in the ending phase of the helping relationship. Briefly, summarize your understanding of the important features of the ending process and the worker's phase-specific helping tasks.

2. Each theoretical framework conceives of the ending process in a different way, and each framework theorizes in its own way about likely issues, concerns, or opportunities associated with guiding the ending or termination activities. See Table 14.1 for a list of fourteen frameworks, the conceptualization of ending for each, and illustrative ending phase issues. Select two frameworks that seem useful to you. Provide some details about how you might use each framework to understand the ending phase dynamics of a particular case and to guide your helping actions.

3. Identify factors that you will consider when selecting a theory-based approach or approaches for use during the ending phase with a particular client, group, family, or larger system. What theory-relevant indicators suggest that the client system is ready to terminate? What might be some identified client system preferences related to the ending phase, and how does your understanding of these preferences direct your selection? What might be some of the positive and challenging aspects of the ending process that your theory-based approach should anticipate? Are client system cultural memberships relevant to your choice of an approach to the ending process? How so? What other factors might you consider?

4. Finally, conclude with reflections on these learning activities. What have you learned that will prepare you to utilize theoretical frameworks to guide the processes of assessment, intervention, and evaluation?

References

Bartle-Haring, S., Glebova, T. and Meyer, K. (2007). Premature termination in marriage and family therapy within a Bowenian perspective. *The American Journal of Family Therapy*, 35, 53–68.

Council on Social Work Education (2008). 2008 Educational policy and accreditation standards. Retrieved June 16, 2010, from www.cswe.org/Accreditation/Reaffirmation.aspx.

Forte, J. A. (1988). Group services for the hard to reach in a new age settlement house. In M. Liederman, M. Birnbaum and B. Dazzo (Eds), *Roots and new frontiers in social group work* (pp. 13–26). New York: Haworth Press.

Forte, J. A. (1989). Restoring positive membership: Group counseling in community based corrections. In J. Lindsay and J. Landriault (Eds), *Proceedings of the 11th Annual Symposium of the Association for the Advancement of Social Work with Groups* (pp. 661–681), Montreal: Coordinating Committee of the 11th Annual Symposium of Social Work with Groups.

Frey, L. A. (1994). The naturalistic paradigm: Studying small groups in the postmodern era. *Small Group Research*, 25 (4), 551–577.

Walsh, J. (2007). *Endings in clinical practice: Ensuring closure across service settings* (2nd ed.). Chicago: Lyceum.

Walsh, J. and Meyersohn, K. (2001). Ending clinical relationships with people with schizophrenia. *Health and Social Work*, 26 (3), 188–195.

Section 3

Multi-theoretical social work across the career

15 Identify and remove barriers to multiple theory use across the career

(EPAS 2.1.1 Identify as a professional social worker; EPAS 2.1.7 Apply knowledge)

Translators can contribute to innovation that makes possible communication and cooperation across social worlds between specialists, novices, and laypersons ... They might help develop curriculums to teach theory users and research users the knowledge, skills, and attitudes necessary for becoming literate and fluent in multiple sign systems.

(Forte, 2009, p. 117)

Now that we have used translation devices and translated fourteen theories for use across each phase of the planned change process, we will consider in this section ways to leap over obstacles to multiple theory use, communicate with speakers of diverse theoretical languages, and develop intentionally an integrative multi-theory practice model. Although the next four lessons and the identified knowledge and skills are not explicitly referenced by the Council on Social Work Education, these lessons will prepare you for a career of competent multi-theoretical social work. We will begin in Lesson 15 by identifying the many barriers to multiple theory use. I will also suggest a set of strategies for removing the barriers.

The challenge of knowledge use

We can identify four major sites for knowledge development and use: the academic university, the research laboratory, the helping agency or organization, and the life space of client systems. Optimally, there would be a smooth flow of knowledge from the ivory tower and research lab to the field to the client's life space, and back from the life space to the field to the lab and ivory tower. However, knowledge translation and exchange is often difficult, and the flow is rarely smooth.

There is some relevant research, for instance, that theory users must overcome many obstacles to learn and apply theories to practice. Norcross and Thomas (1988) reported on a survey of 180 members of the Society for the Exploration of Psychotherapy Integration, an association that promotes communication and cooperation between scientists and therapists who use different theoretical languages. The study participants identified a variety of obstacles to knowledge exchanges including the lack of a common language, definitional confusion, inadequate training in the use of multiple theoretical languages, and partisan zealotry.

The founders of the *Journal of Translational Medicine* (Mankoff, Brander, Ferrone, and Marincola, 2004) reported on why much medical knowledge is "lost in translation" and not used by medical practitioners. They cited as obstacles the infrequent communication between basic science and clinical science groups, the difficulties of translating laboratory discoveries into practice guidelines, the lack of training in translational procedures, the scarcity of exemplars of translational work, and the lack of organizations dedicated to breaking down disciplinary boundaries.

Let's review some of the major factors that may undermine the efforts of social workers to translate and use theoretical knowledge to guide practice. In this book, I have emphasized the communicational aspects of these factors as critical and suggested knowledge translation as a key strategy for social workers. Figure 15.1 provides a summary of the major obstacles.

Obstacles related to differing conceptions of ideal knowledge (language and assumptions of basic science versus language and assumptions of applied science)

Obstacles related to scientific languages (translation difficulties, jargon, scientific communication conventions)

Obstacles related to communication and status differences (status and power battles across disciplines, professions, theoretical traditions)

Obstacles related to organizational context for learning theoretical languages (work demands, lack of support and incentives, disagreements about preferred knowledge)

Obstacles related to education and professional training in multiple theoretical languages (gaps in education, new knowledge issues, lack of continuing education)

Figure 15.1 Barriers to the integration of theory and practice

Obstacles related to communication due to differing conceptions of "ideal" knowledge

Theorizing can be pursued for the sake of knowledge development without reference to knowledge use. The theorizer or researcher is not focused on contemporary and challenging individual problems, public problems, or problems of the social work profession. This is often called *basic science*. Theorizing can also serve practical purposes and contribute to the knowledge development and problem solving necessary for effective social work. Such theorizing has immediate public uses. This is *applied science*. Basic and applied scientists often are socialized and work in vastly different cultures.

Basic scientists, many academic theorists, and laboratory researchers, for example, have very different notions of the features of ideal knowledge than applied scientists, social workers, and clients (Cohen, 1980; Glaser 1978; Lee, 1982; Shoemaker, Tankard, and Lasorsa, 2004; Thompson, 2000). Applied scientists use theoretical knowledge and research to increase their reflective awareness of aspects of a helping situation and to respond creatively and effectively to those in need. Basic scientists create theories and confirm scientific hypotheses to contribute to an ever-growing body of accepted scientific knowledge.

Applied and basic scientists often differ in their stance toward their jobs. The applied scientist attempts to immerse him or her self in the puzzling practice situation, engage with the client and other members of the situation, and use subjective experiences and value judgments to guide theory application. The basic scientist seeks generally a degree of detachment from the puzzling intellectual challenge, maintains personal boundaries relative to the subject matter, and safeguards his or her objectivity while theorizing.

Additionally, the applied scientist accepts that there is a great degree of uncertainty to the knowledge use process and final outcomes can't be guaranteed. It is never certain that X will result in Y. For example, a social work client may not respond positively to a "best practice" theory-informed intervention. The basic scientist assumes a set of predictable steps to inquiry and expects confidently that anticipated outcomes will be realized. It is hypothesized with great confidence that X generally causes Y. The applied scientist expects that resources for theory selection and application will be limited while the basic scientist anticipates funding and other support for theory development and testing.

Applied and basic scientists differ in the particulars of their methods. The applied scientist builds and uses knowledge in natural settings with real life cases. She recognizes that existing knowledge will never perfectly fit the specific practice situation. It has been formulated too abstractly and too independently of any particular time and place (Webster and Whitmeyer, 2001). Received knowledge must be supplemented by professional wisdom, reflection while acting, improvisational creativity, and feedback from the client. Theoretical concepts must be specified and adapted accordingly. The basic scientist prefers knowledge building in experimental laboratories under highly controlled conditions. She feels more assured that the great theories and the accumulated research can fit her abstract, intellectual task. Received concepts are used in accord with the existing literature and used correctly. The applied scientist often generates theory inductively following the accumulation of numerous observations of the PIE configuration. The basic scientist is more likely to use theoretical knowledge deductively moving from empirical generalizations and propositions to specific hypothesis tests.

Applied science and basic science offer different notions of success. The applied scientist is judged for making selective use of theoretical concepts as necessitated by the helping circumstances. To succeed, she asks: can theoretical knowledge predict the achievement of important and desired outcomes in specific and individualized circumstances? Does the knowledge fit with social work purposes, values, and ethics (Roberts, 1990)? The basic scientist is appraised for the precise and full use of the relevant theoretical and research traditions. To succeed, she asks: Does this use advance the intellectual interests of the referenced community of scientists (regardless of social relevance sometimes)? Kudos goes to the applied scientist who has transcended past traditions and created something radically new: a unique and creative response to distinctive personal or collective problems emerging in novel circumstances (Johnson and Svensson, 2005). The basic scientist earns praise by refining scientific knowledge in a way continuous with past scientific problem solving efforts yet adding a new finding or theoretical insight to the corpus. The exception is the scientific genius: an innovator who compels the scientific community toward a new paradigm. The basic scientist often argues that his or her theory or finding improves in some way on those of predecessors, and is considered effective when he or she wins the argument. The effective applied scientist seeks consensus with clients and collaterals about the utility and quality of the useful knowledge.

Social workers are applied scientists. They will have difficulty when they attempt to talk with basic scientists and use basic scientific knowledge. The stances of basic scientists, their scientific methods, their methods of communication, and their notions of success vary greatly from those of applied scientists. Levine (2006) offers a useful summary of some key differences. Basic scientists prefer abstract and general social work theory, theoretical contemplation, and theory advancement respectful of the canon of scientific texts (while standing on the shoulders of giants in their fields). Applied scientists prefer theory related to specific observations and situational factors, theory application, and innovative theorizing that guides inquiry and problem solving in complex and multi factorial practice settings. Effective theory use requires awareness of academic and laboratory knowledge but also the creative, reflective, and responsible translation and application of such basic knowledge and the generation of the special applied knowledge needed for social work practice.

Obstacles related to communication across scientific languages

There are several potential roadblocks to theory use related to the need for communication and cooperation across the four knowledge use sites. The translation of scientific theories and knowledge is difficult. As members of racial and ethnic groups differ in language and language use conventions, the members of different scientific social worlds differ in vocabularies and discourse practices (Duncker, 2001). Scientific concepts have multiple potential meanings (Gottdiener, 1995). For example, the brain scientist, the pharmacist, the clinical social worker, and the support group member may all assign different, and perhaps conflicting, definitions to the word "depression." Such conceptual differences may contribute to failures in effective communication. The processes of taking the perspective of others, gesturing sensibly, coordinating verbal meanings, and using symbolic resources to facilitate the aligning of different lines of action among team members breaks down. Speakers are assigning different definitions to the same word. It is as if the lab scientists speak Chinese, the university theorist speaks Italian, the social work practitioner speaks Arabic, and the client speaks English. Each uses a different sound and set of letters for "depression" and each brings different connotations to the concept.

There are specific differences between scientific English and colloquial or vernacular English. These become especially relevant in circumstances where theoretical novices or non-experts like social workers and their clients attempt to communicate with and use knowledge generated by scientific experts. Scientists use many technical terms. Halliday and Martin (1993) estimate that a particular branch of a scientific discipline may have 50,000 to 100,000 distinctive concepts. Scientists tend to compress much information into one word, and use the word to replace more cumbersome, but perhaps clearer plain English words. Scientists are prone to "lexical density," the packing of many ideas and themes into each passage of a scientific text or turn of a scientific conversation. Scientists change commonsense understandings into technical understandings, and they communicate using terms defined by the interlocking of multiple concepts and by very complex technical taxonomies. Scientists create and use "special expressions" not found in everyday speech or everyday social work practice like "solving the open equation over D." Scientific English is built of "abstractions" and "objectifications" (processes turned into objects named by nouns like "fission"), "complex nominalizations" (the creative naming of phenomena like "energy instability" by blending everyday words, new words, or words from diverse fields of study, and attaching specialized meanings to the blend), and "grammatical metaphors" (the substitution of one image or symbol for another like "cybernetic system" to mean "the family").

The scientific English used in laboratory and academic talk is unlike the English used in everyday language and in practice settings. Roth (2005) reports that spoken science is highly indexical. Speakers refer to tools and laboratory entities, for example, by use of "it", "this", and "that" instead of by using fuller descriptors and nouns. Lab scientists often communicate using incomplete sentences, vague references, and ambiguous sentence structures. Communication difficulties among researchers caused by such patterns are only resolved because participants have a deep grasp of the laboratory as the context for dialogue. Most social workers lack extensive training in the language of lab scientists.

The scientific English used in written reports and textbooks differs greatly from that in non-scientific writing (Lemke 1990). Science writing tends to be verbally explicit, technical, serious, authoritative, and oriented toward causal logic. Science writers tend to avoid informal forms of language, personal feelings, personification, colorful and value-laden phrases, first-person pronouns, reference to fantasy or fiction, and history or historical personalities. Although the conventions of scientific English change over time and varies across science groups, I suspect that many practitioners and laypersons listening to or reading scientific reports would agree with this characterization.

In summary, "language" differences and communication problems can hamper the efforts of social workers to use theoretical knowledge. Increasing our fluency in scientific languages, learning methods of knowledge translation, and using translation products created by leaders of the science translation movement will increase our effective theory use (Forte, 2009; Roberts, 1990).

Obstacles related to communication across status differences

Social status is the importance, honor, and prestige attached to a position. Status can be earned by achievement but status is often assigned simply by placement in a position. Members of different knowledge production and use sites often differ in status. In the United States, for instance, many members of academic and research communities have significantly greater status than members of social work organizations and members of client groups. Such status differences are often associated with negative stereotypes attached to the lower status position holders—social workers as doers not thinkers, as guided by heart not head, and so on. Status issues can become an obstacle to cooperation across ivory tower, lab, field, and life space.

For example, I was employed for a decade at a university with a combined sociology and social work department. The social work educators had very low status relative to their colleagues. The university president attempted to eliminate the entire social work program three times, but he never questioned the importance of the sociology program. The salaries of the social work faculty members were twenty percent or more lower than the salaries of the sociology professors. The sociology professors saw themselves as important theorists and researchers, and castigated the social work faculty as inferior members of the college—practitioners and only knowledge users, not knowledge creators. The sociologists showed minimal interest in knowledge application and doubted that they could learn anything from social workers. At the time of the near demise of the social work program, the sociology leaders refused to even consider saving social work positions by allowing us to teach in the sociology department.

Let's state this more abstractly. Certain high status groups use particular ways of talking or writing to promote their interests and privileges while hindering the interests of others. For example, the stylistic norms and jargon of those "warfare" scientists controlled by the government form a barrier impeding cooperation with citizens. Technocrats use the theories and language of military "science" to perpetuate their status and to assure the dominance of their policies over the viewpoints of a polity not fluent in formal military science (Lemke, 1990). Such ideological use of theories, theoretical knowledge, and theorizing practices blocks collaborative inquiry with peace seekers and cooperative knowledge use for the sake of conflict resolution.

Status and related power differences may also block collaborative inquiry into public problems. In the preface, I reported on Scheff (1995), who studied translation and cooperation across university departments. He likened professors to gang members adopting academic codes similar to the street codes of urban gangs. Professors align themselves with a "theoretical school," their gang, abide by its norms, and pressure other gang members to follow the norms. Academic disciplines are like super-gangs competing for influence in a university. The department is the gang's turf. Members signal loyalty to their group by using its slang and members secure prestige and rewarding attachments by distancing themselves discursively from other gangs. Distancing tactics include hostile and competitive interaction, verbal attacks, and non-recognition directed toward any theory users showing allegiance to enemy gangs. All this undermines interdisciplinary collaboration on community problems. We can add that participants in "using science" ventures such as social workers are in weak gangs, and they rarely have the status, power, or resources equal to those "creating scientific knowledge" (university professors) or "doing science" (researchers), the powerful gangs. Higher status holders therefore can ignore the voices of social workers and of those vulnerable populations that social workers represent. Social workers may decide to avoid painful encounters with prideful "superiors."

In summary, the differences in status and power between partners in knowledge use can undermine theory application. Social workers who can increase the status assigned to social work positions and press for respectful communication and engagement across sites, disciplines, theoretical perspectives, and social roles as equal partners will increase their ability to use theory effectively.

Obstacles related to communication influenced by organizational pressures

A variety of pressures on social work practitioners may reduce the disposition to use theoretical knowledge. Work demands related to a heavy caseload decrease, for example, the limited time available for searching for and making sense of literature on evidence-based practice theories. Overall, time constraints reduce opportunities for theoretical reflection on how well one's theory-based conceptual formulation and intervention plan are serving to ameliorate client problems—before, during, and after the helping process with each client. Many needs of clients have a quality of immediacy. This stimulates the urge to "do something now," sometimes at the expense of "thinking about what I am doing." Standards for worker evaluation may neglect theorizing competencies, and workers who denigrate theory use or pride themselves for non-theoretical practice may earn bonuses and promotions in a theoretical or anti-theoretical organizational cultures, and atheoretical.

Organizational dynamics may undermine inclinations to translate and use theories. There is often a time lag between the knowledge generated by academic theorists and laboratory scientists and the accessing of this knowledge by practitioners and clients. For example, few social workers are expertly aware of the recent advances in biology associated with pioneers in the neurosciences. The agency may do little to facilitate or support the translation and use of contemporary advances in such knowledge. Journals are not purchased. Continuing education events are not offered. Expert consultants are not invited to the agency.

Additionally, important groups and members of a helping organization or clinical business may disagree about the preferred knowledge for practitioners. One camp supports a conventional ego psychology approach. Another camp advocates for the use of critical and feminist theories by the organization. A small but vocal camp argues that the Afrocentric theory makes most sense for the clientele and their problems. This lack of consensus about the preferred and most suitable theoretical orientation and their problems with cooperative interaction despite their differences can confuse novice workers and those with limited knowledge of the strengths and limitations of various practice theories.

The context for social work practice can support or undermine consistent and purposeful theory translation and use. Effective social workers try to help shape an organizational system so that it values and rewards theoretical reflection and creativity and supports communication and cooperation across theoretical boundaries.

Obstacles related to education and professional training for translation work

Effective theory use requires the acquisition of a significant amount of theoretical knowledge, the mastery of a wide range of theorizing competencies, and the cultivation of habits of theory study and reflective theorizing. The advancement toward theoretically sound professionalism takes time, effort, and education. Some elements of our culture and profession divert practitioners from this hard work. Educational institutions, continuing education training centers, social worker leaders, and professional associations vary in their commitment to promoting life-long learning in the areas of knowledge translation and scientific theorizing. Enrollment in social work academic programs and continuing education workshops is expensive. The profession's theory preferences change over time, and organizational administrators may be reluctant to allow practitioners the time to engage in learning activities to keep pace with knowledge advancement. Social workers may become complacent and blind to the limitations of their stale theoretical approaches. Some agents of socialization may hold sexist beliefs and assume that female social workers are poorly inclined to the abstract thinking associated with theory mastery and theorizing (Flax, 1999). Such agents would discourage women from developing theorizing competencies and knowledge.

Without specific knowledge, skills, and dispositions, social workers will not translate and use theory-derived information in practice and theorize effectively. The social worker aiming to maximize all aspects of the professional self—doing, feeling, thinking, talking—will seek to jump over the five barriers to theory exchanges and integration and look continuously for opportunities to learn theory and practice the art and science of theorizing.

Strategies for knowledge translation and use

In the preface, I suggested that multi-theoretical social workers need to venture into *trading zones*, places where exchanges between knowledge creators and knowledge users are frequent, and make use of traders, specialists who facilitate communication across language differences and make possible mutually rewarding bartering and trading activity. The Canadian

Institutes of Health Research (2013) have provided significant leadership to participants in the knowledge translation movement. Although they don't use the language of trading zones, trades, and traders, the institutes offer a set of strategies that can be adapted for my trading zone approach. We will focus on strategies useful to the practitioner and the group or organizational context for practice.

Starting with the organizational context, the institutes recommend that social workers create agency and team cultures that value knowledge translation and knowledge use. Such value preferences should be incorporated into the organization's or group's mission, goal, and objective statements. Social work leaders should also help these organization and teams create communication channels so that interaction across knowledge sites and participation in trading zones is easy and effective. Leaders and other advocates of theory translation need to influence economic processes so there are incentives for knowledge translation and theory use and resources to engage in trades in trading zones. Norms supporting competition between those speaking different languages and conformity to a no-science or one scientific language stance need to be changed to norms supporting communication between knowledge creators and users and mastery of multiple languages. Finally, leaders in the project of knowledge translation need to change the organizational structure. An optimal division of labor allocates the tasks of translating and exchanging in trading zones to some organizational members who become specialists, and these specialists are given the time, flexibility, and support to meet these demands and to share their translation work.

Additionally, all social workers can increase their capabilities and motivation related to knowledge translation and use. The Canadian Institutes of Health Research (2013) recommends training designed to prepare knowledge users, practitioners, for effective trading with knowledge creators, theorists and researchers. Such training would include the following objectives: increase practitioners' awareness of the potential benefits of learning scientific languages and using scientific theories; increase practitioners' understanding of knowledge translation methods and techniques (a focus, also, of this book and my discussions of knowledge translation devices); increase practitioners' skills in knowledge translation; and increase attitudes supportive of translation work and knowledge trading including confidence, perceived outcome efficacy, and overall motivation. With support and training, social work practitioners can become adept translators who enter trading zones, assess barriers to negotiating and exchanging across scientific languages, remove barriers effectively, and bring bargains back to their clients, colleagues, and agencies while providing valuable resources (theoretical insights informed by practice) to their trading partners.

Learning activities and reflections

1. Think about your experiences in your field internship, in the classroom, or as a professional social worker, Reflect specifically on experiences related to the application of theories to practice. Attempt to identify the possible obstacles to using theoretical knowledge as a guide to the planned change process.

2. Theory users differ in their conception of ideal knowledge. Four sources of professional knowledge are very important: academic knowledge developed by the great theorists and their followers, empirical knowledge developed by researchers in laboratories and community settings, practice wisdom gained in helping settings derived from reflection on and study of practice experiences, and the life experiences or everyday knowledge of our clients. Social workers learn theoretical knowledge from reading books and articles, from observing theory experts in action, and from conversations with professors, researchers, colleagues, and clients. What are some of the differences between the various kinds and sources of knowledge, and what features of university and laboratory-derived knowledge might make it difficult to use in practice?

3. To use theoretical knowledge, you must understand the concepts, propositions, and other elements of different theoretical languages. What barriers to grasping and using the languages of different theoretical frameworks might you face in your career?

4. Social workers often participate on interdisciplinary teams or on work groups with social workers varying in their preferred theoretical orientation. We also consult with colleagues who aren't social workers. What are some possible barriers related to cooperation across disciplines, professions, theoretical orientations, or roles (practitioner, academic, researcher, client), and how could these barriers interfere with your theory use?

5. For social workers, theory use generally occurs in an organizational context: a field agency, a social work organization, or a private practice business. What obstacles related to organization processes, structures, dynamics, or resources might impede your effects to use theory to guide your practice?

6. The effective and responsible application of theoretical knowledge requires both mastery of content and mastery of various theorizing competencies. Such mastery takes time and training. What obstacles related to your professional education and post-graduation training might contribute to difficulties in translating knowledge and using theory?

7. To summarize, identify the three or four obstacles that you consider most likely to impede your quest to master theoretical knowledge and become competent at theorizing. Develop a strategy for overcoming each obstacle. You might imagine that your supervisor has asked you to develop a two-year plan to keep up with the latest and most important advances in knowledge? What would you plan? How can you ensure that the plan will be successful?

8. Finally, reflect on this learning activity. What have you learned about social work and the basics of competent theorizing?

References

Canadian Institutes of Health Research (2013). Knowledge translation publications. Retrieved September 29, 2013, from www.cihr-irsc.gc.ca/e/29418.html.

Cohen, B. P. (1980). *Developing sociological knowledge: Theory and method*. Englewood Cliffs, NJ: Prentice-Hall.

Duncker, E. (2001). Symbolic communication in multidisciplinary cooperations. *Science, Technology, and Human Values, 26*, 349–386.

Flax, J. (1999). Women do theory. In M. Pearsall (Ed.), *Women and values: Readings in recent feminist philosophy* (pp. 9–13). Belmont, CA: Wadsworth.

Forte, J. A. (2009). Translating theory and research for interactionist practice: A signs, symbols, and social worlds approach. *Humboldt Journal of Social Relations, 32* (1), 86–122.

Glaser, B. (1978). *Theoretical sensitivity*. San Francisco: The Sociology Press.

Gottdiener, M. (1995). *Postmodern semiotics: Material culture and the forms of postmodern life*. Cambridge, MA: Blackwell.

Halliday, M. A. K. and Martin, J. R. (1993). *Writing science: Literacy and discursive power*. Pittsburgh, PA: University of Pittsburgh Press.

Johnson, E. and Svensson, K. (2005). Theory in social work—some reflections on understanding and explaining interventions. *European Journal of Social Work, 8* (4), 419–433.

Lee, P. (1982). Some contemporary and perennial problems of relating theory to practice in social work. In R. Bailey and P. Lee (Eds), *Theory and practice in social work* (pp. 15–45). Oxford: Basil Blackwell.

Lemke, J. (1990). *Talking science*. Westport, CT: Ablex.

Levine, D. N. (2006). Note on the discipline. *Canadian Journal of Sociology, 31* (2), 235–243.

Mankoff, S. P., Brander, C., Ferrone, S. and Marincola, F. M. (2004). Lost in translation: obstacles to translation medicine. *Journal of Translational Medicine 2*, 1–7.

Norcross, J. G. and Thomas, B. L. (1988). What's stopping us now? Obstacles to psychotherapy integration. *Journal of Integrative and Eclectic Psychotherapy,* 7 (1), 74–80.

Roberts, R. (1990). *Lessons from the past: Issues for social work theory.* London: Tavistock/Routledge.

Roth, W-M. (2005). *Talking science: Language and learning in science classrooms.* Lanham, MD: Rowman and Littlefield.

Scheff, T. (1995). Academic gangs. *Crime, Law, and Social Change, 23,* 157–162.

Shoemaker, P. J., Tankard, J. W., Jr. and Lasorsa, D. L. (2004). *How to build social science theories.* Thousand Oaks, CA: Sage.

Thompson, N. (2000). *Theory and practice in human services.* Maidenhead: Open University Press.

Webster, M., Jr. and Whitmeyer, J. M. (2001). Applications of theories of group processes. *Sociological Theory, 19* (3), 250–270.

16 Participate in multi-theory reflecting teams

(EPAS 2.1.1 Identify as a professional social worker; EPAS 2.1.7 Apply knowledge; EPAS 2.1.10 Engage, assess, intervene, and evaluate)

> *The Clinical Exchange was designed to foster open inquiry and transtheoretical dialogue in terms of actual psychotherapy cases. Specifically, the purpose is for eminent clinicians of diverse persuasions to share, in ordinary language, their clinical formulations and treatment plans of the same psychotherapy patient—who was not selected or nominated by those therapists—and then to discuss points of convergence and contention in their recommendations.*
>
> (Allen, 2005, p. 67)

By necessity, most social workers cooperate with colleagues from different professions, partners educated in varied disciplines, and specialists in diverse roles including researcher, theorist, and practitioner roles. Most partners were not socialized in the language and perspective of the social work profession. Often these partners bring theoretical frameworks to the collaboration different from those of the social workers. I have argued repeatedly that can be a good thing. Team members with different perspectives can reflect together on common practice challenges, and each member can assist colleagues with their individual theoretical puzzles and theory application difficulties. Any client system's PIE configuration is complex, and collaborative teams increase the number of lenses and tools available for the job of understanding and helping these systems.

I believe that the quality of the knowledge base for the social work professions will improve if members of the profession initiate and participate in conversations with adherents to different theoretical schools. If interactionist social workers talk more often with their rivals, the behavioral psychologists, for example, the symbolic interactionists may better identify their theoretical blind spots and make the theory more useful for themselves and others (Forte, 2001).

Additionally, practitioners who collaborate in reflective activities during multiple theoretical team meetings will solve more practical problems and solve them more effectively than those who use only one theoretical tradition. We can refer to these multi-theoretical forums as *reflecting teams* (Andersen, 1987, 1991). These are groups of helpers reflecting on a particular case and talking to each other and to their clients about observations, theoretical perspectives on information gathering, and theoretical ideas about best interventions. Returning to the metaphor of trading zones, the reflecting team offers a place where professionals speaking different theoretical languages can meet to communicate for the purposes of mutually beneficial knowledge exchanges and for the achievement of common goals. Reflecting team work is especially useful for understanding and addressing complex personal or collective change projects requiring the engagement of multiple stakeholders in inquiry and action planning (Canadian Institutes of Research, 2013). Reflecting team leaders might use varied modalities for convening a session: the face-to-face meeting, online discussion boards, teleconferences, and so on. During reflecting team sessions—whatever the modality—practitioners can also generate new knowledge and insights for use by the whole profession.

Modalities for multi-theory team reflection

There are several interesting illustrations of the use of multi-theory reflecting teams. In one novel application, teams of practitioners engaged in collaborative theorizing in front of and with the clients during actual helping sessions (Lax, 1995). Family members, for example, were involved in discussions about the helping process as it occurred. Practitioners carefully translated the scientific language of theoretical frameworks into everyday words familiar to the family. Topics of concern to the family were viewed from multiple perspectives, and the family's personal knowledge of their PIE concerns was considered as important as the practitioners' theoretical knowledge.

Koopmans (1995) involved field interns in weekly reflecting teams and gave them opportunities to observe family therapists using and talking about varying theoretical frameworks. Koopmans also invited guests to the reflecting team meetings (other clients, field liaisons, and special experts) to translate, share, and compare their distinctive languages during the reflection session. Thomlison (1995) required students to develop a multi-perspective case analysis. She helped by introducing social work students on the reflecting team to students from other disciplines. One team included three master's level social work students, a master's level nursing student, an educational psychology student, and a doctoral level psychology student. Students had opportunities to see each other practice and to hear the theory-specific concerns and issues generated during these multi-disciplinary dialogues and reflections. Social workers sometimes bring theory-oriented process records to reflecting team meetings. These include information about the different theoretical frameworks and social science knowledge that was used during the helping work (Forte, 1994) and then, team members can examine the records and comparisons of the utility of varied theoretical frameworks.

An *interdisciplinary team* brings together people from different agencies, disciplines, and professions to work together on shared cases. A family assessment and planning team (FAPT), for example, might include parents, private therapists and other private service providers, and representatives from the community service board, court service unit, department of social services, and the school system. This group theorizes about how to best understand a family and its challenges, about how to best mobilize family strengths and community resources, and about the appropriate service plan.

Walder (1993) developed an interesting approach called the *integrative case seminar* in his Institute for Integrated Training in Psychotherapy. These seminars included students and two faculty members representing divergent theoretical approaches. Such a seminar provides participants an opportunity to integrate theoretical material from the classroom (lectures, readings) with field experiences. Walder moderated the discussion of case materials, resolved issues leading to communication problems, and proposed a set of discussion questions to promote comparative examination of the usefulness of the relevant theoretical frameworks.

The *clinical exchange* is another reflective approach to knowledge building developed for the *Journal of Psychotherapy Integration* to foster cooperative, open inquiry and cross-theoretical dialogue in relation to actual psychotherapy cases (Allen, 2005). Experts in various theoretical orientations are invited to examine the same case. They present a written analysis using everyday language that captures their perspectives on problem formulation, the optimal therapeutic relationship, preferred intervention methods, and the likely progression of the helping process. The written summary allows also for a comparison of the points of similarity and difference between the different theory users. Participants in the clinical exchange also respond to each other with short written commentaries. Readers can easily compare the languages and perspectives of users of different theories and the implications of each theory-based presentation for helping work. Clinical exchanges can also be conducted as face-to-face meetings.

At the Daily Planet Community and Counseling Center, my first social work organizational employer, for example, we met every Wednesday for a staff meeting comparable to a clinical exchange. The meeting included the consulting psychiatrist who was expert in psychopharmacology, a therapist identified with the existential-humanistic perspective, the program and financial manager of our work training business, an art therapist, and me, the social group worker aligned with the mainstream interactionist approach (Forte, 1988). We would identify together five or so difficult cases from our agency membership of deinstitutionalized ex-mental patients. Then we would reflect together on how to best understand and help each focal member.

Multi-theory collaboration: guidelines

Multi-theoretical reflection teams work best when certain attitudes prevail and rules are followed (Canadian Institutes of Health Research, 2008; Forte, 2002; Van de Ven and Johnson, 2006). For one, a commitment to achieving shared purposes reduces interdisciplinary and cross-theoretical allegiance tensions. Team members, whatever their theoretical orientation, can agree to high priority moral, policy, and social change goals, and then dedicate their theoretical and intervention resources toward cooperatively achieving these mutual goals.

Second, collaborative practitioners can best participate in multi-theoretical reflecting teams if they resist institutional and personal inclinations toward parading in-group and out-group distinctions. Contests and controversies about the best theory or the best profession distract practitioners from practical and unified public activity toward professional goals. Exploration of similarities and differences is guided by the commitment to find an integrative framework for conceptualizing and solving the problem at hand.

Third, each participant in the reflecting team event should work hard to translate their specialty theoretical language for understanding by others (Canadian Institutes of Research, 2013). This translation work might include identifying the foundational metaphors and core assumptions of their theory, identifying the key terms of their language and transforming these into plain English, explaining the theory-informed foci and questions guiding their assessment efforts, discussing their preferred theory of change, and converting any jargon associated with theory-based intervention strategies and implementation theory into clearer words. If the team members can interact frequently and over an extended period of time, they will become more familiar with and respectful of their peers' theoretical languages and perspectives. A social worker versed in multiple theories and in translation devices might even serve to facilitate cross-theory communication. Figure 16.1 illustrates this conception of the social worker as translator on multi-theory reflecting teams.

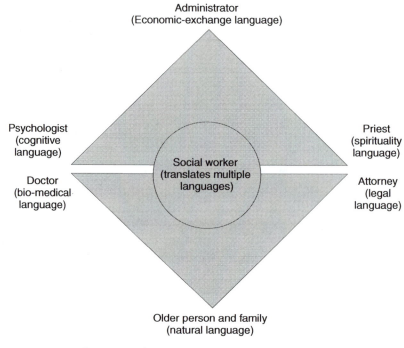

Human service case: elderly person in nursing
home with support of family members

Figure 16.1 The social worker as translator and reflecting teams

Fourth, team members can pledge to seek consensus about group procedures and case formulation decisions. For example, members can seek working agreements about which goals and objectives, guiding conceptions of focal problems, and plans of action will best ameliorate the client's difficulties. The plurality of orientations helps rather than hinders democratically structured group processes if status hierarchies are avoided. Disagreements, for example, become assets in the search for practical solutions to problems not opportunities for status seeking competition. From such disagreements, team members can generate multiple explanations of the problem at hand, varied directives for assessing the person and social situation, and a wide range of solutions and policies. The groups' "working hypotheses" represent the tentative conclusions agreed to by equals in each of these areas. These hypotheses can be publicly verified by the test of their useful and liberating contribution to improving membership processes and conditions.

Fifth, multi-theory reflection teams will work best if all participants are considered equal in potential contributions. Self-reflective practitioners discuss, deliberate, and negotiate as peers not superiors/inferiors while reviewing their alternative theoretical perspectives on the problem and theory-based problem solving strategies. Every member has the right to push the group to think about the meeting issues in richer and more penetrating ways. Ideally, participants bring diverse but complementary theoretical orientations, skills, and background knowledge. Participants might even alternate in sharing their theory-guided insights and working hypotheses about the case as "thought trials" for respectful consideration by the entire team (Van de Ven and Johnson, 2006).

Sixth, group dynamics that value and use differences will enhance multi-theory reflection. Van de Ven and Johnson (2006) borrow a term from the financial community, arbitrage, to characterize this process. In finance circles, arbitrage refers to the exploitation of price differentials in the pursuit of profit. *Multi-theoretical arbitrage*, they suggest, involves exploiting the different perspectives of scholars from diverse disciplines and practitioners with varied practice experiences to address complex problems in ways beneficial to all stakeholders. They add:

> Arbitrage represents a dialectical method of inquiry where understanding and synthesis of a common problem evolve from the confrontation of divergent theses and antitheses ... it is a strategy for triangulating on problems by involving individuals whose perspectives are different.
>
> (Van de Ven and Johnson, 2006, p. 809)

The negotiation of differences during case formulation should be organized according to the same democratic and reflective principles and norms that guide scientific inquiry: ideals such as unimpeded communication, mutual understanding, the decentralization of power, and deliberations free from unconscious constraints or force. Team members should also reflect continuously on the ideals, norms, and interactional patterns that characterize their cooperative inquiry and problem solving and use these reflections to improve the functioning of their reflecting teams.

Seventh, reflecting teams should aim to become a collaborative learning community where members agree to document their collaborative work and share the lessons obtained from multi-theoretical reflection with colleagues and the whole profession. Such documentation can serve as a demonstration of social work translation leadership and an archive for other practitioners interested in multi-theory social work. These collaborative learning communities also provide practitioners opportunities to develop a key practice behavior for the CSWE core competency, "apply critical thinking" including the demonstration of effective oral and written communication in working with clients and colleagues (Council on Social Work Education, 2008).

Learning activities and reflections

1. Observe an interdisciplinary team meeting. What are the different theoretical frameworks represented by the team members? How did members communicate that they are using a particular theoretical approach to understand the case? How well did team members take each other's perspective? What was the quality of multi-theory reflection on the case dynamics? In what ways, did group norms and dynamics help or hinder the multi-theory reflection? What were some missed opportunities for cross-theory communication and collaboration?

2. A clinical exchange is a forum attended by clinical social workers with diverse theoretical allegiances where theory experts unite in the process of case examination and formulation for an identified client. Let's try to simulate the clinical exchange experience. If possible, invite community practitioners with different theoretical orientations to a meeting. If this is not possible, form a student panel. Invite each student to study a particular practice theory and become somewhat expert on this perspective. Ask each panel member to speak as a practitioner and discuss how he or she would approach an agreed upon practice situation (group work with battered women, individual counseling for at-risk high school students, family services to a recently evicted family, organizational development to enhance employees' adherence to sexual harassment policies, or the creation of a neighborhood watch program). Ideally, ideas and opinions are exchanged freely. Each panelist should briefly present a summary of his or her theoretical approach to the practice situation. The panel members should also discuss and debate the relative merits of the different approaches, and the panel members should respond to questions from the others on the panel and members of the audience. Summarize your opinions about the multi-theoretical presentations and reflections shared by panel members.

3. Finally, reflect on what you have learned about theorizing that prepares you to contribute to the advancement of social work knowledge?

References

Allen, D. M. (2005). The clinical exchange. *Journal of Psychotherapy Integration*, 15 (1), 67–68.

Andersen, T. (1987). The reflecting team: Dialogue and meta-dialogue in clinical work. *Family Process*, 26, 415–428.

Andersen, T. (Ed.). (1991). *The reflecting team: Dialogues and dialogues about the dialogues*. New York: W. W. Norton and Company.

Canadian Institutes of Health Research (2008). Knowledge to action: A knowledge translation casebook. Retrieved March 26, 2013, from www.cihr-irsc.gc.ca/e/38764.html

Canadian Institutes of Health Research (2013). Knowledge translation publications. Retrieved September 29, 2013, from www.cihr-irsc.gc.ca/e/29418.html.

Council on Social Work Education (2008). Educational policy and accreditation standards. Retrieved June 16, 2010, from www.cswe.org/Accreditation/Reaffirmation.aspx.

Forte, J. A. (1988). Group services for the hard to reach in a new age settlement house. In M. Liederman, M. Birnbaum and B. Dazzo (Eds), *Roots and new frontiers in social group work* (pp. 13–26). New York: Haworth Press.

Forte, J. A. (1994). The teaching record: A framework for teaching group process. *Journal of Social Work Education*, 30 (1), 116–128.

Forte, J. A. (2001). *Theories for practice: Symbolic interactionist translations*. Lanham, MD: University Press of America.

Forte, J. A. (2002). Mead, contemporary metatheory, and twenty-first-century interdisciplinary team work. *Sociological Practice: A Journal of Clinical and Applied Sociology*, 4 (4), 315–334.

Koopmans, J. (1995). The use of the reflecting team to enhance student learning. In G. Rogers (Ed.), *Social work field education: Views and visions* (pp. 229–233). Dubuque, IA: Kendall/Hunt.

Lax, W. D. (1995). Offering reflections: Some theoretical and practical considerations. In S. Friedman (Ed.), *The reflecting team in action: Collaborative practice in family therapy* (pp. 145–166). New York: Guilford Press.

Thomlison, B. (1995). Student perceptions of reflective team supervision. In G. Rogers (Ed.), *Social work field education: Views and visions* (pp. 234–244). Dubuque, IA: Kendall/Hunt.

Van de Ven, A. H. and Johnson, P. E. (2006). Knowledge for theory and practice. *Academy of Management Review*, 31 (4), 802–821.

Walder, E. H. (1993). Supervision and instruction in postgraduate psychotherapy. In G. Stricker and J. K. Gold (Eds), *Comprehensive handbook of psychotherapy integration* (pp. 499–512). New York: Plenum Press.

17 Choose and implement an approach to integrate theoretical languages

(EPAS 2.1.1 Identify as a professional social worker; EPAS 2.1.3 Apply critical thinking; EPAS 2.1.7 Apply knowledge)

The "comfortable sense" veteran social workers can take for granted stems from their successful development of intellectual scaffolding and conceptual architecture related to the profession. Such intellectual space houses theory, application knowledge, and skill competencies, and enables praxis (the art and science of social work practice). However, this comfortable sense belies the challenging cognitive work of constructing that conceptual space.

(Garner, 2011, p. 255)

Educational Policy and Accreditation Standard 2.1.3 identifies "critical thinking" as a core professional competency. The competency definition indicates that critical thinking "requires the synthesis and communication of relevant information", and the educational policy statement includes "distinguish, appraise, and integrate multiple sources of knowledge" as a practice behavior demonstrating competency in this area (Council on Social Work Education, 2008, p. 4). However, the Council and the social work professional literature offer little guidance on the processes of theory synthesis and integration.

Multi-theoretical social work and theoretical integration

The verb for integration, "integrate," has many synonyms including incorporate, assemble, combine, coordinate, join, consolidate, desegregate, mix, assimilate, blend, unify, and converge. The verb, integrate, has several opposites, too. The list of opposites includes segregate, differentiate, and diverge. You may have used some of these synonyms or antonyms for "integrate" in your everyday conversations. In your practice classes, you may have read about "personality integration," a concept referring to a goal of some counselors and clients. Personality integration involves bringing together and organizing all aspects of the personality including thoughts, feelings, desires, and behavioral tendencies into a harmonious whole. The related concept, "systems integration," is taught in courses on family and organizational practice. It refers to the goal of bringing together the different parts of a family or social work agency so that they are coordinated as elements in a well functioning system.

A major theme of all social work field internships is integration. I am certain that you have heard this term used by your field coordinator, by your field supervisors, and by your practice teachers. In this usage, integration refers to linking what you learned in your academic classes with what you are learning day to day from direct experience with clients, and bringing back your reflections on your field experiences to enrich the lessons at your school.

Social workers can enhance their own practice and contribute to the profession's knowledge base by using multiple theories and by engaging in theoretical integration. *Theoretical integration* refers to attempts, however piecemeal, to transform multiple theoretical frameworks into a unified framework (Forte, 2006). Theoretical integration requires that practitioners "look beyond the confines of single-school approaches to see what can be learned from other perspectives. It is characterized by openness to various ways of integrating theories and techniques" (Stricker, 2010, p. 4). For example, the "person interacting in an environment" metatheory that I have shared in this book invites practitioners to integrate knowledge from fourteen different theoretical approaches. Bernstein, Goodman, and Epstein (1997) also relate the term integration to knowledge application and suggest, "competent social workers do not merely apply a single theory in their practice. Instead, they reflectively integrate multiple theories and values with each of their actions in different, complex, changing contexts" (p. 140). There are four major approaches to theoretical integration.

Theoretical integration: the common factors approach

Common factors are "conditions and processes activated and facilitated by strategies and skills that positively influence practice outcomes across a range of practice theories" (Cameron and Keenan, 2010, p. 63). The common factors approach starts with a process of desegregation (Forte, 2006). The unique contributions of each theoretical approach to practice are separated from the "common factors" or "active ingredients", those elements that contribute to the positive outcomes of the helping process whatever the theoretical perspective. Then a process of reintegration begins and theoretical approaches are aligned on the basis of their possession of these common factors.

Using our comparison of a scientific theory to language, we can think of the common factors approach as the search for and identification of conceptual or cultural universals. These are concepts or key terms found in some form in every human language such as calendar, causality, emotion, family, leader, medicine, property, risk-taking, socialization, toy, trade, and weapon (Brown, 1991). Common theoretical factors can unite diverse approaches to helping across historical periods, cultural groups, social institutions, and theoretical languages. Theoretical integrationists have generated lists of factors common to practice theories. Candidates for the distinction of common factor include catharsis, the worker's personality, consistency of the rationale and conceptual framework for helping, provision of alternative formulations of the bio-psycho-social events troubling the client system, a positive helping relationship or working alliance, an appreciation for certain helper qualities such as empathy and non-judgmental acceptance, a structuring of the planned change process into phases, expectations for positive change, and support (Forte, 2006; Stricker, 2010). Common factors in helping theories, then, are shared theoretical concepts that transcend specific theoretical frameworks.

The *Transtheoretical Model of Change* (TTM) developed by Prochaska and DiClemente (1992) is a very popular and well-researched approach to theoretical integration used in many fields of practice. The current conceptualization suggests that there are common stages to the change process that transcend many different theories. These include precontemplation, contemplation, preparation, action, and maintenance. Calderwood (2011) used this approach to conceptualize the bereavement process and assist social workers facilitating cognitive, emotional, and behavioral processes central to effective grief work. She argued that TTM usefully integrates knowledge across theories such as attachment theory, family systems theory, resilience theory, and cognitive-behavioral theory. McGuire (2004) documented the usefulness of the transtheoretical "common phases" model and its limitations in guiding public housing residents during their welfare to work transition.

Critics wonder how common these factors are to different approaches. They suggest that the specific meanings of particular common factors like empathy can vary significantly across approaches (Forte, 2006). Also, there is little social work research documenting the contribution of common factors to work with different client groups or the challenges of teaching common factors in light of the significant differences between theoretical approaches and their preferred outcomes (Smith, 2012).

Theoretical integration: the eclectic approach

The eclectic approach to navigating across a terrain including many different theoretical communities directs us to look everywhere for specific techniques to help clients. The *eclectic approach* involves a commitment to assembling the techniques, and the concepts and theories supporting these techniques, that work best from a variety of theories (Norcross, 1986). Using our comparison of science to a language, the eclectic practitioner learns the terms for interventions across a range of theories—coaching, cognitive restructuring, consciousness raising, free association, reciprocal perspective taking, role rehearsal, and so on—and selects an intervention term or a set of terms differentially from this collection or dictionary to guide a particular change project. For example, Holland (2006) reports on a case study of social work with survivors of Hurricane Katrina seeking help at an emergency disaster shelter. He used intervention terms and strategies derived from four theoretical frameworks: ecosystems theory, crisis intervention theory, cognitive-behavioral theory, and a spiritual approach.

Those who use the eclectic approach vary in how systematic, planned, conscious, and critical they are in the assembling and use of techniques and procedures (Forte, 2006). There are several variations of the eclectic approach.

Intuitive eclectics select helping strategies and techniques from various theories based on life experiences, practice style, practice preferences, and hunches. They closely monitor their use of helping interventions, and if clients do not respond to one technique, then the worker selects a different one from the toolbox.

Guided eclectics accumulate techniques from different approaches based on the guidelines from each theory. Recommendations from behaviorists and then family systems theorists for when and how to use systematic desensitization are carefully followed, for examples.

Technical eclectics add techniques to their toolboxes based on established efficacy. Most frequently they choose techniques from different theoretical approaches and less often they assemble the theoretical metaphors and assumptions from the different theoretical frameworks. Selection is based on empirical evidence for the effectiveness of the selected techniques. The technical eclectic questions whether a given technique has proven utility before adding it to her or his toolbox. Technical eclectics are sometimes atheoretical, therefore, and focused more on the collection of validated helping tools than on grappling with theoretical diversity or on synthesizing a set of helping theories (Forte, 2006).

Systematic eclectics integrate techniques chosen because of an explicit logic or framework indicating which techniques to use with which client with which particular problems for what desired outcome under what set of specific circumstances (Forte, 2006). The logic for matching techniques to situations may consider any or all of the following variables: stage of the helping process; characteristics of the client system problem; the client's assessment formulation or psychiatric diagnosis; the personality character-istics of the client; the qualities of the practitioner; and the characteristics of the environment and the setting in which helping services are provided. Assessment of the client-worker-environment configuration precedes the selection of the best strategy for aiding the client.

The eclectic approach for theoretical integration directs the practitioner to add many techniques to his or her toolbox and use the techniques that work for the particular helping job whatever the theoretical source. Workers with a toolbox with many techniques will have a large range of intervention choices, and they are more likely to find helping strategies acceptable to client systems than workers with only a few tools. The eclectic approach also directs the prac-titioner to relate to and converse with theory-users from different theoretical communities by asking for demonstrations of their problem solving strategies and techniques. When there is evidence of effectiveness, such practitioners ask for the permission and knowledge necessary to make the technique their own.

Critics of the eclectic approach argue that eclectic social workers can be uncritical when they select and integrate concepts, techniques and prin-ciples from diverse theoretical traditions (Forte, 2006; Thompson, 2000). Concepts and techniques from different theoretical traditions and practice models are often mixed and matched with minimal self-awareness, with insufficient attention to the evidence supporting or failing to support the ele-ments added, and with too little sensitivity to client variables including the client's goals, perspectives and situational constraints. Eclectic practitioners may also juxtapose techniques that are derived from incompatible theo-retical frameworks. Techniques and procedures are theory-specific and each theory provides its own way of explaining reality, assessing and framing client problems, and generating methods to solve problems; techniques can't be mixed and matched in one box like hammers or saws. Eclectic social workers often fail to use a higher order conceptual framework to guide selection and combining of components, and their toolbox of techniques becomes a poorly organized hodge-podge of techniques.

Theoretical integration: the assimilative integration approach

The *assimilative integration* of theoretical approaches requires the creation of a new superordinate or overarching conceptual framework into which other theories will fit (Forte, 2006). The umbrella conceptualization integrates and organizes many theories and capitalizes on the strengths of all the theoretical elements assimilated into the larger framework. The assimilative approach to theoretical integration focuses on the juxtaposing, joining, and eventual merging of different theoretical frameworks into one intellectual system characterized by fewer distinctions. Conceptualizing assimilative integration is like language learning, we can think of the infant learning a native language at home, Spanish, for example. Then, the language learner assimilates a second language, English, during adolescent interactions at school, in the neighborhood, and with television personalities. The ambitious speaker might even assimilate an additional language, Chinese perhaps, through travel and intensive study as an adult.

There are a few examples in social work of the assimilative approach. Ecological theories and systems theories, for instance, have been integrated into a larger ecosystems paradigm that most social workers learn. Ecosystems theorists argue that other theoretical traditions can be assimilated into this superordinate conceptual framework. Advocates of this grand and comprehensive conceptual system want it to serve as a way to incorporate all the knowledge available for social work use. Inspired by Ken Wilber's integral approach to science, Garner (2011) has created the Social Work Integral Model (SWIM). She considers it a "universally applicable conceptual architecture of social work practice" (p. 255) and an "overarching transtheoretical conceptual model" (p. 256). Her model uses diagrams to depict the central relations of HBSE theory, assessment theory, intervention theory, and practice skill and to depict the convergence of the values and ethics of the client, the practitioner, and the profession in every helping project. She recommends the SWIM foundation as a higher-order intellectual system for thinking about and assimilating diverse theories for thoughtful use in given situations. In my own integrative efforts, I have used symbolic interactionist tenets and concepts as my theoretical base, and assimilated ideas from thirteen other theoretical frameworks into this base (Forte, 2001). Selected concepts from each theory were translated into the language of interactionism and assimilated into a broader, expanded synthesis; a richer applied symbolic interactionism.

Assimilative integration involves an additive learning process (Forte, 2006). Theory users learn and maintain allegiance to a first or native theoretical language. Concepts and techniques from other theoretical traditions are incorporated after their meanings are transformed in accord with the dictates of the primary framework. Both the imported theoretical element and the primary theoretical framework change because of the assimilation. The process can be characterized as the selective assimilation of theories, concepts, techniques, and attitudes after transforming the new elements into one's evolving theoretical approach to practice while adding some of the value of the elements original theoretical meaning. Assimilation is only possible when the meanings of imported concepts or techniques are compatible with the meanings (core assumptions, root metaphors, and concepts) of the primary language.

The premise of this assimilative approach to theoretical integration is that theory users generally form an existing base built on one theory. There is a theoretical imprinting and the first framework or language learned influences our later perceptions and our helping work. The assimilative approach directs the worker to seek a clever and useful way to organize his or her theoretical toolbox. In your various jobs as a social work professional, you can collect and integrate various theories into a super and carefully arranged toolbox starting from your first theoretical framework. This framework is assigned to the top sections of the toolbox and elements of other theoretical frameworks are added across your career as they can be fit into the other sections.

Critics of the assimilative approach to theoretical integration warn of problems and obstacles. Integrating theories into a larger framework substantially modifies and usually reduces the meaning and value of the integrated theoretical element. Many theory-specific concepts assimilated into the ecosystems framework, for example, lose rich denotative and connotative meaning in the new thought system. The critical theory notion of oppression, for a specific example, has a much richer meaning and deeper historical heritage than the concept taught as part of ecosystems thinking. Some theories come from traditions with distinct theoretical assumptions and premises and don't mix easily with those based on different assumptions. Critics assert, for example, that humanistic client-centered approaches are incompatible with behavioral approaches and a holistic umbrella theory merges these rival theories at peril (Forte, 2008). There is also the educational problem. Students who are taught integration through assimilation may become expert in one framework, and may borrow terms from other frameworks, but critics have not seen evidence that social workers can easily become masterful in multiple theories assimilated into an overarching framework.

Theoretical integration: the client-directed approach

The *client-directed approach* to theoretical integration is the newest addition to this field (Duncan and Miller, 2000; Duncan, Sparks, and Miller, 2006). Rather than beginning with theoretical knowledge and the search for commonalities, with techniques assembled in a toolbox, or with a theoretical base for assimilating various ideas, the client-directed approach begins with the client. The worker doesn't start with his or her theory integration approach, and then proceed to use it to help the client. A theoretical framework or frameworks should be selected in consultation with the client. The worker starts by asking the client about his or her own theories of PIE challenges and theories of change, and considers carefully the client's preferences regarding theories to guide the inquiry and action planning processes.

If we compare the client-directed approach to language mastery and use, we conceive of the practitioner as learning every language that his or her clients might speak and switching tongues fluently depending on client communication preferences. This achievement is not possible. Instead, we might imagine the practitioner carrying an iPad or other tablet device with language translation software including a database of all languages spoken by typical clients. For helping work, the languages are the languages of scientific theories. The worker activates the translation software package requested by the client.

Caspar (2007) characterizes this theory integration approach as a process of continual co-construction in which the worker and client both play active roles in selecting and using theoretical resources in ways that meet the client's needs and preferences. Client-directed practitioners select and individualize theoretical knowledge with client input and for use in specific helping circumstances. Theoretical choices are modified continuously based on client feedback about progress toward achieved agreed-upon outcomes. Stricker (2010) applauds this new approach for its sensitivity to the cultural preferences of clients. Moreover, this approach ensures that the client not the worker directs the selection and adaptation of theoretical knowledge.

The approach is so new that critics are few. However, I wonder whether clients know enough about alternative theoretical frameworks, their strengths and limitations to make informed requests to service providers. Moreover, this approach suggests that social work practitioners would need to master every conceivable theoretical framework that their clients might prefer.

Learning activities and reflections

1. Review the commentary above on the various approaches to theoretical integration. Consider each a map for traveling through a practice universe filled with many different human behavior theories, human development theories, and practice theories.
    Which approach appeals to you most: the eclectic approach (if so, select your favorite version of this approach), the common factors approach, the assimilation approach, or the client-directed approach? Why? What are the strengths and limitations of your preferred approach?
2. Start with your preferred approach to theory integration. Comment on how you might use this approach to theory integration to assemble knowledge from diverse sources and traditions? How might you prepare for a career in our multi-theory scientific community using your preferred approach?

3. Think about the assimilative integration approach to theoretical pluralism. What is the base theoretical framework or language that you have learned or are learning? What other theoretical frameworks have you assimilated? What do you foresee as some additional theoretical frameworks that you will need to assimilate later in your career? How orderly and coherent is your overarching thought system and its integrated elements?
4. Finally, reflect on what you have learned about theorizing that prepares you to contribute to the advancement of social work knowledge.

References

Bernstein, S., Goodman, H. and Epstein, I. (1997). Grounded theory: A methodology for integrating social work and social science theory. In D. J. Tucker, C. Garvin and R. Sarri (Eds), *Integrating knowledge and practice: The case of social work and social science* (pp. 139–148). Westport, CT: Praeger.

Brown, D. E. (1991). *Human universals.* New York: McGraw-Hill.

Calderwood, K. A. (2011). Adapting the transtheoretical model of change to the bereavement process. *Social Work, 56* (2), 107–118.

Cameron, M. and Keenan, E. K. (2010). The common factors model: Implications for transtheoretical clinical social work practice. *Social Work, 55* (1), 63–73.

Caspar, F. (2007). Plan analysis. In T. D. Eells (Ed.), *Handbook of psychotherapy case formulation* (2nd ed., pp. 251–289). New York: Guilford Press.

Council on Social Work Education (2008). Educational policy and accreditation standards. Retrieved June 16, 2010, from www.cswe.org/Accreditation/Reaffirmation.aspx.

Duncan, B. L. and Miller, S. D. (2000). The client's theory of change: Consulting the client in the integrative process. *Journal of Psychotherapy Integration, 10* (2), 169–187.

Duncan, B. L., Sparks, J. A. and Miller, S. D. (2006). Client, not theory, directed: Integrating approaches one client at a time. In G. Stricker and J. Gold (Eds), *A casebook of psychotherapy integration* (pp. 225–240). Washington, DC: American Psychological Association.

Forte, J. A. (2001). *Theories for practice: Symbolic interactionist translations.* Lanham, MD: University Press of America.

Forte, J. A. (2006). *Human behavior and the social environment: Models, metaphors, and maps for applying theoretical perspectives to practice.* Belmont, CA: Thomson Brooks/Cole.

Forte, J. A. (2008). Making interactionism useful: Translations for social work and sociological direct practice. In N. K. Denzin (Ed.), *Studies in symbolic interaction* (Vol. 32, pp. 219–249). Bingley: Emerald.

Garner, M. D. (2011). Thinking practice: The social work integral model. *Families in Society: The Journal of Contemporary Social Services*, 92 (3), 255–261.

Holland, C. D. (2006). Eclectic disaster social work practice: Spiritual support for evacuees. Paper presented at National Association of Christian Social Workers Convention, Philadelphia, October 2006. Retrieved March 27, 2013, from www.nacsw.org/Publications/Proceedings2006/HollandCDisasterReliefE.pdf.

McGuire, L. S. (2004). The transtheoretical model: Welfare to work as a change process. *Journal of Human Behavior in the Social Environment*, 10 (2), 33–56.

Norcross, J. C. (1986). Eclectic psychotherapy: An introduction and overview. In J. C. Norcross (Ed.), *Handbook of eclectic psychotherapy* (p. 3–24). New York: Brunner/Mazel.

Prochaska, J. O. and DiClemente, C. C. (1992). Stages of change in the modification of problem behaviors. In M. Hersen, R. M. Eisler and P. M. Miller (Eds), *Progress in behavior modification* (pp. 183–218). Sycamore, IL: Sycamore Publishing.

Smith, D. C. (2012). Jacquelines of all trades or masters of some? Negative implications of focusing on common factors. *Social Work*, 57 (3), 283–287.

Stricker, G. (2010). *Psychotherapy Integration*. Washington, DC: American Psychological Association.

Thompson, N. (2000). *Theory and Practice in Human Services*. Buckingham: Open University Press.

18 Build an integrative multi-theory personal practice model

(EPAS 2.1.1 Identify as a professional social worker; EPAS 2.1.7 Apply knowledge)

We contend that the real issue is not whether practitioners operate from theory, but rather "what" theory they use and how they should evaluate its usefulness for practice. For it seems evident that those who feel that they can operate entirely without theory are usually basing their behaviour on vaguely defined "implicit" theory.

(Roland LeComte cited in Roberts, 1990, p. 35)

Core competency EPAS 2.1.1 challenges practitioners to "identify as a professional social worker and conduct oneself according" (Council on Social Work Education, 2008, p. 3). This competency is demonstrated by practice behaviors including "practice professional reflection and self-correction to assure continual professional development" and "engage in career-long learning." There is a tool that will help social workers achieve proficiency in these practice behaviors, the personal practical model.

Overview of personal practice model

Professional theorizing requires a common base of professional mission, knowledge, values, and ethics but this base must also be supplemented by each practitioner with knowledge, skills, and attitudes suited to the specific characteristics of their practice context. Such systematic adjustments have been called personal practice models (Mullens, 1981, 1983, 1988) or personal practice theories (Cornett et al., 1992). A *personal practice model* is an explicit conceptual framework that expresses an individual social worker's distinctive approach to practice and gives orderly direction to work with a specific set of clients under specific circumstances (Mullens, 1983).

One's personal practice model is manifest in all phases of the helping process including engagement, assessment, intervention, evaluation, and the ending phase. The notion of personal practice model has some similarities to "theoretical orientation." However, a personal practice model explicitly summarizes more elements than a theoretical orientation, and the personal practice model includes reasons and evidence justifying the practitioner's preferences and the practitioner's matching of elements to typical helping circumstances.

A professional social worker develops his or her personal practice model carefully and over a career (Mullens, 1983; Spruill and Benshoff, 2000). In the beginning phase, the social work student reflects on the values, beliefs, and motivations related to seeking a helping career. The consequent understanding of personal inclinations can guide the search for theoretical knowledge, research knowledge, and practice wisdom and mastery of the relevant knowledge. Next, the social work student and intern studies various theoretical approaches to "human development" and "human behavior and the environment," and begins to test the fit of these approaches with his or her personal convictions and professional aspirations. Those that fit well merit extra study and refinement. Third, the novice practitioner identifies some of the parameters related to likely employment settings such as problem area and field of practice, and uses classroom and field internship experiences, guidance from field instructors and supervisors, and feedback from clients to begin integrating theoretical knowledge into a personal model suitable to these parameters. The first versions of the model needs pilot testing, and the practitioner starts to try out the model in simulated, experimental, or non-risky settings and begins monitoring and evaluating the implementation of practice guidelines. A field internship is the first educational setting for such testing. After this testing phase, the practitioner with some experience gains confidence in his or her efforts at knowledge integration. Theoretical summarizations and practice guidelines can be more confidently integrated into the practice model and readied for use in helping situations calling for autonomous practice.

Research suggests that developing a preliminary philosophy of social work and a personal practice model takes many years of professional education (Watson, 1994), and new graduates will have to modify their personal practice models repeatedly to account for the particular features of their employing organization (O'Connor and Dalgeish, 1986). Because of the complexity of contemporary social work, some practitioners may even have to develop more than one personal practice model, and create a system for matching their different models to different clients and new career paths. The work at information acquisition and utilization (knowledge adaptation, synthesis, integration, and testing) continues across the professional career providing a way to ensure career-long learning. Effective practitioners may, for example, critically revisit and "check up" on their progress in personal practice model development once a year. Revisions and improvements follow the new information and feedback.

Tailoring the personal practice model to helping context

A personal practice model is a "how to do it" conceptual framework (Reid, 1979) tailored to factors relevant to the particular practitioner and practice context. These factors include the practitioner's qualities (style of helping, values and beliefs, training, personal and work experience, social memberships), client qualities (social memberships such as class and race, degree of motivation, interaction patterns, typical problems and challenges, and so on), relationship qualities including those interaction factors associated with effective intervention, and the characteristics of the agency or other helping setting (auspices, culture, structure, mission, and goals). The personal practice model also incorporates knowledge including "human behavior and the environment" theoretical knowledge, research findings, practice wisdom, and insights achieved from reflection on life events that will be relevant and useful in the helping context.

Benefits of the personal practice model

Mullens (1981) reports on his thinking about personal practice models stating that they are personal statements

> ... the product of rational, conscious consideration of theoretical and empirical information, combined with a sense of values and ethics. These models serve as a device for a summarization of a worker's values, ethics, and knowledge as these are related to the intervener's role. In addition, through their guidelines these models give direction to the social worker's interventions.
>
> (p. 632).

Because it is tailored to particulars, the personal practice model serves as a tool that increases the practitioner's accountability to stakeholders: clients, agencies, the profession, and society (Mullens, 1983). Conscious and continual reflection on the use of this personalized approach to practice also increases the worker's control over helping work, and with critical and evidence-based thinking fosters self-corrective activities that reduce assessment and intervention errors (Carpenter, 2008).

Practically, the development of a preliminary personal practice model prepares practitioners for employment and promotion interviews. For example, it supplies a detailed and coherent answer to the interview question: how would you describe and justify your approach to practice in our kind of organization?

The integrative multi-theory personal practice model

The personal practice model makes the practitioner's theoretical orientation explicit. Mullens (1983) developed this tool before most leaders in the profession began to grapple with the proliferation of theories. I have updated his notions in line with my commitment to multi-theoretical social work and offer a revised name, the *integrative multi-theory personal practice model* (IMTPPM). Figure 18.1 identifies some of the critical elements of this approach to knowledge synthesis that might be referenced in a written or verbal statement of a practitioner's model.

Theoretical knowledge

The model specifies the theories and their theoretical elements (assumptions, metaphors, concepts, propositions, models, and principles) that assist in understanding clients and their problems (explanatory theory) and informing the change process (practice theory). This specification includes information about the strengths and limitations of the theories included in the theoretical synthesis and a review of associated evidence.

The practitioner's view of social work purpose

The practitioner's guiding theoretical framework(s) explanatory (theories to explain) and practice (theories to inform) including:

    Preferred theory-based engagement styles
    Preferred theory-based information gathering markers and questions
    Preferred theory-based problem conceptualizations
    Preferred theory-based goals and objectives
    Preferred theory-based conception of change
    Preferred theory-based interventions
    Preferred theory-based ending and evaluation strategies

The practitioner's assembled research knowledge

The practitioner's preferred techniques, skills, roles

The practitioner's understanding of
    His/her typical clients
    Their characteristics, and the
    Best match of theories to clients

Figure 18.1 Elements of an integrative multi-theoretical personal model

Mullens (1988) suggested a three-step process for incorporating theoretical knowledge: locate the information suitable to your practice parameters; evaluate the quality of the information using standards associated with evidence-based science; and convert the information and appraisal into general summary statements. For example, Mullens reports on several generalizations derived from the literature on the cognitive approach: humans respond primarily to cognitive representations of their environments rather than to the environment directly. Human learning is mediated by cognitive processes. Mullens also developed summaries regarding the limitations or contraindications of the theoretical model. For example, the cognitive learning model has been shown to be less successful with clients unable to identify and verbalize their thinking processes and their thoughts.

Novice social workers might begin to build this knowledge while learning about theory in human behavior, practice, research, and other social work classes. Following graduation, professional journals, professional conferences and workshops, and conversations with supervisors and colleagues will serve as sources of additional theoretical knowledge.

Practice guidelines

The integrative multi-theory personal practice model also specifies theory-informed principles or practice guidelines that will direct the planned change process. These include preferred theory-based styles of engaging client systems, preferred theory-based information strategies and tools, preferred theory-based intervention strategies, and preferred theory-based ending and evaluation approaches. An integrative multi-theory personal practice principle built on a cognitive theory foundation, for instance, might state "I will use cognitive learning principles to better understand and assess clients by considering the effects of maladaptive cognitions on behaviors" (Mullens, 1988, p. 528). The multi-theoretical social worker might also take a humanistic stance toward helping. For an example of a guideline drawn from the client-centered humanistic approach and related research, Mullens (1988) developed the following practice directive: "In practice situations where client self-exploration is desirable, practice responses that reflect accurate empathy should be used to facilitate client self-exploration" (p. 515).

Interventions

Additionally, the integrative multi-theory personal practice model includes information about specific and preferred helping tools (skills, roles, strategies, and techniques). Ideally, these are informed by their particular theoretical sources and supported by evidence. These will be part of the development of a repertoire of practice behaviors distinctive to the practitioner. Continuing with the cognitive theory example, Mullens (1988) identified self-monitoring, covert counter conditioning, cognitive restructuring, coping skills and problem solving training as established and useful techniques to add to a cognitive learning model.

The worker's notes or paper on the integrative multi-theory practice model should include information about the justification of his or her theory choices in relation to evidence, logic, client needs, and agency constraints and opportunities. The worker might also discuss or write about how she has determined that the IMTPPM fits well with her temperament, values, relationship style, and other factors important to the professional use of self. Finally, the practitioner might make an effort to articulate the theoretical integration approach (common factors, eclectic, assimilative, or client-centered) directing the assembly of the theoretical pieces of the model.

Integrative multi-theory personal practice models: Illustrations

My integrative multi-theory personal practice model helps me provide group work with vulnerable populations including persons dealing with homelessness, with chronic mental health issues, and with developmental disabilities in not-for-profit community-based agencies. My model draws heavily from symbolic interactionism and role theory including knowledge obtained from many case summaries and qualitative studies derived from these traditions. The model also draws from the practice tradition called "mainstream group work," a tradition very compatible with my preferred explanatory theory. The model promotes the value of mutual aid and gives emphasis to the use of traditional group work techniques like role play, program activity, democratic deliberations and decision making, and cooperative problem solving. As I have become more aware of the systematic exploitation of vulnerable people in our society, I am integrating critical, feminist, and other empowerment theories and their elements into my own approach.

Ronald Rooney (1992) developed an integrative multi-theory personal practice model integrating Germain's ecological explanatory theory, Reid's task centered practice theory, relevant research, strengths perspective concepts, and his own practice experiences for use in work with involuntary adult clients, specifically chronically neglectful families. Here are a few highlights of his statements of this model. He was working often with clients who must follow a court order to meet with a social worker and with clients facing the threat of a court sentence. The task centered approach seemed a helpful practice foundation. It can be summarized concisely: interventions are to be "short-term, focused on specific, agreed-upon target problems, and to be organized around problem-solving actions or tasks to be carried out by clients and practitioners" (Reid, 1979, p. 222). So, for example, Rooney endorsed the helping principle that clients identify tasks and make commitments to work on these tasks between sessions.

Rooney's (1999) review of research studies for this type of client indicated that there was no family characteristic or ecological factor that predicts success in social work services. Therefore, he chose and affirmed the guidelines that "past failure is not necessarily predictive of current failure" and "the worker should give opportunities and support to each client." This second guideline is derived from a strengths orientation. Rooney (1992) incorporated also the task centered theoretical concept of "motivational congruence" meaning that the outcomes of the helping work are more likely to be successful if there is overlap between the client's perception of the situation and concerns and the perceptions of the practitioner. In his model Rooney (1992) also provided theoretical and research support for a set of generalizations. The first will serve as an example: court-ordered clients can achieve outcomes as successful as those achieved by voluntary clients. Rooney also identified preferred practice strategies, strategies supported by theory and research. These include teaching clients to access contingencies, to generate new alternatives, to substitute positive self-talk for negative self-talk, to examine attitudes and beliefs, and to make commitments to try new behavior.

Learning activities and reflections

1. Begin the process of developing your own personal practice model. The best model is one tailored to the particular circumstances and challenges that you face as a practitioner. You might start by asking yourself and then answering these basic questions about the likely parameters of practice. With what type of clients and what kind of problem areas do you intend to work? In what type of agency or helping setting do you anticipate practicing social work? For example, a student in one of my classes would like to develop an ecologically oriented approach to using horses in the rehabilitation of incarcerated prisoners.

2. Begin to identify the knowledge—theoretical frameworks and practice theories, research studies, and life experiences—that you can integrate into your model. What theoretical framework or frameworks do you anticipate will be most suitable to your practice, and how can you transform this knowledge into usable form as theoretical concepts, theoretical summaries and displays,

theory-based practice principles and guidelines, and theory-informed helping techniques and skills? What research programs and specific research studies will enrich the knowledge necessary for your approach to practice? What life experiences have you had that you might reflect on and incorporate as guiding lessons into your practice model?

3. Plan for your future career. Give your integrative multi-theory personal practice model a name. Write down some of your ideas regarding a systematic model development project describing the continued refinement of your personal practice model. You might identify next steps related to reading relevant articles and books, attending continuing education workshops, regional and national conferences, and conversing with supervisors, colleagues, and theory experts.

4. Every social worker can make a contribution to the advancement of our profession's knowledge base. Comment also on how you will share with the social work profession the knowledge and lessons you acquire as you build, use, and test your integrative multi-theory personal practice model.

5. Finally, reflect on what you have learned about theorizing that prepares you to contribute to the advancement of social work knowledge?

References

Carpenter, D. (2008) Identifying, evaluating and developing personal practice models: A manual for MSW students in the PPM masters project path. Retrieved November 26, 2009, from www.d.umn.edu/sw/MANUALS/documents/PPMS pr08.pdf.

Cornett, J. W., Chase, K. S., Miller, P., Schrock, D., Bennett, B. J., Goins, A. and Hammond, C. (1992). Insights for the analysis of our own theorizing: The viewpoints of seven teachers. In E. W. Ross, J. W. Cornett and G. McCutcheon (Eds), *Teacher personal theorizing: Connecting curriculum, practice, theory, and research* (pp. 137–157). Albany, NY: State University of New York Press.

Council on Social Work Education (2008). Educational policy and accreditation standards. Retrieved June 16, 2010, from www.cswe.org/Accreditation/Reaffirmation.aspx.

Mullens, E. J. (1981). Development of personal intervention models. In R. M. Grinnell Jr. (Ed.), *Social work research and evaluation* (pp. 606–632). Itasca, IL: F. E. Peacock.

Mullens, E. J. (1983). Personal practice models. In A. Rosenblatt and D. Waldfogel (Eds), *Handbook of clinical social work* (pp. 623–649). New York: John Wiley and Sons.

Mullens, E. J. (1988). Constructing personal practice models. In R. M. Grinnell Jr. (Ed.), *Social work research and evaluation* (3rd ed., pp. 503–533). Itasca, IL: F. E. Peacock.

O'Connor, I. and Dalgeish, L. (1986). Cautionary tales from beginning practitioners: The fate of personal models of social work in beginning practice. *British Journal of Social Work, 16* (4), 431–447.

Reid, W, J. (1979). The model development dissertation. *Journal of Social Service Research, 3* (2), 215–225.

Roberts, R. (1990). *Lessons from the past: Issues for social work theory.* London: Tavistock/Routledge.

Rooney, R. H. (1992). *Strategies for work with involuntary clients.* New York: Columbia University Press.

Rooney, R. H. (1999). Working with involuntary clients: Key observations for concurrent planning. Retrieved December 1, 2009, from www.cehd.umn.edu/ssw/cascw/attributes/PDF/childwelfarenews/insert_rooney_14.pdf.

Spruill, D. A. and Benshoff, J. M. (2000). Helping beginning counselors develop a personal theory of counseling. *Counselor Education and Supervision, 40* (1), 70–80.

Watson, C. (1994). Improving the quality of careers guidance: Toward an understanding of the development of personal models. *British Journal of Guidance and Counselling, 22* (3), 357–372.

Section 4

Conclusion

19 Translation and translators for multi-theoretical social work

In this book, I have invited social workers and other human service practitioners to use the resources of fourteen theories to make sense of complex practice situations. However, I have also argued that these major scientific theories represent human behavior, human development, and the environment in specialized languages, ones foreign to our ears. I have introduced a framework for theory translation work with seven theory translation devices. I have also offered selectively my translations of the fourteen theories and indicated how each might guide helping work during the major phases of the planned change process. Additionally, I have linked the eighteen lessons in multi-theoretical social work to the profession's core competencies, especially professional identity (EPAS 2.1.1), critical thinking (EPAS 2.1.3), knowledge application (EPAS 2.1.7), and professional practice (EPAS 2.1.10).

The history of translation in social work

Thomas Kuhn, a philosopher of science, understood the problems of communication across theoretical and disciplinary languages and anticipated the translation science movement by many decades. For advancing science, he recommended "what the participants in a communication breakdown can do is recognize each others as members of different language communities and then become translators" (Kuhn, 1970, p. 202). Early in the history of social work, Jane Addams may have been even more perspicacious than Kuhn (Forte, 2002). Guided by Addams, settlement workers engaged in language translation and attempted to interpret American institutions to immigrants bewildered by the signs and symbols of their new country.

Furthermore, Addams and the settlement workers translated the words used by foreign language speaking settlement members in ways that the privileged and fortunate members of Chicago could understand.

Settlement workers used a translational approach to increase their understanding of and empathic identification with the poor (Forte, 2002). According to George Herbert Mead (1907), an academic at the University of Chicago and frequent collaborator with Jane Addams (their partnership was a demonstration of the value of communication between members of university and field), Addams and other settlement workers lived in the neighborhoods of their clients and discovered the problems of the community by becoming "an understanding part of it" (p. 3). These practitioners worked hard to hone their translation skills. Over time, the language and meanings held central by the immigrants and other struggling neighbors became intelligible to the settlement workers. Settlement workers also learned to translate the words, phrases, and grammar of American society to the help-seeking members of Hull-House. Some even became language instructors and taught English to Hull-House residents and neighbors (Addams, 1910/1990). Successful instruction helped Hull-House members make sense of the bewildering experiences of urban Chicago. Successful language translation made work in factories possible, and decreased the likelihood of starvation and early death. Successful language translation fostered cooperation. Addams (1895/2002) reported, for instance, on a first meeting between Russian Jews who were trained tailors and the American-Irish girls who were moving into this industry without training and for lower wages. She noted "they were separated by strong racial differences, by language, by nationality, by religion, by mode of life, by every possible social distinction." However, Addams added, "The interpreter stood between the two sides of the room" (p. 51), and Addams discusses how the interpreter worked hard to help the two groups understand each other and realize their economic and social interdependence

Beside her innovative work translating natural languages, Jane Addams anticipated the translation science movement. Addams and her creative social work colleagues assembled from residents the *Hull-House Maps and Papers* (Residents of Hull-House, 1895/1970), a comprehensive report on the immigrants living near the settlement house and their living conditions. This was one of the first research studies of its kind and a groundbreaking attempt to translate research for practical use. Jane Addams also translated her practice experiences for an audience of scientific theorists (Forte, 2003). Addams was a "founding mother" of the important theoretical tradition of symbolic interactionism (Deegan, 1988), and she became an exemplary model of the scholarly social worker. Addams taught as a visiting lecturer at the University of Chicago Extension School and lectured at the Chicago School of Civics and Philanthropy. She was a charter member of the American Sociological Society and addressed the group on four occasions.

Addams published five articles in the *American Journal of Sociology*. Major social theorists of the time reviewed her books very favorably. Mead (1907), for example, viewed Addams's book *The Newer Ideals of Peace* as "the expression of enlightened social intelligence in sympathetic contact with men, women and children" (p. 128). He praised her for revealing the reality of life as experienced by immigrants, workers in industrial factories, and poor city dwellers, a reality hid from academics by their "academic and political abstractions" (p. 128). Jane Addams established Hull-House as a trading zone for knowledge, too. She invited sociological and philosophical theorists including George Herbert Mead, John Dewey, and W. I. Thomas to speak to Hull-House residents about their social insights. She also formed teams involving Dewey, Mead, and other scholars to work with social workers on policy advocacy and other change projects for community improvement. Jane Addams and the settlement house workers opened up channels of communication so Chicago's newcomers could become informed, capable, responsible, and active participants in social and political groups and organizations, and so Chicago's established citizens could accept and relate cooperatively to their new neighbors.

The translator role: definition

Like Addams, Martin Bloom (1975) viewed translation as central to social work problem solving. He wrote that "the major task of using theories from the literature is to find them … to know how to understand them, and, finally, to translate them into direct strategy statements" (p. 162). Translation is the act of translating from one language into another, rendering meanings intelligible across languages (Forte, 2002). A translator is a personal agent who takes part in and exerts control over a process of interpretation by making sense out of some text, discourse, or other semiotic phenomena (Colapietro, 1993). The translator becomes adept at finding equivalent terms in a target language for the terms in a source language (Sarukkai, 2002). Following the lead of Addams and Bloom, I propose adding the role of "basic translator" to the roles mastered by generalist social workers and developing the role of "translation specialist" for doctoral level social workers.

The basic translator serves as a mediator between two persons or groups for whom mutual communication might otherwise be problematic (Hatim and Mason, 1990). For example, the practitioner as basic translator mediates between the client and the researcher offering the latest evidence-based knowledge about a problem and its remedy; this is a key focus of the translation science movement. Or the practitioner mediates between the client and theorists providing useful theoretical knowledge to guide the inquiry process and the action planning process; this has been the focus of this book. Basic translators can facilitate communication and cooperation across language

Conclusion

groups and increase the effectiveness of reflecting teams including theory specialists, theory generalists, layperson collaterals, and clients.

Advanced-level social workers can be trained as specialists in translating scientific languages for practical use. Specialist translators are "people who are in touch with the best in theory and research, who can translate this into effective programs, and who can evaluate these programs. Translators are thus social scientists who have a commitment to theory-and-research-based action for people" (Egan, 1979, p. 15). These social workers will take on the tasks of familiarizing themselves with the classic and contemporary theoretical literature, of translating diverse theoretical languages into a language for use by the profession (I advocate for the language of membership), and of disseminating translation dictionaries among practice educators, practitioners, and researchers. These theory interpreters can become the tour guides who will aid multi-theoretical social workers as they travel to new theoretical locations and bring back what they learn to benefit clients (Forte, 2001).

Translator role requirements

There are some requirements for effective translation (Hatim and Mason, 1990; Hatim and Munday, 2004). The social work translator must develop a multilingual capacity and master the sign systems (languages) of basic science (explanatory theoretical languages) and of applied science (practice theoretical languages). The translator must also cultivate a multi-cultural vision and grasp the culture of representatives from diverse social worlds including the knowledge creators from the academy and research laboratory and the knowledge users located in the community such as clients, patients, and citizens. Due to social workers' training for culturally sensitive and competent practice, they should be ready for the work necessary to meet these requirements.

Social work translators must also develop knowledge, skill, and dispositions in three other areas. First, the translator must become capable of understanding a source text including its grammar and vocabulary, its base in a specialized knowledge system, and its intended meaning. For example, the adept educator or supervisor can understand books and articles like those written by the theorist Patricia Hill Collins on intersectionality theory. This translator can relate Collins's writing to feminist, critical, and Afrocentric human behavior theories, and decipher the central meanings of her innovative system of thought.

Second, the social work translator must be able to transform meanings (lexical, grammatical, and rhetorical) for their new uses. The educator and supervisor might teach the novice practitioner the key terms of Collins's theory, the way Collins links these terms grammatically into propositions and systems of propositions, and the powerful images and resonant symbols that

Collins uses to persuade readers of the value of her framework. This translation work will prepare students and supervisees to use Collins's matrix of oppression to assess the interconnected reactions to a person's cultural memberships and identities and to guide the planned change process in ways sensitive to multiple membership identities and processes of oppression.

Third, the translator must be able to create a target text or sign system—this might be a narrative, a diagram, a mathematical formula, or an image—one that is comprehensible, respectful of the representational conventions and practices of the target audience, and adequate for the contracted translational project. One of my colleagues, an experienced HBSE educator, expanded and modified a display of Collins's intersectionality theory for use in the course module on constructionist theories of diversity. Her representation visualized cultural categories (race, class, religion, sexual orientation, physical ability, age, and status as citizen) as slices of a circular pie. There was an inner pie with slice halves representing category memberships privileged in a society and an outer pie with corresponding slice halves representing category memberships often associated with oppression. Students use this translation product to think about the different experiences of persons in privileged and oppressed categories, the likely experiences of persons in multiple oppressed categories, the ways certain categories of privilege like class might override a person's categorization in other groups, and the use of intersectionality theory in practice.

Possible benefits of translating and using multiple languages

In this section, I present provisionally a set of general statements regarding the benefits of theory translation and multi-theoretical social work. I relate these benefits to mastery of a set of the Council on Social Work Education core competencies and related practice behaviors. There is some evidence supporting these claims. More is needed.

Multi-theoretical social work and professional identity (EPAS 2.1.1)

Social work began to emerge more than a century ago as a profession with the distinctive function of "intersystem translation" that is, facilitating communication between persons with needs and troubles and the formal and informal social systems that might ameliorate these needs and troubles (Abbott, 1995). According to Abbott, formal and informal translation work has been central to our history, identity, and conduct since the profession's formation.

The social worker committed to translating and learning multiple theoretical languages advances his or her growth as a person and a professional.

The effort to develop translational capabilities and to appreciate the multiple realities or perspectives shaped by different theoretical languages increases intellectual flexibility. Such efforts also reduce the non-critical thinking associated with personal bias, insularity, and excessive certainty (Greene and Ephross, 1991). Greene and Ephross add that the development of capacities for translating and using multiple theories stimulates creativity because we learn to synthesize and integrate different theoretical terms into our professional vocabulary. Multi-theory training also provides the growth experiences associated with learning deeply about the character and components of the theoretical language(s) that we prefer (Camic and Joas, 2004), especially as we contrast our favorites with other theoretical languages.

Multi-theoretical social work and critical thinking (EPAS 2.1.3)

According to the Council on Social Work Education (2008), critical thinking "requires the synthesis and communication of relevant information" (p. 4). Translation skill and the study of multiple theories lead to effective theory integration and communication about theory-derived insights. The critical thinking competency includes effective communication as an associated practice behavior. By continual translation practice, the multi-theory practitioner will improve in verbal and written communication abilities (Payne, 2002). The practitioner can better use formal theoretical languages with peers to clarify, criticize, and organize ideas about how to help. The practitioner can better communicate wisely in writing and in words to judges, administrators, family members of a client, and colleagues from other disciplines because the practitioner can use the audience members' preferred language but can also translate scientific terminology into a language that these people understand. Multi-lingual practitioners can use the appropriate theoretical languages fluently to explain their professional judgments at case conferences and in supervisory meetings with helpers from other theoretical backgrounds.

Multi-theoretical social work and research–practice reciprocity (EPAS 2.1.6)

Translators can help practitioners and community members who see no use for social work research findings. The translator might work to make evidence-based practice studies accessible and applicable by creating simple and short summaries, for instance. The translator also might work as a member of collaborative teams of researchers, theorists, direct service practitioners, and policy makers and show how empirical information can contribute to the effectiveness of public problem solving activities. Reversing directions, the translator might help practitioners share lessons from the field in terms that informs research and theoretical projects in the academy.

Multi-theoretical social work and knowledge application (EPAS 2.1.7)

The Council on Social Work Education (2008) expects social workers to become competent in knowledge application: "Social workers apply theories and knowledge from the liberal arts to understand biological, social, cultural, psychological, and spiritual development" (p. 6). Translators versed in multiple theoretical languages can provide many services to individual practitioners applying knowledge from diverse sources. The translator might translate a complex theoretical language (neofunctionalism or the world-system theory of globalization, for examples) for use by individual therapists, policy advocates, group counselors, or community organizers who are working to add such theories to their toolboxes (Burr, 1973). The translator might transform the metaphors, concepts, propositions, and models of a theoretical language and the jargon of a professional group into plain English for the sake of clients and their families. The translator might also translate scientific theories used by social workers into language useful to the general public in the form of a press release, a YouTube video, a PowerPoint slideshow, or an educational brochure. Recently, the National Association of Social Workers commended a social worker who translated Goffman's interactionist theory of stigma for use by a magazine and website informing the public about the social difficulties experienced by gay men especially those with the HIV disease. In ways like this, the knowledge and skills developed by social work professionals can be shared with and used by a wide audience (Egan, 1979).

Translators can help members of interdisciplinary teams, interprofessional teams, and other reflecting teams understand and use knowledge. During deliberations, the translator might work to identify the terms and phrases that are clear to members of one language group (the family systems theorists, for example) but cause difficulties when members of different language communities are interacting: the systems theorists and the feminists (Kuhn, 1970). The translator can help participants of work teams and helping groups as they try to take each other's perspective and understand what the other is thinking and trying to say. The translator can help participants learn the basics of each other's language, learn ways to convert the theoretical concepts of one subgroup into the terms of the other group, and develop a pidgin language: a simple, common, and shared vocabulary for exchanging knowledge. The translator can also help the participants in a multi-theory dialogue begin to learn the craft of translation so they can undertake efforts on their own to clarify misunderstandings and enhance cooperation.

Multi-theoretical social work and responses to evolving contexts (EPAS 2.1.9)

Educational Policy and Accreditation Standard 2.1.9 specifies the core competency, "respond to contexts that shape practice." I have shown that theoretical pluralism and the translation science movement are two major contemporary influences on practice. The lessons presented in this book present knowledge and skills equipping social workers to respond to these dynamic forces. The Council on Social Work Education calls for social workers to become proactive in relation to evolving context. For example, they identify the practice behavior "provide leadership in promoting sustainable changes in service delivery and practice to improve the quality of social services".

The social worker committed to translating and learning multiple theoretical languages can provide community and organizational leadership in a variety of specific ways. The multi-theory social worker expands continually his or her breadth of disciplinary knowledge, and thus can provide diverse perspectives on a greater range of the social situations and human troubles and challenges addressed in public change campaigns (Hardiker and Barker, 1991). Multi-theory professionals have knowledge of many theoretical resources for social work projects (Camic and Joas, 2004) and can demonstrate how to translate and make sense of the core assumptions, root metaphors, concepts, propositions, and middle-range theories used by other project members when conceptualizing cases. Use of the multi-theory translation stance increases the quality of communication among community or organizational partners with different theoretical, professional, and disciplinary allegiances. The social work translator can model virtuous knowledge use and exchange. Emulating the social worker, partners in a collective project might embrace a sense of humility about their theoretical knowledge and become wary of those with a sense of absolute certainty. Team members can learn to show respect for those who speak different theoretical languages. Partners from varied theoretical backgrounds can learn to better divide labor and avoid wasteful duplication by going with each member's theoretical strengths. Due to proactive social work leadership, partners from other traditions may develop a greater appreciation for social workers' distinctive contributions as theory borrowers and translators.

Multi-theoretical social work and effective practice (EPAS 2.1.10)

Facility with multiple theoretical languages and a multi-theory orientation enhances professional practice at each phase. Such multi-theoretical fluency and literacy makes possible comprehensive and detailed depictions of the major aspects of the "person interacting in the environment with a challenge" configuration (Greene, 1999). This improves client assessment work. Theoretical multi-lingualism increases the accuracy of inquiry because the worker can select from a variety of theoretical frameworks and practice theories the ones that best guide information gathering in the particular situation and the ones that provide the deepest and fullest PIE understanding (Rosen, 1988).

Practitioners who can translate and speak multiple theoretical languages and use multiple theory-based interventions in intelligent combinations will solve more practice problems and solve them more effectively than those who speak no theoretical language or only one language (Glanz and Bishop, 2010; Wallston and Armstrong, 2002). More theoretical choices for the worker increase the possibilities for identifying or generating ameliorative actions (Payne, 1997), and the likelihood of producing a maximal positive impact based on the differential use of theories and theory-based interventions (Turner, 1996).

The practitioner conversant in many theoretical languages and able to translate the research literature on theory effectiveness can also avoid the theory-informed engagement strategies, assessment tools, interventions, and ending techniques that have been shown to be useless or to cause harm to clients (Turner, 1999). Multi-theory speakers and users, in short, are likely to provide better service to their clients than the theoretically mute and the one-language practitioners (Reid, 1998).

Conclusion

I will conclude with some hopeful predictions. The social work profession will become stronger and more effective as the number of theory translators and multi-theory social workers increases. Our profession's knowledge base will expand while we will develop better metatheories for organizing this knowledge (Turner, 1999). Energy and time spent on fights and rivalries among theoretical subgroups within the profession will lessen. Turner (1999) adds the prediction that boundaries between theory-based associations and professional groups will become more permeable, increasing the opportunity for the cross-theory dialogues and resource development that will benefit practitioners and the profession. Social work's connections to the larger citizenry will improve too when we use both theoretical and non-theoretical languages skillfully to advance causes shared by the profession and sectors of the public.

Social work provides unique opportunities for practitioners and educators to become knowledge translators. Our profession may be the multilingual profession par excellence because it deals with many dialects of lay language, borrows heavily from many basic sciences, uses research findings and methods from a variety of disciplines, is involved in value considerations from diverse points of view, and has chaotic and uncontrolled jargon.

(Bloom, Wood, and Chambon, 1991, p. 530)

Coady and Lehmann (2001) concur, and they "support the long-range goal of translating theories into ordinary English in order to further demystification and to facilitate cross-theory dialogue" (p. 415). What would Jane Addams do as a response to the contemporary complexity of scientific languages and the proliferation of theories? She would call on social workers to learn to translate and use multiple theories for our projects, and thus to extend the good to all members of all societies.

References

Abbott, A. (1995). Boundaries of social work or social work of boundaries? *Social Service Review*, 69 (4), 545–562.

Addams, J. (1895/2002). The settlement as a factor in the labor movement. In J. B. Elshtain (Ed.), *The Jane Addams reader* (pp. 46–61). New York: Basic Books.

Addams, J. (1910/1990). *Twenty-years at Hull-House with autobiographical notes*. Urbana, IL: University of Illinois Press.

Bloom, M. (1975). *The paradox of helping: Introduction to the philosophy of scientific practice*. New York: Wiley.

Bloom, M., Wood, K. and Chambon, A. (1991). The six languages of social work. *Social Work*, 36 (6), 530–534.

Burr, W. R. (1973). *Theory construction and the sociology of the family*. New York: Wiley.

Camic, C. and Joas, H. (2004). The dialogical turn. In C. Camic and H. Joas (Eds), *The dialogical turn: New roles for sociology in the postdisciplinary age* (p. 1–19). Lanham, MD: Rowman and Littlefield.

Coady, N. and Lehmann, P. (2001). Revisiting the generalist-eclectic approach. In P. Lehmann and N. Coady (Eds), *Theoretical perspectives for direct social work practice: A generalist-eclectic approach* (pp. 405–420). New York: Springer.

Colapietro, V. M. (1993). *Glossary of semiotics*. New York: Paragon House.

Council on Social Work Education (2008). Educational policy and accreditation standards. Retrieved June 16, 2010, from www.cswe.org/Accreditation/Reaffirmation.aspx.

Deegan, M. J. (1988). *Jane Addams and the men of the Chicago School, 1892–1918*. New Brunswick, NJ: Transaction Books.

Egan, G. (1979). *People in systems: A model for development in the human-service professions and education*. Monterey, CA: Brooks/Cole.

Forte, J. A. (2001). *Theories for practice: Symbolic interactionist translations*. Lanham, MD: University Press of America.

Forte, J. A. (2002). Mead, contemporary metatheory, and twenty-first-century interdisciplinary team work. *Sociological Practice: A Journal of Clinical and Applied Sociology*, 4, 315–334.

Forte, J. A. (2003). Applied symbolic interactionism: Meanings, memberships, and social work. In L. T. Reynolds and N. J. Herman-Kinney (Eds), *Handbook of symbolic interactionism* (pp. 915–936). Walnut Creek, CA: AltaMira Press.

Glanz, K. and Bishop, D. B. (2010). The role of behavioral science theory in the development and implementation of public health interventions. *Annual Review of Public Health, 31*, 399–418.

Greene, R. R. (1999). *Human behavior theory and social work practice* (2nd ed.). New York: Aldine de Gruyter.

Greene, R. R. and Ephross, P. H. (1991). *Human behavior theory and social work practice*. New York: Aldine de Gruyter.

Hardiker, P. and Barker, M. (1991). Towards social theory for social work. In J. Lishman (Ed.), *Handbook of theory for practice teachers in social work* (pp. 87–101). London: Jessica Kingsley.

Hatim, B. and Mason, I. (1990). *Discourse and the translator*. London: Longman.

Hatim, B. and Munday, J. (2004). *Translation: An advanced resource book*. London: Routledge.

Kuhn, T. S. (1970). *The structure of scientific revolutions* (2nd ed.). Chicago: University of Chicago Press.

Mead, G. H. (1907). The newer ideals of peace [Review]. *American Journal of Sociology, 13*, 121–128.

Mead, G. H. (1907). The social settlement: Its basis and function. *University of Chicago Record, 12*, 108–110. New pages 1–4, Retrieved March 27, 2013, from www.brocku.ca/MeadProject/Mead/pubs/Mead_1907g.html.

Payne, M. (1997). *Modern social work theory* (2nd ed.). Chicago: Lyceum.

Payne, M. (2002). Social work theories and reflective practice. In R. Adams, L. Dominelli and M. Payne (Eds), *Social work: Themes, issues, and critical debates* (2nd ed., pp. 123–138). Basingstoke: Palgrave.

Reid, W. J. (1998). The paradigms and long-term trends in clinical social work. In R. A. Dorfman (Ed.), *Paradigms of clinical social work* (vol. 2, pp. 337–351). New York: Brunner/Mazel.

Residents of Hull-House. (1895/1970). *Hull-House maps and papers: A presentation of nationalities and wages in a congested district of Chicago*. New York: Arno.

Rosen, H. (1988). Evolving a personal philosophy of practice: Towards eclecticism. In R. A. Dorfman (Ed.), *Paradigms of clinical social work* (pp. 388–412). New York: Brunner/Mazel.

Sarukkai, S. (2002). *Translating the world: Science and language*. Lanham, MD: University Press of America.

Turner, F. J. (1996). An interlocking perspective for treatment. In F. J. Turner (Ed.), *Social work treatment: Interlocking theoretical approaches* (4th ed., pp. 699–711). New York: Free Press.

Turner, F. J. (1999). Theories of practice with vulnerable populations. In D. E. Biegel and A. Blum (Eds), *Innovations in practice and service delivery across the lifespan* (pp. 13–31). New York: Oxford University Press.

Wallston, K. and Armstrong, C. (2002). Theoretically-based strategies for health behavior change. In M. P. O'Donnell and Associates (Eds), *Health promotion in the workplace* (2nd ed., pp. 182–201). Belmont, CA: Delmar Thomson/Cengage Learning.

Index

Page numbers in **bold** refer to tables and in *italic* refer to figures.

Made in the USA
Middletown, DE
19 August 2018